Sermons by Jonathan Edwards on the Matthean Parables
volume I

The Wise and Foolish Virgins, by Jan Luyken

Sermons by Jonathan Edwards on the Matthean Parables
VOLUME I

TRUE AND FALSE CHRISTIANS
(ON THE PARABLE OF THE WISE AND FOOLISH VIRGINS)

EDITED BY
Kenneth P. Minkema, Adriaan C. Neele,
and Bryan McCarthy

WITH AN INTRODUCTION BY
Wilson H. Kimnach

CASCADE *Books* · Eugene, Oregon

The *Jonathan Edwards*
Center at Yale University

SERMONS BY JONATHAN EDWARDS ON THE MATTHEAN PARABLES,
VOLUME I
True and False Christians (On the Parable of the Wise and Foolish Virgins)

Cascade Books
A Division of Wipf and Stock Publishers
199 W. 8th Ave., Suite 3
Eugene, OR 97401

www.wipfandstock.com

ISBN 13: 978-1-61097-714-2

Cataloging-in-Publication data:

Edwards, Jonathan, 1703–1758.

Sermons from Jonathan Edwards on the Matthean parables, volume I : true
and false Christians (on the parable of the wise and foolish virgins) / Jonathan
Edwards, edited by Kenneth P. Minkema, Adriaan C. Neele, and Bryan McCarthy.

x + 220 p. ; 23 cm. Includes bibliographical references and index.

ISBN 13: 978-1-61097-714-2

1. Sermons of Jonathan Edwards / Jonathan Edwards. 2 Ten virgins
(Parable)—Sermons. 3. Jesus Christ—Parables. 4. Bible. N.T. Matthew—Criticism,
interpretation, etc. 5. Preaching—United States—History—18th century. I.
Kimnach, Wilson H. II. McCarthy, Brian. III. Minkema, Kenneth P. IV. Neele,
Adriaan C. V. Title.

BX7233.E42 M25 2012

Manufactured in the U.S.A.

CONTENTS

CONTRIBUTORS

Dr. Wilson H. Kimnach is the Presidential Professor in the Humanities (Emeritus), Bridgeport University, and General Sermon Editor of *The Works of Jonathan Edwards*.

Bryan McCarthy is a former editorial assistant at the Jonathan Edwards Center, Yale University, and is now a doctoral candidate at Oxford University.

Dr. Kenneth P. Minkema is the Executive Editor and Director of the Jonathan Edwards Center, Yale University, and Research Scholar at Yale Divinity School.

Rev. Dr. Adriaan C. Neele is the Associate Editor and Director of the Jonathan Edwards Center, Yale University, Research Scholar at Yale Divinity School, and Professor Extraordinary at the University of the Free State, Bloemfontein, South Africa.

PREFACE

THIS FIRST VOLUME OF *SERMONS BY JONATHAN EDWARDS ON THE Matthean Parables* contains a previously unpublished series by Edwards on Jesus' Parable of the Wise and Foolish Virgins, as found in Matthew 25. Edwards preached these sermons in 1737–38, in the lull between the Connecticut Valley Revival of 1734–35 and the Great Awakening, which started in Massachusetts in late 1740. Not only does this series have significance for its place in the Protestant evangelical awakening of the eighteenth century, but it is also an important index of Edwards' developing thought on the nature of sainthood and related topics of theoretical and practical Christianity, particularly in the context of widespread spiritual renewal. To assist the reader, preceding the series are two introductions that describe Edwards' preaching style and method and provide an historical context for the series itself.

A NOTE ON EDWARDS' TEXT

Edwards' sermon series, *True and False Christians*, is printed here in full for the first time from the original manuscripts as transcribed and edited by the staff of the Jonathan Edwards Center at Yale University. In presenting these texts, the editors have followed the conventions of the Yale Edition of *The Works of Jonathan Edwards* (26 volumes, 1957–2008), regularizing spelling, capitalization, and format. Preserved here are Edwards' own words, punctuated in an eighteenth-century style. Because the manuscript was largely uncorrected by Edwards—it was, after all, for his personal use for public delivery—there are inconsistencies in number, style, and tense, which, as a rule, are left as they are; any changes are footnoted. In any given manuscript there are a great number of deletions, so here only deletions of significant textual importance are footnoted. Readers may find Edwards' manner of writing challenging at first, but we believe the effort to understand Edwards in his own terms, in his own idiom, and to get a sense of the immediacy of his preaching, will be rewarded. Finally, Scripture quotes are rendered according to the King James Bible, which was the version Edwards used.

One feature of the text presented below bears special explanation: cases of editorial interpolation. These are of two types. First, outright omissions by Edwards, and lacunae in the manuscript, are filled by insertions in square brackets ([,]). Secondly, one aspect of the outlinish nature of this sermon series is easily seen in the many dashes of varying lengths that Edwards drew at the beginning, in the middle, and at the end of statements. These dashes represent repeated words or phrases, as well as connective pieces of sentences that Edwards would have provided extemporaneously. Where these dashes have been editorially amplified, they are surrounded by curly brackets ({,}).

The manuscripts are in the Edwards Collection, Beinecke Rare Book and Manuscript Library, Yale University. Transcripts may be viewed on the Jonathan Edwards Center's website, edwards.yale.edu. The Introduction by Wilson H. Kimnach is adapted from his larger discussion of "Jonathan Edwards' Art of Prophesying" in *The Works of Jonathan Edwards, 10, Sermons and Discourses, 1720–1723* (New Haven, Yale University Press, 1990), 21–27, 36–42.

INTRODUCTION
Edwards the Preacher

Wilson H. Kimnach

EDWARDS' THOUGHTS ON PREACHING

JONATHAN EDWARDS WAS IN FULL AGREEMENT WITH HIS TEACHERS RE-
specting the exalted status of the preacher. For though his writings
occasionally contain references to "earthen vessels" and sometimes emphasize the preacher's humble situation as a son of Adam, it is much
more common for Edwards to see the preacher as a man exalted and
even transfigured by his calling. Indeed, in some of the earliest entries
in his "Miscellanies" (nos. mm, qq, and 40) Edwards attempts to define
to his own satisfaction the nature of the call, the limits and quality of a
minister's influence in society, and the power in preaching or teaching
the divine Word.

> Yet it is clear that those that are in the New Testament called min-
> isters are not every private Christian, and consequently if [any]
> such remain now as are there spoken of, they are distinct from
> other Christians. 'Tis clear they are born undistinguished; from
> this 'tis clear they are distinguished afterwards. 'Tis also evident
> that they are distinguished some way or other by Christ . . .[1]

1. "Miscellanies" no. *mm*, in *Works of Jonathan Edwards, 13, "Miscellanies," a-500*,
edited by Thomas A. Schafer (New Haven: Yale University Press, 1994), 187. After initial citation, volumes in *The Works of Jonathan Edwards* (New Haven: Yale University
Press, 1957–2008) will be referred to as "WJE" plus volume and page numbers. Texts
by JE published in the Jonathan Edwards Center's website (edwards.yale.edu) will be
referred to as "WJEO" plus the volume number.

This earliest entry on the office of the preacher calls attention to the essentially aristocratic bias of Edwards, which is quite in keeping with his upbringing, while it also demonstrates his characteristic propensity to rethink every important aspect of his life "from the ground up," regardless of his background and training. He may not seriously question the assumptions of his heritage, but he will insist upon a personal formulation of that heritage in his own written words.

The preacher is, then, a "chosen one" with a distinct charisma as a result of his call to serve Christ. He is invested with a capacity and right to instruct, lead, and judge his people;[2] he has no pretension to civil authority, but in the all-important moral and spiritual realms he is, of all human beings, supremely authoritative. "Miscellanies" no. 40 contains early speculations upon the powers that would inhere in the effective preaching of the Word, specifically:

> Without doubt, ministers are to teach men what Christ would have them to do, and to teach them who doth these things and who doth them not; that is, who are Christians and who are not
> . . .
>
> Thus, if I in a right manner am become the teacher of a people, so far as they ought to hear what I teach them, so much power I have. Thus, if they are obliged to hear me only because they themselves have chosen me to guide them, and therein declared that they thought me sufficiently instructed in the mind of Christ to teach them, and because I have the other requisites of being their teacher, then I have power as other ministers have in these days. But if it was plain to them that I was under the infallible guidance of Christ, then I should have more power. And if it was plain to all the world of Christians that I was under the infallible guidance of Christ, and [that] I was sent forth to teach the world the will of Christ, then I should have power in all the world. I should have power to teach them what they ought to do, and they would be obliged to hear me; I should have power to teach them who were Christians and who not, and in this likewise they would be obliged to hear me.[3]

As in a daydream, the student-preacher toys with the mystery of the call, and at least by implication ponders the limits and possibilities of the role of a preacher. Could he command the people, or even the

2. WJE 13:188.
3. WJE 13:222.

world, as a divine messenger? Obviously, there must be some immediate sign, some quality of utterance, that would in itself attest to the supernatural ordination. In this early passage Edwards is already pondering aspects of sermonic style, but characteristically he begins on the most general and profound, most philosophical level. Puritan ministers had always been urged to "preach powerfully," but in this meditation there are new undertones, and "power" clearly relates to a divine investiture that transcends conventional sectarian sanctions. Certainly it seems that Edwards was as well fitted to study the art of preaching under the imperious Solomon Stoddard—his grandfather and predecessor as the pastor of Northampton, Massachusetts—as any man.

Edwards did not pretend to eloquence or a fine style. Indeed, from the first he seems to have made a point of proclaiming his lack of a fine style.

> [T]he practical discourses that follow . . . now appear in that very plain and unpolished dress in which they were first prepared and delivered; which was mostly at a time when the circumstances of the auditory they were preached to, were enough to make a minister neglect, forget, and despise such ornaments as politeness and modishness of style and method, when coming as a messenger from God to souls deeply impressed with a sense of their danger of God's everlasting wrath, to treat with them about their eternal salvation. However unable I am to preach or write politely, if I would, yet I have this to comfort me under such a defect; that God has showed us that he don't need such talents in men to carry on his own work, and that he has been pleased to smile upon and bless a very plain, unfashionable way of preaching. And have we not reason to think that it ever has been, and ever will be, God's manner to bless the foolishness of preaching to save them that believe, let the elegance of language, and excellency of style, be carried to never so great a height, by the learning and wit of the present and future ages?

This passage, from the Preface to *Discourses on Various Important Subjects* (1738),[4] is characteristic of the tone of most of Edwards' prefaces, though the discussion is a little more explicit and fully developed. It is defensive, condemning wit and style out of hand as irrelevant to

---

4. P. v; *The Works of Jonathan Edwards, 19, Sermons and Discourses, 1734–1738*, edited by M. X. Lesser (New Haven: Yale University Press, 2001), 797.

effective preaching, while also suggesting an incapacity for stylistic excellence on his own part.

Part of this may be explained by Edwards' cultural background that would have taught him to think of rhetoric or eloquence as a thing separable from the logical structure of an argument.[5] Since he was consciously developing a heart-piercing manner of writing that would be as spare and efficient as an arrow, he assumed that "style," being an adventitious decoration, would have to be left out. It would not have struck Edwards that that efficacious verbal expression for which he constantly strove and "style" might be the same thing. Thus he really could spend much of his lifetime studying the theory and practice of language and metaphor without "paying any attention to style." Of course, part of the problem is also that, as in the seventeenth century, preaching styles were associated with theological positions. In Edwards' day many of the most eloquent preachers of the East were suspect in Edwards' eyes of being rationalist, Arminian, or just theologically jejune. He would therefore rather deny excellence in his carefully wrought sermons than be thought—perhaps even by himself—to be a creature of wit and style. He was too serious, too full of thought, and too honest for *style*.

Indeed, if Edwards claimed brilliance of any kind it was the more essential and "substantial" excellence of thought, and once again he saw himself as being out of tune with the times:

5. The peculiar attitude that assumes substance and expression to be distinct and separable was quite widespread in the seventeenth century and occasioned the birth of the "plain style" among preachers and "mathematical plainness" in the Royal Society. While a detailed survey of this significant aspect of JE's cultural background is beyond the scope of this introduction, it should be stated that the crucial factor in that background seems to have been the philosophy of Peter Ramus. With the aid of his colleague, Omer Talon, Ramus devised a new formulation of the relationship between logic and rhetoric, involving the transfer of the classical (Ciceronian) invention, disposition, and memory from the province of rhetoric to that of dialectic. This left only style, apprehended as a matter of figures and tropes, and delivery to rhetoric; rhetoric became the sideshow to thought, a crowd-pleasing (or even crowd-deluding) device. Thus, those who were intent upon the intellectual substance of their expression or were intensely earnest, such as Puritan preachers and the new scientists, tended to condemn and avoid "style" as something adventitious and frivolous. Moreover, those who cultivated rhetoric during the seventeenth century actually did tend to artificiality and ornateness, as might be expected when figures and tropes are seen more or less as ends in themselves. For a detailed discussion of the history behind JE's attitude, and an investigation of the long groping toward what we should today call an organic style, see Wilbur S. Howell's *Logic and Rhetoric in England, 1500–1700* (Princeton: Princeton University Press, 1956).

> Our discovering the absurdity of the impertinent and abstruse
> distinctions of the School Divines, may justly give us a distaste
> of such distinctions as have a show of learning in obscure words,
> but convey no light to the mind; but I can see no reason why we
> should also discard those that are clear and rational, and can be
> made out to have their foundation in truth.

In the same Preface,[6] in a sustained argument of two pages, he defends
the virtue of "real" fine distinctions in elaborating the "mysteries" of religion. If, as Cotton Mather contended in *Manuductio ad Ministerium*
(1726), his instruction manual for aspiring ministers, that reason is natural to the soul of man, then Edwards would have him test this capacity,
as he would fully exercise the heart, in the quest of a valid apprehension
of divine truths.

Edwards may have been inspired by the example of his father
Timothy Edwards, minister of East Windsor, Connecticut, to use the utmost rigor in making convicting arguments, and Stoddard undoubtedly
provided the pattern for a potent, "psychological" rhetoric for which
Edwards had no name. But having a finer mind and more imagination
than either Stoddard or Timothy Edwards, Edwards outperformed each
at his specialty while combining elements of both their strategies. His
intense interest in the mysterious power of language, however, was apparently innate.

Edwards' matured vision of the ideal preacher is most completely
delineated in his ordination sermon on John 5:35, entitled *The True
Excellency of a Minister of the Gospel* (1744).[7] There, he insists that a
minister must be "both a burning and a shining light"; that "his heart
burn with love to Christ, and fervent desires of the advancement of his
kingdom and glory," and that "his instructions [be] clear and plain, accommodated to the capacity of his hearers, and tending to convey light
to their understandings." This peculiar combination of head and heart,
he insists, is absolutely necessary to the success of a preacher:

> When light and heat are thus united in a minister of the gospel,
> it shows that each is genuine, and of a right kind, and that both
> are divine. Divine light is attended with heat; and so, on the other

6. P. iii; WJE 19:795–96.

7. *The Works of Jonathan Edwards, 25, Sermons and Discourses, 1743–1758*, edited
by Wilson H. Kimnach (New Haven: Yale University Press, 2006), 82–102.

hand, a truly divine and holy heat and ardor is ever accompanied
with light.

That both heat and light may be acquired by the aspiring preacher,
Edwards urges him to be "diligent in [his] studies," "very conversant
with the holy Scriptures," and "much in seeking God, and conversing
with him by prayer, who is the fountain of light and love." All in all,
Edwards' ideal does not seem to be very different from that of the tradi-
tional preacher of the time, except that in the full context of the sermon
and through the extensive use of light imagery, he suggests a standard
of transcendent dedication and nearly mystical fervor that is rare in any
age. And like Stoddard before him, Edwards cultivated a subtle personal
tone in his rhetoric that, more than any stated principle, demonstrates
the risk-taking commitment demanded of the good preacher.

Edwards is best known for his defenses of passionate emotion,
including "hellfire," in revival preaching. And, indeed, in *Religious
Affections* he argues that "such means are to be desired, as have much of
a tendency to move the affections."[8] Moreover, in *Some Thoughts on the
Revival of Religion in New England*, he emphatically insists that

> Though . . . clearness of distinction and illustration, and strength
> of reason, and a good method, in the doctrinal handling of the
> truths of religion, is many ways needful and profitable, and not
> to be neglected. . . . Our people don't so much need to have their
> heads stored, as to have their hearts touched; and they stand in
> the greatest need of that sort of preaching that has the greatest
> tendency to do this.[9]

As for "hellfire" preaching in particular, Edwards argues:

> Some talk of it as an unreasonable thing to think to fright per-
> sons to heaven; but I think it is a reasonable thing to endeavor to
> fright persons away from hell . . . 'tis a reasonable thing to fright
> a person out of an house on fire.

As for the style or manner of "hellfire" preaching, he makes this observation:

> When ministers preach of hell, and warn sinners to avoid it, in
> a cold manner, though they may say in words that it is infinitely

8. *The Works of Jonathan Edwards, 2, Religious Affections*, edited by John E. Smith
(New Haven: Yale University Press, 1959), 121.

9. *The Works of Jonathan Edwards, 4, Great Awakening*, edited by C. C. Goen (New
Haven: Yale University Press, 1972), 387–88.

terrible; yet (if we look on language as a communication of our minds to others) they contradict themselves; for actions, as I observed before, have a language to convey our minds, as well as words; and at the same time that such a preacher's words represents the sinner's state as infinitely dreadful, his behavior and manner of speaking contradict it, and show that the preacher don't think so; so that he defeats his own purpose; for the language of his actions, in such a case, is much more effectual than the bare signification of his words.[10]

Edwards might well have extended this comment to include the "gesture of language"—specifically, images and metaphors employed in making an argument concrete—in the case of printed sermons.

In summary, it should be observed that, while Edwards placed no limits on the intensity of emotion that a preacher might attempt to evoke through his preaching, he insisted upon a constant balance and aesthetically pleasing harmony between emotion and thought. Indeed, he insisted that without a duly precise and comprehensive body of theological concepts in the sermon, there is no religion at all.[11]

Edwards' ideal preacher is, then, a figure of commanding intellectual rigor and overwhelming rhetorical power; he strikes a blow for religion simultaneously in the heads and hearts of his auditors, though with an emphasis upon the heart. In the performance of his duty, he shows that he is the peculiarly designated servant of his Master:

> They should imitate [Christ] in the manner of his preaching; who taught not as the Scribes, but with authority, boldly, zealously and fervently; insisting chiefly on the most important things in religion, being much in warning men of the danger of damnation, setting forth the greatness of the future misery of the ungodly; insisting not only on the outward, but also the inward and spiritual duties of religion: being much in declaring the great provocation and danger of spiritual pride, and a self-righteous disposition; yet much insisting on the necessity and importance of inherent holiness, and the practice of piety . . . wonderfully adapting his discourse to persons, seasons and occasions.[12]

10. WJE 4:247–48.

11. For an extended discussion of JE's ideas on the necessity of intellectual substance in sermons, see his sermon, *The Importance and Advantage of a Thorough Knowledge of Divine Truth*, in WJE 22:80–102.

12. *Christ the Example of Ministers*, WJE 25:339.

If a congregation could "hear and stand it out" under such preaching, there would probably be little hope for the English language as an instrument of salvation.

The Sermon in Edwards' Hands

The development and ultimate deterioration of the sermon form in Edwards' hands will be discussed shortly, but now an attempt must be made to define the formal limits of the Edwardsean sermon at the zenith of its development during the late 1720s, the 1730s, and the very early 1740s (and whenever Edwards had an important preaching occasion in subsequent years and returned to that form and style).[13] This sermon is a formal literary unit consisting of three main divisions, Text, Doctrine, and Application. There is only one significant variation in the form, which is called a "lecture." The lecture is differentiated from the sermon only through the altered proportions in the Doctrine and Application. For whereas in the sermon the Application is usually a little longer than the Doctrine and often several times as long, in the lecture the Doctrine is substantially longer than the Application. Perhaps the best-known instance of the lecture variant is *A Divine and Supernatural Light* (1734), which has a doctrine of twenty-three pages, and an Application of a little over three pages in the first edition.

Otherwise, so far as *form* is concerned, a sermon is a sermon—whether pastoral, imprecatory, occasional, doctrinal, or whatever.[14] Of course, this does not mean that the form was ever so fixed as to restrict variations; indeed, there were always so many variations that the very identity of the sermon as a literary form seems at times threatened. If the variations possible within the three main divisions are considered, however, it is evident that Edwards never lost sight of the paradigm.

13. The recovery in the early 1980s of JE's original MS of the *Farewell Sermon* (1750) provided confirmation that, though he employed scrap paper in all late sermons, JE returned to writing out all sermons he considered important.

14. Sermons based upon Old Testament texts tend to have longer Doctrines than those based upon New Testament texts, resulting in some lessening of emphasis upon Application in Old Testament-text sermons. This phenomenon seems to result from a necessity for relating Old Testament materials to the gospel message, which is effected in the Doctrine.

Text

The Text begins the sermon, invariably with the Scripture passage upon which the formal structure of the sermon rests. Indeed, it is the verse citation of the initial Scripture passage, rather than a word or phrase from the doctrine, that identifies a sermon when it is referred to in Edwards' notebooks. There is no exordium or introduction before the reading of the Scripture text, and there need not be any explication or exegesis after it, if the meaning is obvious, in order to have a complete Text. In the vast majority of sermons, however, there is a brief passage (a page, more or less) of comment and explication following the scriptural passage which Edwards designates the Opening of the Text. The Opening consists of several brief, numbered heads, frequently designated "Observation" or "Inference," in which Edwards defines difficult terms, cites other Scripture passages that parallel or complement the textual passage, and generally explains its meaning. In explication, he is never pedantic, even on those rare occasions when he introduces Hebrew or Greek words to clarify definitions; he explains carefully, but does not belabor small points. Indeed, some students of Edwards have felt the Opening of the Text to be the finest part of the sermon because of Edwards' remarkable ability to narrate the statements and events of the text as immediate experience, and in his narrations he not infrequently displays the talent of a first-rate journalist or novelist. But his narrations present concise sketches rather than murals, and the Text is never long.

Doctrine

Following the Text is the Doctrine, a major portion of most sermons and, structurally, often the most complex. The Doctrine usually begins with a single statement of doctrine, carefully labeled "Doc[trine]." In his inclination to formulate the entire doctrinal message of the sermon in a single statement of doctrine, Edwards was, it seems, a little unusual for his day. Most contemporary preachers tended to formulate two or more equally important statements and list them in parallel at the head of the Doctrine. Although it is Edwards' custom to draw two, three, or four Propositions or Observations from the doctrine immediately after its statement, thus dividing it for "clearing" or full discussion in the body of the Doctrine, the single statement of doctrine brings the entire sermon into a sharp thematic focus, like light rays passing through a lens, if only for a vivid moment.

But there need be no formal statement of doctrine at all. Sometimes, when the Scripture text is a clear, concise statement of thesis in itself and in need of no explication, Text and Doctrine elide and the Scripture quotation becomes the statement of doctrine, or, as Edwards puts it, the doctrine is "supplied." At other times, though rarely in Edwards' best days of preaching, there is no statement labeled "Doc[trine]," but only one or two propositions.[15] In such cases, the Proposition differs not at all from the usual statement of doctrine, unless it be a little less assertive in tone.

After the statement of doctrine and the division of the statement into Propositions, Edwards takes up the propositions, explaining the import of each and developing its implications through Inquiries, Observations, Arguments, and plain numbered heads. Each Proposition is also "proved" through Reasons. The term "reason" is actually a generic term for all "proofs" under the Doctrine, and Edwards does not frequently use it as the name for a particular head. The proofs of the doctrine are of two basic types: citations of Scripture (often attended with interpretation), and appeals to human reason and commonplace experience.

Most of the time, particularly in the shorter and middle-length sermons, the Doctrine ends with the giving of various reasons or proofs. However, each Proposition may have its own Use, Improvement, or Application, especially in the longer sermons. This occurs most often when the various propositions have quite different practical implications, and Edwards feels compelled to spell out the different duties implied by each Proposition. However, these uses are within the division of the Doctrine and are not to be confused with the third main division of the sermon. In sermons where such "doctrinal uses" are employed, Edwards often differentiates them from the third main division by calling it the "Application of the Whole."

15. A hallmark of the Stockbridge Indian sermons is that, whether written out or in bare outline, they have nothing labeled "Doc[trine]," but only Propositions or Observations, despite being virtual synopses of earlier sermons which had formal statements of doctrine.

Application

The Application (or Improvement or Use) is the largest of the three main divisions of the sermon (except in the lecture variant), and in long sermons it may be several times as long as the Text and Doctrine together. It is usually marked by a significant alteration in tone and rhetoric, and by a comparatively simple structure; for whereas the Text and Doctrine are concerned with theory, principle, and precept, the Application is concerned with experience and practice. The Application is directed to specific thoughts, attitudes, and actions of living human beings, and it gives specific advice on these attitudes and actions, in poignant language, in the light of the sermon's doctrine. But as employed by Edwards, the Application also has a subtler use as is indicated by his own statement in this transitional passage between the Doctrine and Application of Genesis 19:14.

> The Improvement we shall make of this doctrine shall be to offer some considerations to make future punishment seem real to you.

In effect, then, the Application is a period of hypothetical experience for Edwards' auditory, a time of living imaginatively, through a "willing suspension of disbelief," a series of fictive experiences created and controlled by the preacher.

Uses

The Application or Improvement is generally structured by division into several Uses. Most of the time, the term "use" is restricted to serving as the categorical name for main heads under the division of "Application" or "Improvement," paralleling "reasons" in the Doctrine. (The two division names, incidentally, are used interchangeably, though "Application" appears to be the favored term after the first few years of preaching.) Thus, there is frequently a Use of Self-examination, or a Use of Consolation, and up to four or five such "specialized" uses, though the concluding use is most often the Use of Exhortation. Each Use is subdivided by Inquiries, Considerations, and plain numbered heads, and a list of Considerations or Directions generally concludes the Use of Exhortation.

There are several "paired" heads, such as Objection-Consideration, Enquiry-Answer, and Positive-Negative, that may appear under any one of the three major divisions of the sermon as they are needed, as may such heads as Inference, Observation, or Inquiry. In fact, it should be noted that the minor heads are generally employed in a very flexible way, and are inserted wherever they fit. Few are used only in the Text, Doctrine, or the Application.

In order to have a complete Edwardsean sermon, then, there must be an identifying passage of Scripture at the beginning and an Application (of the whole) at the end; in the middle, there must be a doctrinal discussion of the Bible text, though not necessarily an Opening of the Text or an explicitly labeled "Doc[trine]." The minimal requirements are comparatively easy to describe; the difficulties arise when one attempts to define the "outer limits" of the sermon form.

First, there is the problem of literary form versus pulpit performance. Edwards sometimes speaks of a single preaching session in the pulpit, and that portion of a long sermon that might be preached in one session, as "a sermon"; but he also speaks of a complex literary unit, which includes several clearly marked preaching units within it, as "a sermon." Apparently he was not alone in his ambiguity, for in several eighteenth-century editions his longer sermons are printed as a series of sermons (according to preaching units) rather than as the single long sermons that, according to the form, they are. Such printing conventions preserve the root sense of the Latin *sermo* which means "talk"; moreover, they preserve the spirit of the seventeenth-century New England sermon as a speech act only incidentally preserved in print. When editing his own sermons for the press, however, Edwards scrupulously called sermons of more than one preaching unit "discourses," as in *Discourses on Various Important Subjects*, where some pieces are of one preaching unit and others of more. Modern readers especially must treat the Text-Doctrine-Application unit—however long—as a literary unit: otherwise, they will probably miss theme, logic, and form altogether.

Even when one admits that a sermon may be of any length, as long as it is carefully constructed, without losing its formal unity, there is the complication created by the "paired sermons" and the sermon series. In the case of the paired sermons, Edwards may write two sermons on the same text to be preached in series; however, they share nothing, not even the Opening of the Text, beyond the initial Scripture text. Obviously they are two sermons, though they may, if they are brief, be delivered on the same day. Then there is the variant in which Edwards announces two doctrines in two sermons, but develops only the first doctrine in the first sermon and only the second doctrine in the second sermon. Again, though the sermons are obviously meant to go together, they are formally separated. Such variations, when multiplied, led to the several sermon series which Edwards wrote and preached in the 1730s, including the one presented here.

Obviously, somewhere between the morning-and-afternoon sermon, divided between the Doctrine and the Application so that it could fill the entire Sabbath-day services, and the over-two-hundred-page, thirty-preaching-unit sermon series, the form of the sermon begins to disintegrate. Edwards became a master of his inherited sermon form, but in the 1730s, at the zenith of his mastery, he began experimenting artistically with the sermon. He apparently did everything he could do without actually abandoning the old form entirely, and the only possible conclusion one can draw from the manuscript evidence of his experiments is that he was searching, consciously or unconsciously, for a formal alternative to the sermon itself.

INTRODUCTION
Historical Context

Bryan McCarthy

A TIME BETWEEN REVIVALS

THE YEARS BETWEEN THE REVIVALS OF 1734–35 AND 1740–41 CONSTI-
tute an important, though often overlooked, period in the life and
thought of Jonathan Edwards. For one, as historian and Edwards editor
Ava Chamberlain notes, this stage marks the beginning of the mature
Edwards' practice of preaching treatises from the pulpit in the form of
extended sermon series, including the series presented here, *True and
False Christians*, a nineteen-unit discourse on the Parable of the Wise
and Foolish Virgins.[1] This, and other factors, makes these years instructive for the study of Edwards' life and thought in the context of the years
that preceded and followed it.

In 1734, the First Church of Springfield, Massachusetts, located
fifteen to twenty miles south of Edwards' church in Northampton,
sought to replace its recently deceased minister with Robert Breck, a
young Harvard graduate with a reputation for questionable behavior
and liberal theology.[2] In response to this development, Edwards and

1. Ava Chamberlain, "Editor's Introduction," in *The Works of Jonathan Edwards, 18,
The "Miscellanies," 501–832* (New Haven: Yale University Press, 2000), 6.

2. WJE 18:3–4. See also the "Editor's Introduction" in *The Works of Jonathan
Edwards, 12, Ecclesiastical Writings*, edited by David D. Hall (New Haven: Yale
University Press, 1994), 4–17, and George M. Marsden, *Jonathan Edwards: A Life* (New
Haven: Yale University Press, 2003), 177, the latter of which notes that Breck had been
dismissed for stealing books, to which he later confessed, and had publicly speculated
concerning the possibility of heathens being saved out of love for virtue itself without

five other members of the Hampshire Association of clergy would later lobby against Breck's ordination. For the time being, however, Edwards addressed the problem more generally, penning his two-part lecture on justification, in which he sought to counter Arminian ideas associated with Breck and others.[3]

Then, in December 1734, Edwards preached on the preciousness of time, exhorting young people and others to awaken from their slothful and wicked condition and look to eternal matters.[4] Shortly thereafter, revival ensued in Northampton. In his 1737 chronicle, *A Faithful Narrative of the Surprising Work of God*, Edwards described the situation thus: "[T]he Spirit of God began extraordinarily to set in, and wonderfully to work amongst us; and there were, very suddenly, one after another, five or six persons who were to all appearance savingly converted, and some of them wrought upon in a very remarkable manner."[5]

This spiritual awakening was not to endure, however. Just five months later, in May 1735, Edwards' Northampton congregation witnessed what he later identified as the gradual withdrawal of God's Spirit.[6] This withdrawal, Edwards surmised, was evident in the suicide of his uncle, Joseph Hawley, as well as in the "strange enthusiastic delusions" of two church members in nearby towns and in the general spiritual decline of the region.[7] To Edwards' mind, subsequent temporal concerns like Governor Jonathan Belcher's visit to make peace with several Indian tribes, the ongoing controversy over Breck's ordination, and plans for a new meetinghouse further distracted his congregation from religious matters.

---

faith in or knowledge of Christ.

3. *Justification by Faith Alone*, in WJE 19:147–242.

4. *The Preciousness of Time*, in WJE 19:246–61.

5. *Faithful Narrative*, in WJE 4:149. JE's phrase "to all appearance" here betrays his belief that many of those who were seemingly converted during the revival but subsequently "fell away" were never, in fact, so wrought upon, a theme to which this study will devote considerable attention.

6. WKE 4:206.

7. WJE 4:206–7. One such delusion involved a layman in South Hadley feeling divinely instructed to have a friend in dire circumstances pray Ps. 116:4. Edwards emphatically believed that such "extraordinary" or "miraculous" gifts, which St. Paul describes in I Cor. 12, had ceased with the close of the apostolic age and had no reason to return. See the second, fourteenth, and fifteenth sermons of *Charity and Its Fruits*, in *The Works of Jonathan Edwards, 8, Ethical Writings*, edited by Paul Ramsey (New Haven: Yale University Press, 1989), 149–73, 351–97.

Though absent of spiritual vigor, the following years were fairly eventful for Edwards and Northampton. The minor pamphlet exchange over Breck's ordination culminated in a 1737 tract by Edwards and his brother-in-law, Samuel Hopkins of Springfield, entitled, *A Letter to the Author of the Pamphlet Called an Answer to the Hampshire Narrative*. Moreover, December of that year saw the completion and dedication of a new meetinghouse whose seating arrangement gave priority to affluence rather than age and "usefulness," a development Edwards criticized. Then, in March 1738, Northampton voted to build a town hall for precinct and court sessions. This maneuver separated church and state affairs and, along with the new meetinghouse's disputed seating plan, signaled a departure from tradition, where ecclesiastical and political spheres were intertwined. Last, Edwards published his final texts commemorating the Connecticut Valley revival of 1734–35: *Discourses on Various Important Subjects*, a collection of five sermons from the awakening, and the third, definitive edition of *A Faithful Narrative*, corrected by Edwards and published in Boston.

The spiritual respite that settled in in 1735 continued until 1740, when the itinerant preacher George Whitefield circulated throughout the region, inciting churches to revival. Within those years lies a formative period for Edwards, centered on late 1737 to early 1739. During these months, he sought to galvanize his indolent, backslidden congregants with forceful, increasingly ambitious and extended sermons, among them the sermonic treatises on the virgins parable as well as the familiar *Charity and Its Fruits*.[8]

THEMES IN 1737–38

Since the concerns and issues of foregoing years naturally informed Edwards' sermons during this period, it is somewhat artificial to segregate a fifteen-month or so piece of his preaching life for study. Nevertheless, a few prominent and distinctive themes do emerge from this time and form the groundwork for much of Edwards' later ministry. The first, intimated above, is his emphasis on the danger of "falling away" or "backsliding." The spirituality of the 1734–35 converts was evaporating and Edwards worked to counteract the problem in

---

8. Also in 1738, JE revised and republished *Justification by Faith Alone*, his two-part lecture preceding the revival of 1734–35; WJE 19:143–242.

both major sermon treatises as well as various stand-alone sermons throughout the year.[9] As he put it in his August 1738 sermon on Neh. 2:20, "Throughout this land and also in the other England, great notice has been taken of the great work that was here wrought and the profession we make. And the account that was sent over to London of it has already had two impressions." "But," he later wonders, "have there not been many things amongst us that have tended to pull [the city of God] down? . . . If we strictly examine all our behavior this two or three years past, have we not done more to pull down than to build up?"[10] To address this predicament, Edwards counseled his congregants to "examine wherein you are guilty of declining or backsliding" and, for "those that are awake, take care; don't fall asleep."[11]

A second theme also surfaces continually in Edwards' sermons of 1737–38: that of distinguishing worldly, carnal happiness from divine happiness. Worldly fulfillment, Edwards says, lies in self-interestedness, in attaining worldly enjoyments and carnal interests: food, drink, clothing, status, wealth, sex. In contrast, the latter, proper happiness, which conversely entails self-denial and world-renunciation, is "that rest and delight that an intelligent being has in the absence of evil and possession of its proper good." In humanity's case, this good is Christ as Savior and portion, an infinitely more excellent prize than the temporal fulfillments humans normally pursue.[12] For Edwards, true happiness has its origin, authorship, and continual source in God, "a being possessed of the most absolutely perfect happiness" by virtue of being absolutely free of evil and in absolute possession of himself, his own proper good. In and from this fountain of goodness and grace, humankind finds its own happiness.[13]

---

9. For explicit mentions of Northampton backsliding, often in light of the 1734–35 revival, see below, p. 96; sermon two in *Charity and Its Fruits*, WJE 8:149–73; MS Sermon on I Pet. 1:19 (no. 456, Jan. 1738); MS Sermon on Gen. 39:12 (no. 464, Mar. 1738); MS Sermon on Prov. 9:12 (no. 474, May 1738); MS Sermon on Jer. 2:5 (no. 468, Apr. 1738); and MS Sermon on Neh. 2:20 (no. 484, Aug. 1738), in WJEO 53.

10. MS Sermon on Neh. 2:20 (no. 484, Aug. 1738), in WJEO 53. The "account" JE refers to here is his *Faithful Narrative*.

11. See below, pp. 96, 100.

12. MS Lecture on Matt. 10:39 (no. 466, Mar. 1738), in WJEO 53.

13. MS Sermon on I Tim. 6:15 (no. 494, Nov. 1738), in WJEO 53. See also *The Terms of Prayer*, WJE 19:774, where JE states, "Nor is it possible that the happiness of any creature should be in any proportion to the happiness of God, because God's

Edwards further distinguishes these fulfillments according to their respective ends: temporal and eternal ruin for those seeking worldly pleasure, temporal and eternal good for those seeking godly pleasure. In this regard, Edwards' sermon on Prov. 9:12 cautions, "Such is the nature of those ways [contrary to God's directives], that they don't only deserve ruin but also naturally tend to bring it on."[14] The point becomes even clearer in his comments on Matt. 10:39, where he calls attention to the irony that, in seeking happiness through worldly enjoyments and carnal interests, one "brings on himself the reverse of what he seeks": destruction rather than salvation; pain instead of pleasure; vexation and disquiet rather than ease and peace; bondage instead of liberty; inflammation of thirst instead of quenching it.[15] The ruin is not merely eternal, however, for Edwards points out that "Many of those ways [contrary to God's directives] tend to men's temporal ruin and, very commonly, are the occasions of it, but they have an inevitable tendency to his spiritual ruin, supposing that his being be continued and God is not pleased to annihilate him to his eternal ruin." In other words, self-interestedly pursuing worldly enjoyments and carnal interests rather than Christ as Savior and portion results not only in an unfulfilled existence in this life, but also in the eternal misery of hell.

Conversely, Edwards teaches that following God's directives in pursuit of Christ as the proper good leads to temporal and eternal contentment. For example, in his sermon on Prov. 19:12 he argues that God's commands ultimately aim for our safety, preservation, and prosperity. "In all that God requires of us and counsels us to in religion," Edwards states, "he does but direct us to be friendly to ourselves"; and later, "the practice of the duties God requires of us naturally tends to our prosperity . . . tends in its own nature to our happiness." As with pursuing

---

happiness is infinite, and the happiness of a creature cannot be any more than finite." See also the same sermon (WJE 19:779–82), and the seventh sermon of *Charity and Its Fruits* (WJE 8:269), where JE offers an extended discussion on the proper pursuit of happiness: "When you are required not to be selfish you are not required, as has already been observed, not to love and seek your own happiness. You are required not mainly to seek your private and confined interest. But if you place your happiness in God, and in glorifying him and serving him by doing good, in this way, above all others, will you promote your own wealth, and your own honor and pleasure, and durable riches, and obtain a crown of glory, and pleasures forevermore."

14. MS Sermon on Prov. 9:12 (no. 474, May 1738), in WJEO 53.
15. MS Lecture on Matt. 10:39 (no. 466, March 1738), in WJEO 53.

worldly pleasure, however, the result is not merely temporal; practicing the duties required of us "will, by God's free promise, issue in our eternal happiness and glory."[16] Self-denial, denying the world in pursuit of Christ, brings both temporal fulfillment and an eternity of contentment in heaven.

In addition to these two themes of falling away and worldly versus godly happiness, there is a third, even more prominent theme: the need for distinguishing true and false Christians. Edwards devotes the whole of *True and False Christians*, his series on the parable of the wise and foolish virgins, to this purpose, and further elaborates on it in *Charity and Its Fruits* and a number of the stand-alone sermons that surround them.

TRUE AND FALSE CHRISTIANITY: THE WISE AND FOOLISH VIRGINS

In the series delivered on the parable from Matthew 25 during the winter of 1737–38, Edwards is at pains to distinguish true Christians from hypocrites who pretend to Christianity but do not have the Spirit of grace operating within them.[17] He was eager to win back lapsed converts, or show them they were never truly converted in the first place. Thus, while he first acknowledged, and lamented, that true and false Christians were comparable in certain respects, he subsequently proceeded to set the two apart.

Edwards was by no means the only preacher in colonial New England to hold forth at length on this parable. Most influential for

16. MS Sermon on Prov. 9:12 (no. 474, May 1738), in WJEO 53. See also MS Lecture on Matt. 10:39 (no. 466, Mar. 1738), where JE speaks of "how great a thing it is to be a Christian indeed"; and MS Sermon on Ps. 23:2 (no. 483, July 1738); and MS Sermon on I Tim. 6:15 (no. 494, Nov. 1738), in WJEO 53.

17. As Norman Fiering (*Moral Philosophy at Seventeenth Century Harvard* [Chapel Hill: University of North Carolina Press, 1981], 172) and Paul Ramsey (WJE 8:61, n. 8, and 181, n. 8) point out, in referring to false Christians as "hypocrites," JE does not accuse them of deliberate falsification but of not knowing their own hearts. Furthermore, Edwards stresses that it is not the presence of hypocrisy that characterizes a hypocrite but its exclusive presence, i.e., the absence of any sincerity. As he puts it in the third sermon of *Charity and Its Fruits* (WJE 8:181), "Doubtless if we examine ourselves aright, we may see abundance of hypocrisy; but is there any sincerity? . . . Though there be a great deal of hypocrisy, yet if there be any sincerity, that little sincerity shall not be rejected because there is so much hypocrisy with it." Ramsey (WJE 8:182, n. 8) suggests this is indicative of JE's view that the Christian life is always one *on the way* to holiness.

Edwards was *The Parable of the Ten Virgins Opened & Applied*, preached by Thomas Shepard at his church of Cambridge, Massachusetts, from 1636 to 1640, and posthumously published in 1660. Those familiar with New England religious history know that Shepard's delivery coincided with the so-called Antinomian Controversy, which began when Anne Hutchinson, a member of John Cotton's church at Boston, began to teach laymen and women. Purporting to explain Cotton's sermons, she taught that justification and assurance are based only on Christ and not dependent on obedience to God's commandments, and that the recipient of grace, by virtue of the presence of the Holy Spirit, was beyond the law. Her following grew to the point that the authorities, feeling threatened for theological and political reasons, put her on trial and banished her.[18] Shepard's *Parable of the Ten Virgins* was a critical response to antinomianism, pointing out the differences between saints and "evangelical hypocrites," and the characteristics of saving and common grace. With the rise of a new kind of antinomianism during the eighteenth-century revivals, Shepard's discourse was formative not only for Edwards' *Treatise Concerning Religious Affections* of 1746, but also for his own, earlier series on the parable.[19]

Edwards begins his discourse on the parable by asserting a distinction between true Christians and hypocrites, noting that while both will rush out to meet Christ "after the midnight cry" at the end of days, only the former will be received. An extended explication of how Christ is espoused to the church, the sermons comprising the introduction use the analogy of a marriage covenant to show how Christ is the bridegroom of the parable, with professors of Christianity represented by the two sets

18. The literature on Hutchinson, the Antinomian Controversy, and the prominence of antinomian, familist, and radical thought within the puritan movement is large; for representative studies, see *The Antinomian controversy, 1636–1638: A Documentary History*, edited by David D. Hall (Middletown, CT: Wesleyan University Press, 1968); Eve LaPlante, *American Jezebel: The Uncommon Life of Anne Hutchinson, the Woman who Defied the Puritans* (San Francisco: Harper, 2004); Theodore Dwight Bozeman, *The Precisianist Strain: Disciplinary Religion and Antinomian Backlash in Puritanism to 1638* (Chapel Hill, NC: University of North Carolina Press, 2004); Michael Winship, *Times and Trials of Anne Hutchinson: Puritans Divided* (Lawrence, KS: University Press of Kansas, 2005).

19. William K. B. Stoever, "The Godly Will's Discerning: Shepard, Edwards, and the Identification of True Godliness," in *The Writings of Jonathan Edwards: Text, Context, and Interpretation*, edited by Stephen J. Stein (Bloomington: Indiana University Press, 1996), 85–99.

of virgins. Edwards goes on to apply this union by demonstrating that the saints' oneness with Christ—or justification—is achieved through faith. But how to distinguish the true saint from the false within the visible church, which is made up of both? This is the question that Edwards pursues through much of the series.

Inevitably, as Edwards asserts in the first proposition, the visible church is made up of both the elect and "false professors." Hypocrisy and self-deception in the human heart, and an inability to search the hearts of others, insure this earthly commingling. Only when Christ appears as the head of the church at the Day of Judgment will the true saints be fully revealed and gathered in, and the reprobates confirmed in their sins. Consequently, those who "go about to make a separation between true and false Christians in the world" make a grave mistake, because they presume to act the part of God. The present state of the church is not its last state; therefore, the concern of individuals should be to see to their own souls.

Edwards moves on to consider similarities and differences between the two sorts. Under the second proposition, he observes that they are alike and unalike in both godliness and ungodliness. They agree in profession and external duties, in sharing the same society, entertaining the same hopes, seeking the same heaven. Even Judas, who betrayed Jesus, resembled a true saint in these regards. True and false Christians sometimes agree in their appearances of godliness, such as a profession of special experiences, or having many religious affections, or being exact in their "walk," confident of their good estate and of their being received into the charity of true Christians. "Improving" these points, Edwards warns his hearers that they must be careful with respect to the grounds of their hopes of salvation. "[A] man, that moment that he settles it with himself that he is in a good estate, he may eternally undo himself, and as effectually as he would have killed his body, if he had that moment run a sword through his own throat." He then embarks in a long list of things that believers should not rely on as signs of their election, including profession, duties, society, and affections.

Edwards then embarks on a series of points, each with its own Application, on the similarities of true and false Christians. Sometimes, he observes, they agree through the infirmities and failings of true Christians. There is, after all, still an "abundance of corruption" in the hearts of Christians, even after they are converted. "Corruption,"

Edwards asserts, "is done away no further than grace prevails." Godly individuals still have love to sin; they have "two principles" warring in them. As Chamberlain puts it in her study of this discourse, "Hypocrites resemble saints because they are capable of a wide variety of religious beliefs and actions; saints resemble hypocrites because 'there is abundance of corruption in the hearts of true Christians as well as others.'"[20]

So true Christians may sometimes resemble false in the "corrupt frames that they are in," motivated primarily by "natural principles" and feeling no different from when they were unconverted. Also, the two may agree in the "ill acts they commit." True Christians are not immune to falling into transgression and walking in evil ways. These realities should drive home the importance of circumspection: do not "cast others out of our charity too quickly" or be prejudiced against them for having the same flaws.

Another way in which true and false Christians are similar is that they can both "slumber and sleep," especially in "a time of decay of religion." At such times, individuals experience a cessation of sense and of action, both because God withdraws his Spirit and because humans influence each other in their behavior. In applying this point, Edwards becomes particularly specific in speaking to the supposed converts of the late revival, telling them to examine how they are guilty of backsliding, how they have discredited the town and the cause of religion, how they have allowed themselves to go on in practices that before they would have abhorred, and how they justify things they used to condemn. Rouse out of sleep, Edwards cries; to those that are awake, he says, stay awake, and wake those around you that are slumbering.

The sheer length of time that Christ, the Bridegroom, is taking to arrive is a "great reason" why both the wise and foolish are inattentive. But this is no excuse to be lackadaisical, Edwards tells his hearers. When Christ does come, the time spent waiting for him will seem to have been but a moment. You do not know when the Bridegroom will come, so keep alert and active. Perhaps Christ is tarrying in order to give his elect ones longer to be prepared for his coming.

20. Ava Chamberlain, "Brides of Christ and Signs of Grace: Edwards's Sermon Series on the Parable of the Wise and Foolish Virgins," in *The Writings of Jonathan Edwards*, edited by Stein, 9. In the latter half of this explanation, Chamberlain quotes the first point JE makes in support of his contention that true and false Christians are alike "through the infirmities and failings of true Christians," to which he commits the whole of his MS Sermon on Matt. 25:1–12(c) (no. 455, Jan. 1738), in WJEO 53.

Though Christians have long heard of and expected Christ's coming, the "midnight cry," which will sound when he does come, will nonetheless be "unexpected" to many, both wise and foolish. A cry, Edwards observes, is something loud, earnest, and important. But a cry at midnight is even more so, for that is the time when no one expects such a thing, when people are in the deepest sleep and least active. Thus the midnight cry will be surprising to both sinners and to slumbering saints.

Having shown how true and false Christians agree in this world, Edwards moves on to show how they will agree in another world. They will then "agree in the conviction that they have of the truth of divine and eternal things," and agree in the "value and importance of such things." Natural and godly persons will then agree in wishing to be in the same state as the godly, being ready to seek it, and in bewailing their lack of opportunity to do so. Edwards exhorts listeners to apply this to their own lives, to examine themselves to see if they will think differently of their lives in another world than they do now. If they are not convinced of divine truths now, they will be then. But having knowledge in another world will only aggravate misery. Come to a right judgment now, while there is time, Edwards counsels, and while there are "advantages" (i.e., a time of the work of the Spirit) for doing so.

The rest of the series concerns the differences between true Christians and hypocrites. First, the wise have oil in their spiritual vessels, their hearts, while the others do not. This oil represents a principle in their heart that is spiritual and abiding. It brings a new nature to the soul by virtue of things it "tends to" and the things that agree with it, as much as the things it "resists and opposes." This oil identifies their Christian spirit, which guides their judgments and choices. While this oil or principle is a gift of the Holy Spirit, it is also something saints "procure" by seeking it. Having this oil, in the end, makes a "radical difference," such that the two greatly differ in their general character. The consequences of having this oil respect one's behavior, present state, and state of glory. With respect to behavior, true Christians' external religion will not fail in times of trial, which comes with the nature of the new principle and the nature of God's covenant to believers. With respect to the present state, true Christians will see their hopes endure, brightened, and brought to fruition. After applying these consequences, Edwards considers their difference with respect to a state of glory, a state to which true Christians will be admitted to enjoy the approval, power, and glory of Christ, and to enter into the heavenly feast. False Christians, on the other hand, will be shut out, with no part or portion in Christ, cast into darkness, abhorred and rejected by Christ. Edwards warns foolish virgins in his congregation to seek that glory of true Christians, who shall have perfect rest, bounty, kingly glory, perfect satisfaction, and perfect assurance of the eternity of their happiness.

Edwards ends his discourse by distinguishing the general character of true Christians from that of hypocrites.[21] The former, he says, keep oil in their lamps, prepare for the coming of Christ, and attain grace, whereas the latter eschew all of these endeavors. The one is gracious and steadfast, the other ungrateful and fickle—in a word, wise and foolish.

CHARITY AND ITS FRUITS

Edwards most likely finished his series on the wise and foolish virgins sometime in March, and promptly took up his second extended sermon series, *Charity and Its Fruits*, on 1 Corinthians 13, from April to October 1738. The text of this series is widely available and a number of good studies of its meaning and significance exist.[22] For our purposes here, it is important to discuss *Charity and Its Fruits* because it echoes the central concern of *True and False Christians*, and therefore is instructive to understanding Edwards' discourse on the wise and foolish virgins.

Edwards opens his second sermon series where he left off with the first, offering the following Doctrine in sermon one of the Charity Discourse: "All that virtue which is saving, and distinguishing of true Christians from others, is summed up in Christian or divine love."[23] With this statement, Edwards constructs the framework for interpreting Paul's highly celebrated meditation on Christian love in terms of his prior concern for distinguishing true and false Christians. For Edwards, it is not so much *duty* that characterizes the New Testament ethic, but

21. MS Sermon on Matt. 25:1–12(i) (no. 463, Feb./Mar. 1738), in WJEO 53.

22. See, for example, Paul Ramsey, "Editor's Introduction," in WJE 8:1–121; Roland A. Delattre, "The Theological Ethics of Jonathan Edwards: An Homage to Paul Ramsey," *Journal of Religious Ethics* 19 (Fall 1991), 71–102; John E. Smith, *Jonathan Edwards: Puritan, Preacher, Philosopher* (London: Geoffrey Chapman, 1992); and John E. Smith, "Christian Virtue and Common Morality," in *The Princeton Companion to Jonathan Edwards*, edited by Sang Hyun Lee (Princeton: Princeton University Press, 2005), 147–66.

23. WJE 8:131.

love.[24] Thus, professions of faith that merely assent and do not involve the heart's consent are not saving or indicative of a genuine disciple. Similarly, if a supposed virtue lacks the Spirit of love as described in 1 Corinthians 13, it is hypocritical and not truly Christian. By such assertions, Edwards means to say that faith professions and virtuous action should emanate from love of God. True Christians profess trust in God because they love God. In the same way, they act virtuously towards other human beings because the latter are like God, if only in the sense of being made in his image, or are children of God, whom true Christians love.[25] Thus, in applying the first sermon of *Charity*, Edwards says one can tell a genuine disciple by the presence of love for God and people, even enemies, and the absence of proud, revengeful resentment.[26]

In the third sermon, Edwards continues his campaign against dutiful but loveless action as a phenomenon characteristic of false Christianity: things of a moral nature, he declares, are nothing without charity. As paradigmatic evidence, he cites the religious performances of Paul before his conversion and the willingness to suffer and even die exhibited by martyrs of false religions. Mere external performance is unacceptable. Rather, Edwards suggests, one must have an internal "sincerity of heart," a love of God and his creatures that motivates the things one says and does. As he puts it in the sermon's doctrinal exposition, "Whatever is done or suffered, yet if the heart is withheld, there is nothing really given to God."[27] Even stronger, "Let what may be done and suffered, if there be no sincerity of heart, it is all but an offering to some idol."[28] Edwards ends his discussion of hypocritical action in the sermon by delineating the features of the sincerity he recommends instead: truth, freedom, integrity, and purity. What appears outwardly should also appear in the heart.

Edwards' burden for distinguishing true and false Christians remains throughout the rest of the series, sometimes as a secondary point, sometimes as the principal concern. For example, in sermon four, he

24. WJE 8:143.

25. WJE 8:133–34. This is not to say JE never stresses duty; he often does, indeed, several times in *Charity*. He never intends mere observance, however. Rather, the desire to do the right thing must flow from love for God.

26. WJE 8:142ff.

27. WJE 8:179.

28. WJE 8:181.

reiterates his emphasis on internality, prominent in the third *Charity* sermon and in *True and False Christians*: the meek forbearance of injury indicative of true Christianity must not be merely external but occur with and because of love in the heart.[29] Later, Edwards treats the true and false Christian theme more fully, devoting the whole of sermon thirteen to it. There, he offers the Doctrine, "True Christian grace is that which nothing that opposes it can overthrow."[30] False grace, he says, is superficial, allowing it to wither, but true grace reaches the bottom of the heart, consisting in a new nature, and therefore perseveres. In his Application, he accordingly reasons, "Hence, we may infer that those whose seeming grace fails, and is overthrown, may conclude they never had any true grace."[31] This verdict of Edwards', like many others in 1738, was probably aimed at those who seemingly converted during the 1734–35 revival but were, by now, backslidden.

Even when the consideration of true and false Christians is neither a secondary point nor the principal concern, it is often present as an implicit force determining the language Edwards uses to address another subject. For example, he frequently qualifies terms like "Christian love," "lovers of God," and "greatness of soul" with adjectives such as "true" and "sincere."[32] Edwards' doctrine for the fifth *Charity* sermon, an exposition on the biblical declaration "charity envieth not," for another example, states that "A *truly* Christian spirit is opposite to an envious spirit."[33] Similarly, in sermon six, Edwards states that "when God is *truly* loved, he is loved as an infinite superior."[34] Further still, sermons eight through twelve present a litany of such qualifiers. Edwards' incidental use of words like "true," "saving," and "sincere" reinforces the dichotomy of true and false Christian that he delineates more explicitly at other points in *Charity*.

Moreover, in describing what is inconsistent with truly Christian love, Edwards often uses the word "hypocritical": "Whatever performances or seeming virtues there are without love are insincere and

---

29. WJE 8:190.

30. WJE 8:341.

31. WJE 8:349.

32. Among many passages in *Charity*, see WJE 8:184, 195, 200.

33. WJE 8:219 (ed. italics). See I Cor. 13:4 for the scripture.

34. WJE 8:245 (ed. italics).

hypocritical."[35] Similarly, heaven is a "world of love," "where there is no hypocrisy or dissembling, but perfect simplicity and sincerity."[36] In other words, where true Christian love is absent, there is only hypocrisy, and where there is only true Christian love, hypocrisy is absent. Hypocrites do not love in the truly Christian sense. This language parallels that which Edwards uses to characterize false Christians in both treatises. In *True and False Christians*, he says, "though the godly may be guilty of great declinings in times of trial, yet their religion can't be said to fail as the religion of hypocrites is wont to do at such times. . . . [A] man comes to leave strict religion out of a real dislike and distaste of it, and to quit the laborious parts of religion and those things in it that are contrary to his own interest."[37] Then, in *Charity and Its Fruits*, Edwards dwells on the Apostle Paul's assertion that love "beareth all things" by saying something quite similar about love's opposite: "Hypocrites may and often do make a great show of religion in profession and words which are cheap, and in those actions in which there is no great difficulty or suffering; but they have not a suffering spirit. . . . They do all which they do in religion from a selfish spirit, and commonly very much for their temporal interest, as the Pharisees did."[38]

All of this analysis suggests that, in *Charity and Its Fruits*, Edwards attempts to present Christian love as the spiritual telltale, winnowing hypocrites from true Christians. In such a light, *True and False Christians* and *Charity* form complementary homiletical efforts that explore the distinctions between true and false Christians and then show those distinctions to hinge on love. It becomes evident, then, that rousing the Northampton congregants to consider whether they were true believers was Edwards' main concern in 1738. This conclusion finds further support in the manner in which the true-and-false-Christian dichotomy also surfaces in an abundance of the regular, stand-alone sermons Edwards gave that year.

35. WJE 8:137.
36. WJE 8:368, 385.
37. See below, p. 191.
38. WJE 8:315.

TRUE AND FALSE CHRISTIANS IN A SAMPLING OF
OTHER SERMONS

The series presented here is, by itself, a considerable and important statement by Edwards. However, seeing it in context with other sermons,
such as *Charity and Its Fruits* and other shorter ones from the period
illustrates Edwards' modulation and extension of themes developed in
True and False Christians. Here, we will review just a few representative
sermons to show how they interact with the longer discourse.

A sermon on Gen. 39:12, preached just after the completion of *True
and False Christians*, expounds on the story of Joseph and his master's
wife. According to this pericope, Joseph one day enters the house to work
and no one is home except the master's wife. When she sees Joseph, she
grabs him by the robe and implores him to sleep with her, an offer he
declines, saying he does not want to injure the master. He quickly slips
out of the garment, leaving it in her hand, and flees the premises.

Edwards begins his sermon on Joseph by emphasizing the magni-
tude of the temptation Joseph faced and lauding the exemplary character
he displayed in resisting it. In response to such behavior, Edwards offers
the doctrine, "'Tis our duty not only to avoid those things that are themselves sinful but also, as far as may be, those things that lead and expose
to sin." Iniquity, he says, is contrary to God's honor and glory, and if we
love God, we ought to avoid things that can lead us to dishonor him. "If
we han't a spirit so to do it," he furthermore offers, believers "show that,
whatever we pretend, we are not God's sincere friends and have not true
love to him."[39] In so proposing, he bolsters the distinction made in *True
and False Christians* and foreshadows a point he will later emphasize
in *Charity and Its Fruits*, according to which truly Christian action, as
distinct from hypocrisy, emanates from love of God.[40]

In his Application, Edwards confronts what he sees as the danger-
ous customs of young people in the community, encouraging the congregation to remember the revival of 1734–35. Would any "wise persons
that have truly the interest of religion at heart," he asks, rejoice if such
customs arose during the last outpouring of the Spirit, or would they
not look darkly upon them as a great danger, taking people's minds off

39. MS Sermon on Gen. 39:12 (no. 464, Mar. 1738), in WJEO 53.
40. See part two above, and the first sermon of *Charity*, in WJE 8:129–48.

of religion?[41] Edwards thus calls his people back to the true piety of the past revival for righteousness in the present.

In another sermon from March 1738, on Jer. 5:21–22, Edwards urges his congregants to cultivate a reverential rather than a sinful fear of God, the difference being that a sinful fear makes one afraid to come to God, while a reverential fear makes one afraid to go away from him. In the Application, he considers potential objections to the idea that Christians should fear God at all. One objection asserts that, once converted, believers are safe and need not be afraid of anything when it comes to God. Edwards counters that "it may be the thing that you take for granted is not true; it may be you are not converted as you suppose." Similarly, he later reminds his hearers that "there are those that think themselves to be converted and ben't converted; for as long as they remain settled on that false foundation, they are out of the way of those convictions and tremblings necessary in order to the conversion."[42]

Edwards more explicitly utilizes the language of true Christianity in his sermon on Rom. 14:8, in which he provides a host of assertions regarding "all true Christians" or "every true Christian." According to one such declaration from the third point of the Doctrine, "Every true Christian dies unto the Lord in some respect." Later in the same point, Edwards observes that those who live and die unto Christ belong to him in both their living and dying, since they have a special union with God that death cannot dissolve. And "who are these persons that are in such a happy case?" The answer: "All true Christians," and "especially those who have been eminent in the graces and labors of a Christian."[43] While he does not, in this sermon, directly discuss the true Christian's hypocritical counterpart, the great number of statements concerning the truly faithful suggests the false Christian looms large in his mind also.

As in his sermon on Gen. 39:12, Edwards alludes in his sermon on Jer. 2:5 to the revival of 1734–35, which he addresses to the Northampton congregation in April 1738. Here he speaks of a people who "formerly seemed to cleave to God and manifested a high esteem of him" but subsequently departed from faithfulness. While explaining that worship entails esteem, respect, and honor beyond what is due to

41. MS Sermon on Gen. 39:12 (no. 464, Mar. 1738), in WJEO 53. JE again alludes to the revival of 1734–35 in *Indicting God*, in WJE 19:749–67; the allusion is on p. 764.

42. MS Sermon on Jer. 5:21–22 (no. 465, Mar. 1738), in WJEO 53.

43. MS Sermon on Rom. 14:8 (no. 467, Mar. 1738), in WJEO 53.

mere creatures, he cautions that not all appearances of such esteem are truly faithful: "sometimes a professing or covenant people do in a special manner make a show of a very high esteem of God . . . either by their abounding very much outward duties of worship . . . or by their seeming affection and engagedness of heart in duties."[44] This warning hearkens back to Edwards' mistrust of the merely external Christianity of hypocrites in *True and False Christians* and anticipates the third and fourth sermons of *Charity and Its Fruits*.[45]

In April, Edwards also delivered a sermon on Heb. 13:8. The Application of this immediate precursor to *Charity and Its Fruits* explicitly evokes the dichotomy between true and false Christian in the language of the parable of the wise and foolish virgins: Christ "often denounces woe to hypocrites, and threatens . . . that those who are foolish virgins, that take their lamps and no oil with them, shall at last be shut out from the marriage when others enter in with the bridegroom."[46] He then outlines some implications of this for various categories of people. Among them are "all that have entered into the bonds of the Christian covenant and proven false to it," "those that have been seemingly pious but are fallen away," and the "truly godly . . . that have been guilty of great declension in religion." Each of these categories reinforces Edwards' true-and-false dichotomy, elaborated in the upcoming Charity Discourse.

In a two-part sermon on Neh. 2:20, a brief hiatus from *Charity and Its Fruits* half-way through its completion, Edwards encourages his congregation to build up the city of God, that is, to promote the prosperity of the church at large and foster peace between its members. Part one lists several reasons why congregants should heed this exhortation, one being that those who have no concern for the city thereby show they are not truly inhabitants of it. In other words, the people in the pews can know they are true Christians and not hypocrites if they apply themselves to furthering the church's cause. Accordingly, Edwards' Doctrine for the second part reads: "Those that are not God's true servants, and don't join in building up his church and kingdom, have no portion nor memorial in God's Jerusalem."[47]

44. WJE 19:751, 749–67.
45. See part two above, and WJE 8:174–217.
46. MS Sermon on Heb. 13:8 (no. 470, Apr. 1738), in WJEO 53.
47. MS Sermon on Heb. 13:8.

The language of true Christianity continues as he explains what he means by "portion" and "memorial." For Edwards, having a portion in God's Jerusalem denotes having a dwelling in heaven and, more fundamentally, in God:

> It is said of true Christians that God has made to set together in heavenly places in Christ (Eph. 2:6), but such persons as those [who are not God's true servants] have no dwelling place; they have none of those mansions assigned to them. God himself is said to be the dwelling place of his people; he is, as it were, a temple and a tabernacle under the court of which they dwell.[48]

Since God himself is the dwelling place, Edwards says, those who are not God's true servants "have no portion in God." Similarly, they have no memorial. That is, their names are not written in the rolls of the spiritual Jerusalem:

> Those that were of Israel . . . had a memorial in Jerusalem. They had their names written in the rolls of that city. And so have all true Christians their names written in the roles of the spiritual Jerusalem . . . Though [persons who are not God's true servants] have been written and reckoned amongst God's visible people, yet if they continue in wickedness, their names shall be blotted out.[49]

The sermon thus warns false Christians of their fate without a dwelling place in heaven and God or vestige in his memory.

A post-*Charity* on Is. 65:20 is one amongst a scattering of sermons in which Edwards addresses different age groups in the Northampton congregation.[50] Here, Edwards focuses on the elderly, asserting that the spiritual age of congregants should match or exceed their physical age. That is, he wants them to be as knowledgeable and wise, committed, and fruitful in religious matters as one would expect them to be, or more so, given their age. In the Application, he suggests this as a criterion to

---

48. MS Sermon on Heb. 13:8. In addition to citing St. Paul's letter to the Ephesians directly, JE here alludes to John 14, on which he preached eight months earlier, when the Northampton congregation seated its new meeting house (*The Many Mansions*, in WJE 19:736–46), as well as several years earlier (MS Sermon on John 14:2[a] [no. 317, Mar. 1734], in WJEO 49).

49. MS Sermon on Heb. 13:8 (no. 470, Apr. 1738), in WJEO 53.

50. MS Sermon on Is. 65:20 (no. 496, Dec. 1738), in WJEO 53. JE identified the four age groups as "childhood," "youth," "middle age," and "old age." Kenneth P. Minkema, "Old Age and Religion in the Writings and Life of Jonathan Edwards," *Church History* 70 (Dec. 2001), 681, 685.

discern the presence or absence of grace in their hearts: "Let [those that are advanced in years] examine themselves, whether or no they have any true grace. To be old and without any true grace is to be an infant of days in the worst sense; for their attainments are so small that they never yet [attain] to anything more than common." To guide the elderly in this endeavor of self-examination, Edwards lists several phenomena that might seem indicative of properly grounded faith yet actually evidence no such thing. One of these, he says, is being long settled and firmly established in one's faith: "Without doubt, many old people will be disappointed when they come to die, that had long looked on themselves to be true converts, and expected to go to heaven when they died, with an hope that had become as habitual to 'em as their mother tongue." Here again, Edwards emphasizes his distinction between true Christians and those who do not know their own unfaithful hearts.

Edwards continues to stress the dichotomy in his penultimate sermon of the year, on Matt. 11:16–19.[51] In elaborating on the Doctrine, "Wicked men are inconsistent with themselves," he says, "their outward show disagrees with their hearts." He then repeats and alludes to this point throughout the rest of the sermon, filling his exposition with terms such as "hypocrites," "dissemblers," "pretenders," and "false professors." Fairly representative of this language is his statement, "A true saint is sanctified throughout in soul and body and spirit . . . but hypocrites are monsters; they have one member like a child of God and another like a child of the devil: they may have a saint's tongue and a devil's hands; the members don't well consist together."[52]

Edwards' final sermon of the year, and the final one in our sampler, interprets 1 John 4:12 according to the categories of true and false Christians so prevalent throughout the year. Expositing on the text, he says, "The special design of this epistle seems to be to give some distinguishing marks, whereby the true Spirit may be distinguished from false spirits." Edwards supplies three of these: one who has the true Spirit confesses and testifies "that he that appeared in the flesh and was crucified, Jesus Christ, was the Christ, the Son of God"; adheres to and follows the doctrine of the apostles; and loves God and the brethren. Taking his

51. MS Sermon on Matt. 11:16–19 (no. 497, Dec. 1738), in WJEO 53, published as *Wicked Men Inconsistent with Themselves*, in Sereno Dwight, *The Works of President Edwards* (10 vols., New York, 1829), 8:320–54.

52. WJE 8:174–217.

cue from the Apostle John, Edwards concentrates on the last of these and affirms Christian love as the sum of all Christian graces, which false Christians lack by virtue of the false spirit within them. Though the latter "go a considerable way towards" having God's love really accomplished in them, being "not far from the kingdom of God and from true grace," their love ultimately fails, showing their spirit untrue.[53] Such a conclusion is fitting for Edwards, given that he has spent the year distinguishing true and false Christians in his discourse on the wise and foolish virgins, and identifying Christian love as the definitive characteristic of this endeavor in *Charity and Its Fruits.*

CONCLUSION

While the interrelated themes described in Edwards' preaching underscore his thinking from late 1737 to early 1739, a close reading of the material nevertheless suggests he was particularly concerned with one of them, namely, that of the distinction between true and false Christians. Indeed, it would not be an exaggeration to say this was his *principal* concern in that period between the awakenings. This is understandable, however, given the situation confronting him, a time when his once ardent congregation had cooled to a complacent lethargy and had not been rejuvenated by a new awakening—at least, not yet.

53. MS Sermon on 1 John 4:12 (no. 498, Dec. 1738), in WJEO 53.

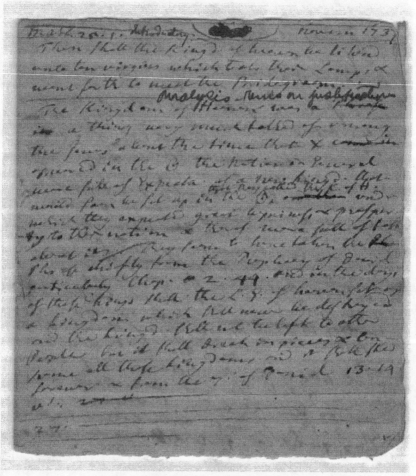

Sermon on Matthew 25:1-2, booklet 1, page 1

Courtesy Beinecke Rare Book and Manuscript Library, Yale University

TRUE AND FALSE CHRISTIANS
(On the Parable of the Wise and Foolish Virgins)

Matthew 25:1.[1]

Then shall the kingdom of heaven be likened unto ten virgins,
which took their lamps, and went forth to meet the bridegroom.

THE KINGDOM OF HEAVEN WAS A THING VERY MUCH TALKED OF AMONG the Jews about the time that Christ appeared in the world. The nation in general were full of expectation of a new kingdom that would soon be set up in the world, that they called "the kingdom of heaven," under which they expected great happiness and prosperity to their nation, and therefore were full of talk about it.

They seem to have taken the phrase chiefly from the prophecy of Daniel, particularly ch. 2:44, "And in the days of these kings shall the God of heaven set up a kingdom, which shall never be destroyed: and the kingdom shall not be left to other people, but it shall break in pieces and consume all these kingdoms, and it shall stand for ever"; and from Dan. 7:13–14, "I saw in the night visions, and, behold, one like the Son of man came with the clouds of heaven, and came to the Ancient of days, and they brought him near before him. And there was given him dominion, and glory, and a kingdom, that all people, nations, and languages, should serve him: his dominion is an everlasting dominion, which shall not pass away, and his kingdom that which shall not be destroyed"; v. 27, "And the kingdom and dominion, and the greatness of the kingdom under the whole heaven, shall be given to the people of the saints of the

---

1. Dated by JE, "Novem. 1737."

most High, whose kingdom is an everlasting kingdom, and all domin-
ions shall serve and obey him."

There being at that day so much talk among the Jews about the
kingdom of heaven, and so much expectation of it, it seems to have been
one great reason why Christ so often took occasion to speak of the kingdom of heaven, and to instruct the Jews and his disciples in particular
concerning it.

John, when he came, he preached that the kingdom of heaven was
at hand, which seemed to increase the Jews' expectation of it: for all held
John as a prophet.

And so when Christ came, he preached the same; as Matt. 4:17,
"From that time Jesus began to preach, and to say, Repent: for the kingdom of heaven is at hand."

And when Christ sent forth his disciples to preach, it was with the
same message. Matt. 10:7, "And as ye go, preach, saying, The kingdom of
heaven is at hand."

And because there was so much talk of the kingdom of heaven,
therefore Christ took occasion to tell the Jews who should have a part in
the kingdom when it came, as in the 5th chapter of Matthew, where he
mentions qualifications quite different from their notions: v. 3, "Blessed
are the poor in spirit, for theirs is the kingdom of heaven"; v. 10, "Blessed
are they which are persecuted for righteousness' sake: for theirs is the
kingdom of heaven"; v. 19, "Whosoever therefore shall break one of
these least commandments, and shall teach men so, he shall be called
the least in the kingdom of heaven: but whosoever shall do and teach
them, the same shall be called great in the kingdom of heaven"; [and v.]
20, "For I say unto you, That except your righteousness shall exceed the
righteousness of the scribes and Pharisees, ye shall in no case enter into
the kingdom of heaven." And so also where he teaches them how they
must become like little children, or they "will never enter the kingdom of
heaven" [Matt. 18:3]; that rich men hardly² enter the kingdom of heaven
[Matt. 19:23]; that "the publicans and the harlots go into the kingdom of
God before you" [Matt. 21:31]; "that many will come from east and west,
and recline at the table with Abraham, Isaac and Jacob in the kingdom
of heaven" [Matt. 8:11]. But it would be very tedious here to mention all
that Christ says about the kingdom of heaven, or the kingdom of God,
which were phrases indifferently used among the Jews to signify that

2. I.e., with difficulty.

kingdom spoken of by Daniel, when he says the Lord "God of heaven set up a kingdom, which shall never be destroyed" [Dan. 2:44].

But I would observe how that Christ very often takes occasion to instruct the Jews on the nature of the kingdom of heaven in his parables, as Matt. 13:24, "The kingdom of heaven is like a man which sowed good seed in his field"; [v.] 31, "the kingdom of heaven is like to a grain of mustard seed"; v. 33, "the kingdom of heaven is like unto leaven, which a woman took, and hid in three measures of meal, till the whole was leavened"; v. 44, "the kingdom of heaven is like unto treasure hid in a field"; v. 45, "the kingdom of heaven is like a merchant man, seeking goodly pearls"; v. 47, "the kingdom of heaven is like a net"; ch. 18:23, "the kingdom of heaven is like a certain king, that would take account of his servants"; [ch.] 20:1, "the kingdom of heaven is like unto a man that is an householder, which went out early in the morning to hire laborers into his vineyard"; [ch.] 22:2[-3], "The kingdom of heaven is like unto a certain king, who made a marriage for his son, and sent forth his servants to call them that were bidden to the wedding." So here in the 25th chapter, the kingdom of heaven is likened unto ten virgins. V. 14, "For the kingdom of heaven is as a man travelling into a far country, who called his own servants, and delivered unto them his goods."

Touching what is said of the kingdom of heaven in this parable of the ten virgins, we may observe that Christ is wont in his parables to make use of things known and familiar amongst the Jews for similitudes, wherewith to represent spiritual things; and so he does here in the similitudes he here uses, alluding to the manners of the Jews at their weddings.

It was the custom among them to have their weddings in the night; and the male guests, they gathered together at the bridegroom's house to attend on him. But the young women and virgins that were invited, they gathered together at the bride's house.

And it was customary for a number of those young women or virgins, when they expected the bridegroom, to go forth to meet him. And because it was in the night, it was the custom for everyone to take a light in their hands, and go forth with their lamps to meet the bridegroom, and so to attend him back, and light the way to the bride's house where the marriage was to be attended.

Here the kingdom of heaven is compared to such a wedding and the customary solemnities of it. And accordingly, the king of this kingdom is compared to the bridegroom, and the visible subjects of it to the virgins that go out with their lamps to meet him.

The Doctrine that I would at this time observe from the words is this, viz.,

DOCTRINE.

The church is espoused to the Lord Jesus Christ.

Christ is the bridegroom, and his true invisible church is the bride. The relation or union between Christ and his church, is compared to many earthly relations and unions: sometimes to that which is between father and children; sometimes to that which is between friends and companions; sometimes to that which is between brethren; sometimes to that which is between head and members; sometimes to that which is between stock and branches. But none is so commonly made use of as that of espousal or marriage.

The Holy Ghost seems peculiarly to delight in this relation above all others, as a similitude and representation of that between Christ and his church. 'Tis abundantly made use [of] throughout the Scriptures, in both Old Testament and New.

It was made use of by Moses; and therefore when God's visible church forsook God and found other gods, Moses calls it "whoredom," comparing it to a woman's forsaking her lawful husband. Num. 14:33, "And your children shall wander in the wilderness forty years, and bear your whoredoms." And with respect to this, 'tis supposed that God gave that law about the marriage of the wife, whereby he was forbidden to marry any but a virgin, Lev. 21:13. David makes use of this representation, as in the 45th Psalm especially.

Solomon makes use of it throughout that Song of his, which is concerning the spiritual union between Christ and his church.

And the prophets do abundantly make use of it, representing God as the husband of his church, and reproving the jubilation of Israel as the whoredom or adultery of that church.

John the Baptist made use of it. John 3:29, "He that hath the bride is the bridegroom: but the friend of the bridegroom, which standeth and heareth him, rejoiceth greatly because of the bridegroom's voice."

Christ himself often makes use of it. So he does in the text. So he does in the 22nd chapter, at the beginning: "The kingdom of heaven is like unto a certain king, which made a marriage for his son"; and Matt. 9:15, "Can the children of the bridechamber mourn, as long as the bridegroom [is with them]?"

The apostles in their epistles made much use of it, as II Cor. 11:2, "I have espoused you to one husband"; Rom. 7:4, "Ye are become dead to the Law, that ye should be married to another"; I Cor. 6:16–17, "For two, saith he, shall be one flesh. But he that joineth unto the Lord is one spirit." Yea, the Apostle seems to speak of it as one end of the appointment of marriage, to be a type of the relation of Christ and his church. Eph. 5:30–32, "For we are members of his body, of his flesh, and of his bones. For this cause shall a man leave his father and mother, and shall be joined unto his wife, and they two shall be one flesh. This is a great mystery: but I speak concerning Christ and the church."

And that new-testament prophet John, in his Revelation, abundantly makes use of this similitude, often calling the false church "the great whore," but calling the true church of Christ "the bride," "the lamb," in places too many to be mentioned.

The following things seem to be held forth to us, in Christ's being represented as the bridegroom of his church.[3]

I. It supposes that Christ and his church are first in a state of separation or distance one from another, i.e., Christ[4] and those persons of which the church is constituted. The relation of parents and children, and so the relation of brethren, begins with the being of one of the parties related. There never was a time wherein the parent and his child both had a being, that there was no such relation subsisting between them.

But [it] is not so in the relation between husband and wife: there is no natural relation, but a relation that always has a state of separation preceding it.

The relation of bridegroom and bride is a new relation, lately established between the parties, that supposes that a little before they were not nearly related. Marriage is forbidden between all that are near of kin, whereby it is the more lively image of the union between Christ and his church, that is, an union made between those that before were not near of kin, but in a state of great alienation and difference one from another.

3. JE's shorthand notation indicates that the following section was preached a second time from Cant. 3:11 at an unspecified date.
4. MS: "that X."

This may be one reason why so many women in Christ's genealogy, those that were the remote mothers of Christ, were aliens or strangers to the nation of Israel.

It is to be observed in Matthew's genealogy, that no more of the mothers, except Mary, the most mediate mother of Christ, are there mentioned than those that were aliens and harlots; as in the third verse, "And Judas begat Phares and Zara of Thamar." Now Tamar was both a Canaanite and a harlot.

And again, v. 5, "and Salmon begat Boaz of Rahab." Rahab also was another harlot and Canaanite; she was an alien from the nation of Israel, and belonged to that cursed city, Jericho. And again, in the next words, "and Boaz begat Obed of Ruth." Ruth was another that was an alien from the nation of Israel, for she was a Moabitess, and seems also to have played the harlot with Boaz before marriage.

And again, v. 6, "David the king begat Solomon of her that had been the wife of Urias." Here again, one is mentioned that had been first the wife of an Hittite, not an Israelite by nation, but one of the Hittites, one of the accursed nations of nations, and was also one that committed adultery with David.

Here, no more of the mothers of Christ are mentioned, but only aliens, and those that had played the harlot. When it is said, "Abraham begat Isaac," it is not said, "Abraham begat Isaac of Sarah, and Isaac begat Jacob of Rebekah," though these women were as worthy to be mentioned as the other.

Those souls that are the spiritual mothers and spouses of Christ, are first aliens and strangers and harlots that have wickedly forsaken God for other lovers; and the church is brought into union with Christ from a state of great alienation, and in order to it forsakes those that before she was united to. Ps. 45:10, "Forget also thine own people, and thy father's house."

When God speaks of the church of Israel under the resemblance of a woman that had been married to him, in the 16th chapter of Ezekiel, she is represented as being first of all an alien, and out of the nations of Canaan. V. 3, "Thus saith the Lord God unto Jerusalem, Thy birth and thy nativity is of the land of Canaan; thy father was an Amorite, and thy mother an Hittite."

II. There is a mutual dear love between Christ and his church. The love that is required to be between husband and wife exceeds that to all earthly friends; and therefore it is said in the institution of marriage, "a man shall leave father and mother, and shall cleave to his wife" [Gen. 2:24].

So the Apostle teaches that there ought to be a most dear love [of] husbands to their wives. Eph. 5:28, "So ought men to love their wives as their own bodies. He that loveth his wife, loveth himself." And the Apostle is in this place comparing the love of Christ to his church, to that which ought to be between husband and wife; as you may see, [v.] 25, "Husbands, love your wives, even as Christ had the church." So wives are commanded to love their husbands.

Correspondent hereto, there is a most dear love between Christ and his church, as is represented abundantly in the Book of Canticles. The love of Christ to his church is that which transcends all the love of earthly lovers; for he loved us and laid down his life for us [I John 3:16]. This love is spoken of as passing knowledge, Eph. 3:19.

On the other hand, the love of the church to Christ is a dear love. Christ is altogether lovely in her eyes; she has an high and adoring esteem of him, and sets him high in her heart.

There is a mutual great love of benevolence. Christ greatly sought the church's good, he loved her with a love of pity, and bore dreadful misery for her, that she might be delivered; and he greatly sought her happiness and purchased eternal glory for her by his blood. And the church has also a great love of benevolence to Christ; she rejoices in Christ's happiness and glory, and desires and seeks his declarative glory.

So there is a great mutual love of complacence. Christ delights in the beauty of the church that he has put upon [her], and speaks of his heart's being ravished with her graces. Cant. 4:9, "Thou hast ravished my heart, my sister, my spouse; thou hast ravished my heart with one of thine eyes, with one chain of thy neck." The church, on the other [hand], takes a superlative delight in the beauty and excellency of [Christ]; he is precious to her. I Pet. 2:7, "To you that believe he is precious." She places her happiness in him, and hath a transcendent pleasure and delight in contemplating his glory.

III. The love that is between Christ and his church, is an electing and distinguishing love. As the love ought to be between husband and wife in their affections: they ought, each of them, to forsake all others for the sake of one another. They should choose one another above all, and should give their hearts to each other, rejecting all others; they should in their hearts and love cleave to those they are espoused to, and to them alone. The husband cleaves to the wife as his chosen consort or companion above all in the world.

The husband is required to leave father and mother and all other friends, and to cleave to his wife.

So is the wife to forget her own people, and her father's house, for the sake of her husband.

The love of parents to children, or the love of brethren, may be equally divided amongst many, but it is not so here. Conjugal love suffers no rival or partner.

So it is in the love between Christ and his church. Christ's love to his church is an electing and distinguishing love. The church is a chosen generation, a peculiar people. Christ hath chosen 'em above all people that are on the face of the earth, and hath set 'em apart for himself; he hath chosen 'em, and carried their names in his heart, and rejected others; he hath chosen them, and rejected multitudes; he hath set his heart on them, but despised others.

So is the love of the church towards Christ: he is her chosen lord and friend above all in the world; he is in her eyes "fairer than the sons of men" [Ps. 45:2], the "chief among ten thousands" [Cant. 5:10]; her beloved is more than other beloveds in her esteem. For his sake she rejects all others, she loves Christ above all, sets him on the throne of her affections. He is that one pearl of great price, for the sake of which she sells all. She tolerates no rival with Christ, but her heart is a garden enclosed, a spring shut up, a fountain sealed. She forsakes all the world for Christ. Christ requires this of his church. Cant. 8:6, "Set me as a seal upon thine heart, as a seal upon thine arm: for love is strong as death; jealousy is cruel as the grave: the coals thereof are coals of fire, which hath a most vehement flame."

IV. There is a very near relation and strict union established between Christ and the church. The relation constituted by marriage is the nearest of all earthly relations, and is so spoken of in its institution: "a man leaves father and mother"—i.e., all other friends—"and cleaves to his wife, and they twain shall be one flesh" [Matt. 19:5], intimating that they twain shall be nearer than all other friends.

So near a relation is established, that it makes 'em one; as the Apostle says, "He that loveth his wife loveth himself," in the aforementioned place in Eph. 5:28.

In this respect, 'tis like the union between Christ and his church: they are so united, that they are one. So is the church one with Christ. I Cor. [6]:16–17, "two, saith he, shall be one flesh." But "he that is joined unto the Lord is one spirit" [I Cor. 6:17]. Husband and wife, in many things, are looked upon one in law, so that the debt of the wife is the husband's discharge or the wife's discharge.

So is Christ and his church one in law. The church's debt, that she owed to divine justice, Christ has taken upon him, and the payment that he has made is reckoned to her. The wife is so united to her husband, that she is reckoned as a child of the same parents; and his father becomes her father, and his relations her relations. So it is between Christ and his church: the saints being united to Christ, his Father is become their Father. "Go tell my brethren, behold, I ascend unto my Father and your Father" [John 20:17].[5]

The husband and wife are so one, that the inheritance or estate of the one, is the estate of the other; they have communion in each others' possessions. So it is between Christ and his church: the church has fellowship with Christ in his possessions, partaking of his inheritance, for they are joint-heirs with Christ, Rom. 8:17. They shall live and reign with him, sitting on his throne.

Christ being the Son of God, the saints partake with him in her filial relations; they also become the children of God. Gal. 4:4–6, "But when the fullness of the time was come, God sent forth his Son, made of a woman, made under the law, to redeem them that were under the law, that we might receive the adoption of sons. And because ye are sons, God hath sent forth the Spirit of his Son into your hearts, crying, Abba, Father." The wife is so related to the husband, that she has his name. So doth the church bear the name of Christ: she is called Christ's.

V. Christ is first in seeking this union. Christ is first in love to his church. I John 4:19, "We love him, because he first loved us." And he first sought the love of the church, and to bring her to union to him. Christ hears his beloved; by the calls and invitations of the gospel, he comes and stands at her door and knocks. Cant. 5:2, "'Tis the voice of my beloved that knocketh, saying, Open to me, my sister, my love." And not only so, but he powerfully persuades or draws her by the influences of his Holy Spirit. He draws her love to him, and makes her willing to accept of the proposals he makes her.

5. MS: "Matt 28.10."

VI. The manner of coming into this union is by free consent. 'Tis so on both sides: Christ's love to the church is free, and he freely receives her into so near and honorable a relation and union to himself. And so it is on her side. None can come into a true and spiritual union with Christ, but by his free consent. Christ must be freely received, received of mere choice; and not as being driven by threats of damnation, but as being drawn from a sense of Christ's excellency and worthiness. Ps. 110:3, "Thy people shall be willing in the day of thy power." The church never does anything with greater delight, than she receives Christ and gives up herself to him; 'tis an act that she rejoices in.

VII. This union is mutually established by covenant, as it is in a marriage union. 'Tis entered into and established by a mutual covenant, or covenant engagements on both sides. Mal. 2:14, "wife of thy covenant"; Prov. 2:17, "forget not the covenant of thy God." So it is between Christ and his church. Christ enters into covenant with his church; he binds himself to her by firm and immutable promises. In Is. 55:3, Christ says, "I will make with you an everlasting covenant, even the sure mercies of David." Christ promises forever to cleave to her and never to forsake, and that his love to her shall never fail, and that he will provide for her, and take care of her, and be her everlasting friend and portion. And on the other hand, the church is also strictly engaged to Christ in a firm covenant, that she hath consented to and sealed, to be Christ's, and his only, never to depart from him, to take him for her everlasting Lord and friend and portion, and to love and obey and follow him forever. Ezek. 16:8, "Now when I passed by thee, and looked upon thee, behold, thy time was the time of love; and I spread my skirt over thee, and covered thy nakedness: yea, I sware unto thee, and entered into a covenant with thee, saith the Lord God, and thou becamest mine."

VIII. This union is in order to mutual communion, cohabitation and enjoyment as friends and companions. As has been observed already, by virtue of it Christ and his church have fellowship in the same benefits and enjoyments, the same inheritance.

So it is in order to a cohabitation. The church is received into this union with Christ, as a wife is to dwell with her spouse in his house; he receives her into his house. The church shall be received up to Christ; the king shall bring her into his chamber, that where he is, there she may be also, there to have a joint possession of his glorious inheritance, to behold his glory and to enjoy his love forever, and to enjoy the most free and intimate converse with [him]: wherein she shall converse with [him], not merely as lord—though he be her Lord and infinitely above her—yet he has taken her nature upon him, to that end, that he might make way for a mutual converse and enjoyment, more free than the infinite distance of the divine nature would admit of. And therefore, Christ tells his disciples that he called 'em not servants but friends [John 15:15], and they are called his brethren and companions, Ps. 122:8.

A specimen of the intimacy of the saints with Christ, when they shall dwell with him, is given in Christ's manner of converse with his disciples on earth, when he eat and drank with them and [a disciple] leaned on his bosom, and were admitted to great freedom and boldness in their communion with him. In this intimacy shall the church forever be glad and rejoice in and with Christ, and continue everlastingly in the full enjoyment of him.[6]

IX.[7] This union is of such a nature, that the church is united to him as her friend and companion, yet she is subject to him as a lord. Herein it is more like the marriage union, than any other earthly union: for in the relation of parents and children, the children are subject to the parents. But there can't properly be said to be an union between them as of companions.

Brethren are united as companions, but have not authority one over another; but in the conjugal relation, both meet together: the husband is companion of his wife, but yet has authority over her. I Pet. 3:5–6, "For after this manner in the old time the holy women also, who trusted in God, adorned themselves, being in subjection unto their own husbands: even as Sara obeyed Abraham, calling him lord: whose daughters ye are, as long as ye do well, and are not afraid with any amazement." Wherein 'tis is a lively image of the union of the church with Christ: for Christ is the Lord of his church. Ps. 45:11, "He is thy Lord; and worship thou him." And yet, Christ tells his disciples that he don't call 'em servants but friends, John [15:15]; and they are called his companions, Ps. 122:8.

And, however, Christ is called both the Father and the brother of believers. He is their Father, which betokens his authority. Heb. 2:13, "Wherefore in all things it behoved him to be made like unto his

6. This point marks the end of first preaching unit. In the next paragraph JE recapitulates the main points (omitted here) before proceeding.

7. MS: "1 sepera. 2. Love. 3 Electing. 4 union. 5. X is first. 6. Consent. 7 covenant 8. communion & 8."

brethren." And he is their brethren, which betokens their being in some sort fellows and companions, Heb. 2:11.

X. The church, in her union with Christ, receives him as one she depends on for guidance, protection and provision. A woman, when she takes anyone as an husband, she takes him as a guide; Prov. 2:17, "Forsaketh the guide of her youth." And she commits herself to his protection; I Pet. 3:7, "Likewise, ye husbands, dwell with them according to knowledge, giving honor unto the wife, as unto the weaker vessel." And she commits herself to him, to be provided for by him; Ex. 21:10, "her food, and her raiment, shall he not diminish."

Herein, this relation is an image of that which is between Christ and his church: for the church, in closing with Christ, receives him, and depends upon him as a prophet to teach and guide her, and as a savior to protect and defend her from [the] devil, from the wrath of God, and from her spiritual enemies; and commits herself to him to provide for her, to procure for her, and bestow upon her all those things needful, to make her happy here and forever. She lives by faith in Christ, and looks to him for spiritual food and [the] supply of all her wants.

XI. The church is thus espoused to Christ, that she may bring forth fruit unto God. Rom. 7:4, "Wherefore, my brethren, ye also are become dead to the law by the body of Christ; that ye should be married to another, even to him who is raised from the dead, that we should bring forth fruit unto God."

Chosen souls, that are truly espoused to Christ, are not barren souls, but fruitful in good works, which they bring forth through the seed of divine grace which they receive by the Spirit. For of his fullness they receive, "and grace for grace" [John 1:16], by which they are enabled to bring forth those fruits that are amiable in God's sight. And the church, by this grace of Christ, is enabled to bring forth many children to Christ.

By her labors and endeavors for the good of souls, she as it were travails in birth with souls, and is the instrument of propagating the church. One saint is the means of the conversion of another, especially faithful ministers in the church. The church of Christ is the mother of particular believers. Gal. 4:26, "But Jerusalem, which is above, is free, which is the mother of us all."

XII. There is an appointed time for the church to be received to cohabitation with Christ, and the perfect enjoyment of him, that is in Scripture represented as her wedding day, Rev. 19:7. The saints at their conversion, are sometimes spoken of as an espousal to Christ; but 'tis rather the betrothing the soul to Christ, than the consummating the marriage. The Jews had a custom of betrothing before marriage. Thus we read of the Virgin Mary's being espoused to Joseph before they came together. So the soul is as it were betrothed or espoused to Christ in conversion, but the wedding is when the soul is brought to celebration with Christ in his glorious palace, there to enjoy perfect communion with him.

This, with respect to particular souls, will be at the soul's departure from the body and reception into heaven, but to a more full and complete degree at the day of judgment, which will the wedding day of the whole elect church. And therefore, Christ's coming, by death and judgment, are in the text spoken of as his coming as a bridegroom to a marriage.

The happiness that will attend and succeed this is often in Scripture compared to a marriage feast. Matt. 22, at [the] beginning, "The kingdom of heaven is like unto a certain king." Rev. 19:9, "Blessed are they which are called unto the marriage supper of the Lamb."[8]

APPLICATION.

Use I of this Doctrine, may be of *Instruction.*

First [*Inference*]. Hence we may learn the nature of justifying faith.[9] The Scripture teaches us that faith is that grace, by which especially [the soul] comes into saving union with Christ, as is evident by faith's being often called coming to Christ. Matt. 11:28, "Come unto me, all ye that labor and are heavy laden, and I will give you rest"; and John 5:40, "And ye will not come to me, that ye might have life"; and 6:37, "All that the Father giveth me shall come to me; and him that cometh to me I will in no wise cast out"; and in many other places.

And we have heard the nature of this union, that it is a kind of conjugal [relation] or marriage. And therefore, from the nature of union, we may also infer the nature of faith, that is that act by which we come into this union, or which is the uniting act; that it is analogous to the act of a woman towards him that seeks her in marriage, whereby she comes into

8. JE skipped the equivalent of seven lines before resuming.

9. Note the parallels with JE's discourse, *Justification by Faith Alone*, in WJE 19:155–56, the expanded version of which would be published in 1738.

a marriage union with him; or that which is the uniting act on her side, which is no other than her yielding to his suit by consenting to have[10] him for her husband, and to be his wife; or by receiving of him as her husband, and giving herself up to him to be his wife in a covenant way.

She receives him to be hers, and in the same act gives up herself to him to be his.

And she receives him in such a manner as therein to reject all others. She receives him, and him alone, in that relation, because, as we observed before, this relation bears no rivals; and so she gives up herself to be his and his only, and that forever, or as long as they both live. And in receiving him as her husband, she receives him as her nearest friend, as a lord, for a protector and guide, and one that will provide for her, and gives herself up to him to be protected and provided for and guided.

Now this may give us light into the nature of justifying faith: it is no other than the heart's yielding to Christ's suit. Christ calls and invites and woos the sinner he finds at his door, and knocks when the heart of the sinner is gained and brought to yield and goes out after Christ, and receives him in that relation in which he offers himself. She[11] receives him alone, and so as to reject all others; and in the same act heartily gives up herself to Christ to be his, and that forever. Then she[12] receives Christ by faith.

In faith, the soul receives Christ as its nearest and best friend, and as an everlasting portion, as a guide and a lord and possessor, as a protector from misery, and a provider of spiritual food and raiment and eternal happiness.

And Christ is thus received, and the soul thus gives up to him in covenant; or, by an hearty consent to the covenant of grace, the soul in faith does as it were set its seal to this covenant.

And this is not only done in profession, nor is it done in a forced manner; but it is done with the heart. The heart does it, and so it is done really freely and with delight. This is that act of faith, which is the act of the heart and whole soul, whereby it comes into union with Christ.

Second [*Inf.*]. Hence also we may learn after what manner faith justifies: that it don't justify as a work or good deed or any worthy act in the

10. MS: "to be have."
11. MS: "he."
12. MS: "he."

believer, but only as it is that which brings into union with Christ, and so to an interest in Christ's satisfaction and merits.

To be justified is to be accepted as free from the guilt of sin, and as having a righteousness belonging to us that entitles to life.

He that is accepted as having an interest in Christ's satisfaction and merits, must be so justified or accepted. For by his satisfaction he had done away the guilt of sin, and by his righteousness he has merited life. Now all that is needful, in order to the having an interest in Christ's satisfaction and merits, is to be in Christ, as to be united to him: for they that are united to his person, so as to be looked upon as one with him, will of necessary consequence have an interest in his satisfaction and merits. If Christ has satisfied and merited, and we are one with him, then it is all one, as if we had satisfied and merited.

But now the nature of faith, as we have just now heard, is to unite to Christ as to make one with him. 'Tis the very act by which we close with him. And thus it is that faith justifies and gives an interest in Christ's satisfaction and [merit], not any goodness or worthiness in the act of faith.

Justification is not given for faith properly as the reward of faith, to reward any goodness that is in the act; but it rather results from the nature of faith, which is to unite to the Mediator through whom justification is to be had.

To illustrate this from the similitude in hand: when a man seeks a woman in marriage, he offers himself to be in a marriage relation together with joint interest in his estate and what he has; which she necessarily has if she has him, because the person and estate go together.

Now he don't offer his person and estate to her on condition of anything that she is to do, any worthy deed in her which he will reward in case she does; but all the condition is her consenting to have him, or yielding to receive him in that relation. And when she does yield to his suit, and at his offer takes him in marriage, her accepting of him, or uniting herself to him in marriage, is the condition of her having him in marriage. But it would be utterly improper to say that he gives himself to her to be her husband in *reward* for her taking him to be her husband, as though her accepting him in marriage at his offer was a worthy deed in her, that he rewarded by his giving himself in marriage. No, but it is the condition of her having him in that union, no otherwise than as it is the very act in her soul by which she is united and married to him, and has him for her husband, and so she comes to have an interest in him as an husband, and so in his estate. In like manner does faith give an interest in Christ as a savior and an interest in his benefits: they ben't offered in reward for any good deed whatsoever, but they are offered and given only on the soul's acceptance.

Third [*Inf.*]. Hence we learn the wonderful grace of the Lord Jesus Christ, that he should receive such poor, unworthy creatures as we are into such a blessed union with him. How wonderful is that condescension of such a person of divine and infinite glory, that he should seek to espouse worms of the dust, and should advance a little, feeble, poor insect to be his bride!

What could Christ have to move him to do this, but mere grace? The elect church has no dowry; she is wretched, miserable and poor in poverty, in nakedness, in contempt, a poor outcast and vagabond.

He gets no wealth by espousing her. She has nothing wherewith to enrich, being herself in the extremest indignity and penury, standing in need of great things from him, but having nothing to bestow upon him.

What will Christ be the richer or the better for taking one for his spouse in beggarly poverty, who, if she had something, Christ would stand in no need of it, being infinitely rich in himself?

Christ doth not espouse her for the sake of her portion, or that he may be enriched by her, but that he may enrich her, that he may bestow his riches upon her.

The church indeed is rich: but how comes she so, but by Christ's espousing her and bestowing himself and his riches upon [her], by admitting her to a joint interest in his estate? He makes his spouse rich by the wealth he bestows upon her.[13] Thus Christ says to the church of Laodicea, "I counsel thee to buy of me gold tried in the fire, that thou mayest be rich," Rev. 3:18.

Christ don't match with the church that he may make himself rich; but on the contrary, he, being rich, has for her sake become poor, that she through his poverty might be rich, II Cor. 8:9. She that Christ seeks for his bride is, in herself, no honorable one. The King of glory don't advance himself or get honor, as earthly princes often do,[14] by the honorableness of their match. Christ found the church in most disgraceful, abject circumstances.

13. MS: "him."
14. MS: "to"

No, it could be nothing but mere grace that could induce Christ to espouse such an one. Christ did not find her beautiful or comely, but makes her so. The church of Christ is indeed spoken of in Scripture as one that[15] is become exceeding beautiful and comely in Christ's eyes, as the lily among thorns, as beautiful as the light of the morning, fair as the moon and clear as the sun, and one whose beauties ravish Christ's heart. But she had none of this beauty till she was espoused to Christ, and Christ had put it upon her. Christ did not set his love on her and espouse her for the sake of any beauty: for Christ loved her when she had none, but was in the grossest deformity and filthiness, a sordid, odious creature. The bright Light of heaven was pleased to set his love on a clod of earth, yea, a mass of filthiness, and to seek to unite it to himself and make it his lovely bride. And he hath so done: he hath taken this dirty clod, this lump of filthiness, and changed it, and beautified and put his own beauty upon it, so that she is sanctified and elevated in her nature, and appears with ravishing heavenly and divine comeliness, in his image, and is become his bride.

It is not for the sake of any ornaments he finds in her, that he has set his love upon her, for he found her clothed with rags. But he has chosen her for his bride in these circumstances, and hath taken and clothed [her] with white raiment; he hath adorned her with resplendent graces, that are ten thousand times more precious, and more bright and beautiful, than gold or diamonds.

And these things has he done for [her] at great expense. Such was her circumstances, that she could not become his spouse unless it was greatly at his cost. She has fallen into doleful circumstances, sunk into a dreadful abyss of misery, and he could not come to unite her to him, without wading through a sea of blood, without himself descending from heaven and as it were leaving the bosom of his Father. [He did] quit his high station in glory there, and empty himself, and descend as it were himself into this abyss of woe, in order to fetch her thence, to bring her to himself.

She was a poor, lost creature in a dreadful wilderness, amidst lions, leopards and other wilds beasts. And he, in order to obtain her to be his spouse, himself must leave the palace of his Father's glory and the glorious city of that [that] was his regal seat, and go into the wilderness, even the wilderness of this sinful, miserable world, and there become a

15. MS: "one is that."

pilgrim, and suffer great and long fatigues and sore hardships, seeking her that is lost there, that he may bring her home to be his bride, to bring her out of the wilderness to the pleasant land, to the glorious city, new Jerusalem, and to his glorious palace,[16] there forever to dwell with him in sweet and everlasting fellowship as his consort. This Christ has done: he comes, and calls her from the wilderness, and from the lions' dens, and the mountains of the leopards. Cant. 4:8, "Come with me from Lebanon, [my spouse, with me from Lebanon: look from the top of Amana, from the top of Shenir and Hermon, from the lions' dens, from the mountains of the leopards]."

But, in order to bring her from those lions' dens, where she was carried by those lions to be their prey, ready to be devoured by them, Christ must go himself and fetch her thence. And this he did: he himself entered the lions' den, and there had a terrible conflict with those roaring lions, to deliver her from their teeth, and so obtain her for his spouse.

Such were her circumstances, that she was not to be obtained for his bride without his being at vast expense to purchase her: for she was a captive in the hands of divine justice for that debt which she owed to that justice, which was more than ten thousand talents; it was an infinite debt. And so she, having nothing to pay, was held close prisoner, in miserable circumstances, and none could redeem her without paying her debt. And this debt was infinitely too great to be paid by silver and gold; all the wealth in the world would not pay it; it could be answered with nothing short of Christ's own precious blood. If Christ would have her that he sought for his spouse, he must purchase her by his blood, he must pay down his life for her price, he must offer up his precious soul: nothing short of this could satisfy. And this he did; so great was his love, that he paid down this great price, and redeemed and purchased his bride at such expense as this, to redeem her out of the hands of justice, that he might have her for his own. Acts 20:28, "Feed the church of God, which he hath purchased with his own blood." He bore the vengeance of justice himself; he suffered the wrath of God that she was exposed to, and so obtained her. How was any that sought a spouse, whom it cost so dear, to obtain her? Inexpressible were the labors and difficulties that he went through for her. She was taken captive by Satan, and was a miserable slave in his hands; but Christ left the habitation of his glory, his vast and infinite pleasure and happiness, and went into the enemy's country,

16. MS: "that."

and had a terrible conflict with the enemy that had been in possession, wherein he conflicted with anguish, amazement and sorrow unto death, and the combat was great, [so] that it occasioned him to sweat blood: and so did he conquer the enemy, and obtain his bride. In this way did Christ seek the love of his church; and this did he do to obtain her in marriage.

And all this, when she had no loveliness, but was deformed, and filthy, and hateful, a poor, abject, outcast vile creature, and deserved Christ's hatred; and all when she had no love to him.

Indeed the church, when brought into union with Christ, loves Christ, and loves him above all: but her love is the fruit of his; 'tis because he has sweetly and powerfully drawn her, by enlightening of her, to see his glory and beauty. And all that Christ has bestowed upon her, has cost Jesus Christ his blood; nothing could be obtained for her at any other price, than that of his blood. It was at this price he procured that holy and heavenly beauty which he puts upon her, to fit her for his presence and cohabitation; it was by the price of this blood that he purchased those excellent ornaments which he adorns her [with], that he might present her to himself a pure, beautiful and glorious church. Eph. 5:25–27, "Husbands, love your wives, even as Christ also loved the church, and gave himself for it; that he might sanctify and cleanse it with the washing of water by the word, that he might present it to himself a glorious church, not having spot, or wrinkle, or any such thing; but that it should be holy and without blemish."

Christ has subjected himself to great expense, difficulty, disgrace and suffering to obtain his church, And how unspeakably and infinitely does the church gain by it, what honor is she advanced to by his ignominy, what glory does she arrive at by his obscurity, what joys and pleasures does she obtain by his pains and torments, by Christ's humiliation, and his becoming a servant! She becomes glorious, powerful, a queen. Ps. 45:9, "Upon thy right hand did stand the queen in gold of Ophir." By his having his body smeared with the spittle of his enemies, and with his own blood, she becomes attired in glorious apparel. Ps. 45:13, "The king's daughter is all glorious within:[17] her clothing is of wrought gold." Christ bore agonies, that she might have ease and rest; he was cast into

17. MS: "whether."

the furnace of God's wrath, that he might bring her into the garden of God's delights, and to drink of the river of his pleasures.[18]

Fourth Inf. Hence we may learn how far the godly are [from] having any cause to be afraid of death, or the day of judgment. For as has been already observed, there is an appointed time for the church to be received to cohabitation with Christ, and the perfect enjoyment of him, that in Scripture [is] represented as her wedding day, as Rev. 19:7.

[We learn from Scripture] that by conversion, she is as it were betrothed to Christ; but that there is another day appointed for the wedding, and that this, with respect to particular souls, will be the day of the soul's departure from the body and the reception into heaven, the day when the souls depart to be with Christ, though in a more full and glorious degree and manner at the day of judgment, which will be the wedding day of the whole elect church.

And therefore Christ coming by death and judgment, proclaimed by the midnight cry which is spoken of in the text and context, is spoken of as the coming of the bridegroom to the marriage.

Now if it be so, what occasion have the saints to be afraid of Christ's coming either to death or judgment? Need the bride be afraid of the coming of her glorious and lovely bridegroom, when he comes to her wedding, when he comes to receive her as his bride into an everlasting union and cohabitation with himself?

As has been already observed, the church, and every true member of it, has a most dear love to the Lord Jesus Christ. Need the bride, therefore, that dearly loves the bridegroom, be under any terrors concerning the coming of her beloved bridegroom?

Do lovers fear a wedding day? Are they not wont, on the contrary, to wait and hope for it with earnest expectation; not looking on it as a day that is terrible, but as a day of gladness and rejoicing?

What need a truly believing soul be afraid to depart from the body, to be received into the arms of Christ as his bride, to go home to him, to dwell with him in his house, which is heaven, and there eternally to enjoy him? Death indeed, in its own nature, is very terrible; but Christ has quite changed the nature of it with respect to all that are his: he has raised the day of death from a dark into a lightsome day; he has changed

18. This point marks the end of the second preaching unit. Before resuming, JE noted "Math 25. 1. / doc. / Use I of Instruction."

[it] from a terrible into a joyful and happy day; he has changed it as it [were] from a dying day into a wedding day.

Death is a joyful and happy change to the godly. The soul then is received out of a world of sorrow, and into everlasting and perfect joy and blessedness. It is then stripped of its old rags and all its filthy garments, and is adorned with glorious robes, as a bride is adorned for the bridegroom.

The soul then leaves all its pollution, has all its corruption purged away from it, and ascends up to Christ, to be presented to him without spot or wrinkle or any such thing; and there is brought unto the King, as it is expressed in Ps. 45:14–15, "in raiment of needle work," and with gladness and rejoicing enters the King's palace.

And so the saints have no cause to be afraid of the day of judgment, when Christ shall come in the glory of his Father, with all the holy angels with him: for that will be the wedding day to the church, and the most joyful day to her that ever she saw. And all the saints are called upon to be glad and rejoice at the coming of that day. Rev. 19:7, "Let us be glad and rejoice, and give honor to him, for the marriage of the Lamb is come, and his wife hath made herself ready."

The glory that Christ will then appear in, though it will be terrible to the wicked, yet it will be joyful to the godly: for it will be to them the glorious attire of a bridegroom.

And then shall the whole church be adorned with glorious beauty in both body and soul, to fit her for cohabitation with Christ, and shall appear shining forth at his right [hand] as it were in robes of glory, and then ascending up with songs of joy with him to enter into the palace of his glory, there to enjoy everlasting, full and perfect communion with him.

Fifth [*Inf.*]. Hence we may learn the greatness of the happiness of heaven: for that is the place of the everlasting cohabitation of Christ and his spouse; that is the place that is provided and prepared for the eternal, perfect communion of Christ beloved[19] and his church.

This is the place that this glorious, loving bridegroom has prepared everlastingly to entertain her that he has chosen to be his bride, and the place where the bride shall everlastingly enjoy this bridegroom. Surely, therefore, the happiness of heaven must be exceeding great.

Use II may [be] of *Exhortation.*

19. MS: "beloved spouse beloved bride."

First. To natural men, to exhort them to hearken to the invitations of Jesus Christ.

This glorious person that you have heard of, to whom the church is espoused, invites you to an espousal with him. He offers himself to you, and has long been wooing of you. He uses many means to prevail upon you; he offers himself with all his glory, and with his ever-eternal inheritance; he offers to admit you jointly to inherit with him.

He offers himself to you freely, as glorious as he is, and as glorious as his possessions are. He requires no money or price; he requires no other conditions, but only that you would accept of him.

He uses many arguments to persuade you; he tells you what he has done and suffered for sinners, and what plentiful provisions he has made for you. Matt. 22:4, "I have prepared my dinner: my oxen and my fatlings are killed, and all things are ready: come unto the marriage."

He tells you what he will do for you: if you will yield yourself to him, he will come and sup with you, and you with him, Rev. 3:20. He "will give you rest," Matt. 11:28. He will give you "that which is good, and your soul shall delight itself in fatness"; and he "will make an everlasting covenant" with you, "even the sure mercies of David," Is. 55:2–3, to induce you to yield to Christ's suit.

Consider particularly what a great difference there is between Christ and those other lovers that you have hitherto yielded yourself to. Though you have not hearkened to Christ, yet there are other lovers that have solicited your heart, that you have hearkened and yielded to; there are others that you have entertained in your bosom, and have been very fond of, and devoted lovers that have been Christ's rivals, that have set themselves in opposition to him.

Your lusts and corruptions have solicited you, and you have yielded yourself to them.

There are many worldly things that have bought your heart, and you have given your heart to them, and have been pursuing after them.

Satan hath been incessantly tempting you and courting you; he has put on a fair vizor.[20] You have yielded your heart to him and have followed him.

And for the sake of those lovers, you have stopped your ears to Christ's calls, you have rejected Christ's suit: for the sake of those, you

---

20. A reference that comes from a time when men of high rank wore armor; the vizor was a metal piece that covered the eyes, with slits, fixed by a hinge to the helmet.

have suffered Christ to stand knocking at the door of your heart in vain, because you have not been willing to part with those for Christ's sake, but have preferred them far before them; for these you turned your back upon Christ: from your high esteem of these you have cast contempt upon the Lord Jesus Christ.

And [you] do so still: you still hearken to these lovers, and cleave to them, and so will not hearken to the invitations and wooings of Christ.

Now consider the great difference there is between Christ and these other lovers:

1. Consider how excellent and worthy Christ is, and how worthless [are others]. That glorious person that seeks your love is a divine person; he is one that is infinitely above all creatures, above the highest angels.

But those other lovers that you have cleaved to, are mean things, and vile in their nature.

Christ is an heavenly one, yea, he is the King of heaven; he is infinitely above heaven itself. But those other lovers are either of the earth, and earthly in their nature, or of hell, and hellish.

Though there be a seeming beauty and loveliness in these lovers that you have hearkened to, yet 'tis nothing real; it is only a mask that they put on, and will be found to be a shadow without substance.

But in Christ is real, substantial excellency. The more acquaintance you have with him, the more excellency will you see in him, to delight and ravish your heart.

Christ is one in whom is the happiness of angels; he is the darling of heaven, and the eternal delight of God himself. But those things that you set your heart upon and cleave to, are the proper enjoyments of the brute creatures.

2. If your soul were espoused to Christ, how profitable a match would it be you; and on the other [hand], how unprofitable those other lovers are to you.

This glorious person, that seeks your love and invites you to a spiritual espousal to him, is one that is of unsearchable riches.

He is infinitely rich in himself; he possesses infinite riches in his glorious, divine nature, for he has the nature of the Godhead. The Godhead has an infinite fullness in it.

And he is unspeakably rich in his external possessions, for he is the heir of all things. For being the Son of God, he is the natural heir of God, he is the great possessor of heaven and earth.

And if you will yield to his suit, and your soul becomes his spouse, his riches shall be yours. You shall have the possession of all that he is, and joint interest in all that he has. How gloriously then will you be endowed! How rich will you become!

Though Christ will gain nothing by such a match, yet you will [be] an unspeakable gainer. He will be never the richer for matching with your soul, for you are a poor vagabond that have nothing to bestow upon him; but you will be an infinite gainer by being espoused to him.

But as to those other lovers that you have followed after, and for whose sake you have rejected Christ, they are poor and empty; they have nothing to bestow upon you.

They flatter you with fair promises of much, but they promise more than they can perform, for they have nothing to endow you with.

If you cleave to them still, and continue to reject Christ for their sake, you will find yourself sadly disappointed at last.

Christ has wherewithal to feed you, and to feast you, and satisfy your soul; and he has wherewithal to clothe you; he has change of raiment and glorious robes to adorn you.

But as to those other lovers, they have nothing to feed your poor, hungry soul. Indeed, they offer you bread, they exhibit something to you under the appearance of bread, but 'tis but a shadow; in pursuing after it, you follow after "that which is not bread," and spend yourself for that which profits not. But if you will hearken diligently unto Christ, you may eat that which is good, and your soul may "delight itself in fatness" [Is. 55:2].

Those lovers have nothing wherewith to cover your naked soul. If you still follow after 'em, you are like still to remain in rags and nakedness as you are.

If you will hearken to Christ and match with him, he is able [to] do great things for you. He is the Lord strong and mighty; he is able to defend you from all that mighty army, to stand against all your enemies, and set you above their reach; he can help you out of all difficulties; he can promote you to great honor, and can bring you to the possession of a kingdom.

But what can these other lovers do for you? They can't save or defend you from any of those awful calamities you are in danger of. If you still cleave to them, you'll be utterly undone, for all that they can do for you.

3. In cleaving to those lovers, you debase yourself; but if your soul be espoused with Christ, you will be greatly honored by it. What can be a greater honor to a poor worm of the dust, than to be espoused to the King of kings? If your soul be thus espoused to Christ, it will thereby be advanced to exceeding dignity and glory. 'Tis wonderful, and [you] will be so affected by all saints and angels to all eternity, that God ever should put such honor upon a creature.

But by your cleaving to those other lovers that you have hitherto followed after, you debase yourself below the proper dignity of the human nature, you sink yourself down to the level of the brute creature, as though you thought you was made for nothing higher than they; or else you match your soul with those who might lower [it], viz., to those that belong to the infernal world.

And will you reject so honorable a match, by which your soul might be dignified and exalted, for the sake of that which is so dishonorable, and will end in everlasting disgrace and contempt?

4. Christ has an exceeding and everlasting love to all those that close with [him]. But those that you now cleave to as your lovers, are indeed your enemies. Christ has a dear love to all that believe in him: he loved them from eternity; he loved them with a dying love.

No lover ever gave such evidences of the sincerity and strength of his love as Christ has done, in doing and undergoing so much for all that accept of him. Nor is there any love to be equalized with the love of Christ.

If you hearken to Christ's calls, then you will hear that which may be a sure evidence of your being the object of this love.

But those others that you are so fond of, and for the sake of which you reject Christ, are indeed your enemies. They seek your love, but indeed they have no love to you, but a mortal enmity.

Christ seeks the eternal blessedness of those souls that are espoused to him, and will bestow it upon 'em. But those that you follow as your lovers seek your destruction, and evermore bring those to ruin that finally cleave to 'em; and that, however they may flatter them, and however fair and tempting their pretenses and promises are.

But this brings me to the next thing to be considered:

5. Christ is a faithful lover, but those other lovers that you have followed are very treacherous and unfaithful. If you cleave to them still,

they will finally fail you; though they promise much, they will fulfill nothing.

Though they may please and flatter you for the present, and by that means keep up a violent pursuit in you after them, yet when you come to extremity, and you stand in the greatest need of help, they will utterly fail you. Then that shall be verified of you in Hos. 2:7, "And she shall follow after her lovers, but she shall not overtake them, and she shall seek them, but shall not find them."

They evermore deceive those that trust in them. What the world, and the flesh, and the devil promises to their votaries, they never fulfill.

Consider how often they have failed you in times past: how often have you been flattered by one worldly enjoyment and another that you have given your heart to, while you have denied it to Christ, and have been woefully frustrated.

But if you will hearken to Christ, and yield your heart to him, he won't frustrate you. His love to you shall never fail: for whom he loves, he loves to the end, John 13:1; and [those other lovers] never "shall be able to separate you from the love of God, which is in Christ Jesus your Lord, neither life, nor death, nor angels, nor principalities, nor powers, nor things present, nor things to come, nor height, nor depth, nor any other creature," Rom. 8, two last verses.

And though Christ's promises are so many and great, yet he never will fail of any of them; they are the sure mercies of David that he promises, Is. 55:3; and all the promises of God in him are "yea, and Amen," II Cor. 1:20.

Secondly, the *Exhortation* may be to the godly.

1. I would hence exhort such to love the Lord Jesus Christ. If you are one that is truly godly, you are one of that church of Christ that you have heard of, that is the spouse of Christ, and your soul is espoused unto Christ, and Christ is your bridegroom, and your soul his bride. And therefore, be exhorted to love him.

Surely, love is becoming such a relation as this, especially considering the gloriousness and dignity of the person with whom your soul is brought into such a relation, and his great love to you.

Indeed, those I now speak to are such as do truly love the Lord Jesus Christ, and do love him above all the world. But yet your love is very little in comparison of what it ought to be; 'tis small in comparison of the excellency of the beloved, and the obligations he has laid upon you to love, small to what such a relation as your soul requires.

O! therefore seek after more love to Jesus Christ, abhor yourself for your coldness and deadness, humble yourself before Jesus for it, and earnestly seek of him more of a spirit of love to Christ.

And militate against everything that is inconsistent with a spirit of love to Christ, and diligently use all proper means for the promoting of love.

Don't forget Christ. Be much in meditating of him, and what he has done and suffered, and in his calls and invitations and promises. And seek to be much conversant with Christ in several duties, and in retirement from the world.

The more you seek of this principle and spirit of love to Christ in your heart, the greater accordance will you have of a real union between Christ and you, and that your soul is indeed espoused to him; and the more pleasantly will you live, the more will you anticipate the pleasures and joys of the future state of celebration in, and full enjoyment of, Christ in heaven; the more will you have of the foretastes of the joys of the wedding day.

2. Be exceeding careful to avoid all falseness and treachery towards Jesus Christ, by harboring other lovers. Surely this will be false treatment of so glorious a person, that has so condescended as to bring such a poor, worthless creature in an espousal with himself.

Shall the King of glory himself become your lover and your husband, and won't you be contented with him? Won't you esteem him sufficient without other lovers, and so go after mammon, and after the objects of your lust, forsaking Jesus Christ?

What ungrateful treatment will this be of him who has so laid out himself, and spent so much and suffered so much to bring you to him, not for his profit, but yours, not to make himself happy, but you!

And hereby you will be guilty of breach of covenant with Christ: for in that covenant by which you are espoused to him,[21] you have engaged yourself to cleave to him, and him only.

There are many on every side of you that are seeking to draw your heart away from Christ. You had need to keep a strict watch over yourself, and to keep your heart with all diligence, to see that your heart don't run out after those lovers to whom it don't belong; and so grieve the

---

21. MS: "you."

Lord Jesus Christ and provoke him to withdraw, and so deprive yourself of much sweet communion with your spouse.

3. Earnestly seek that your soul may be more and more purified and adorned, to fit you for cohabitation with and the enjoyment of Jesus Christ. Christ is a person of infinite purity; he is of purer eyes than to behold spiritual filthiness, and therefore you had need to be clean in order to be fit for Christ's presence and his embraces.

He is a person of infinite dignity and glory, and therefore you had need to be adorned with excellent ornaments in order to your being fitted to go to him, to enter unto his palace, and to enter into his chambers, forever to dwell with him as his spouse. Christ seeks to have his spouse purified and adorned, to fit her to be presented to himself; and therefore he has done great things in order to it, as we are told, Eph. 5:25, "even as Christ also loved the church, and gave himself for it."

How are persons wont to adorn themselves, when they go to appear in the presence of a king. How then should you seek to have your soul adorned to fit you, not only to be in the presence of this glorious King of kings, but to dwell with him in most infinite and perfect communion forever?

Brides are wont to adorn themselves, so to fit them for the bridegroom. But certainly you need the best ornament to fit you for a wedding with such a bridegroom.

And according as you love and esteem the Lord Jesus Christ, will you desire to have your soul adorned to fit it for him. The more you love him, the more worthy will he appear in your eyes of your adorning yourself for him.

But, alas, how far are you from being fit as you are now? How much filthiness do you have, how little of that true grace that is the ornament of the soul in the sight of Christ?

Labor therefore to purge yourself more and more from all filthiness of the flesh and spirit, to mortify those hateful lusts and cleanse yourself from all those hateful ways that defile you and pollute your soul, and to grow in all grace, to be more and more of an holy, humble, meek, and heavenly spirit: for those are the ornaments that make a soul amiable in Christ's eyes.[22]

22. This point marks the end of the third preaching unit and the first booklet; JE designated and dated the next booklet, "No 1 decem 1737."

[DOCTRINE RESUMED.]

[The text we are upon is] Matt. 25:1–12.

The first words in this chapter evidently refer to something forego-ing: "Then shall the kingdom of heaven be likened unto ten virgins." The second "then" refers to some time that Christ had just before been speaking of; and in order to know what time that is, we must look into the preceding chapter: and there we shall find that the time Christ speaks of, is the time of his coming to judgment. You may see, in the 30th verse: "then shall appear the sign of the Son of man in heaven: and then shall all the tribes of the earth mourn, and they shall see the Son of man com-ing in the clouds of heaven with power and great glory." And so he goes on to speak of that day, to the end of the chapter. V. 36, "But of that day and hour knoweth no man, no, not the angels of heaven, but my Father only." [Vv.] 40–41, "Then shall two be in the field; the one shall be taken, and the other left. Two women shall be grinding at the mill; the one shall be taken, and the other left." [V.] 42, "Watch therefore: for ye know not what hour your Lord doth come." [V.] 50, "The lord of that servant shall come in a day when he looketh not for him, and in an hour that he is not aware of." So that this is the time referred to, when it is said here, "Then shall the kingdom of heaven be likened unto ten virgins, which took their lamps, and went forth to meet the bridegroom."

In the parable that I have now read, I would at this time observe two things in general:

1. That the company that goes forth to meet the bridegroom, is made up of two sorts of virgins.

2. That these two sorts of virgins agree in some things, and in others do exceedingly differ. They agree in that they go forth together; they are of the same company; they all take their lamps; they go forth together all upon the same design, viz., to meet the bridegroom.

And they agree in this, that while the bridegroom tarried, they all slumbered and slept. They all heard the midnight cry, wherein they were told that the bridegroom was coming; they were all called upon to go out to meet him, and accordingly all arise and trim their lamps.

But they greatly differ in other things. They greatly differ in what they are: some of them are wise, and others foolish.

They greatly differ in what they do: the one sort takes oil in their vessels with their lamps, and the other takes lamps and no oil with them. And they also greatly differ in the event and issue of things respecting them. They differ in that when the midnight cry was heard, the lamps of one sort were gone out, but the lamps of the other continued burning still. And so they greatly differed: the one were ready to meet the bridegroom, and the other were not.

And this occasioned a great difference in their behavior on occasion of that cry, "Behold, the bridegroom cometh." One are much more put into a fright than the other. One is put into a woeful hurry to seek oil out of season, while the other are prepared for that which is the proper business of the time, viz., not to buy oil, but to go forth to meet the bridegroom, and enter in with him into the marriage.

The one enters in with the bridegroom into the marriage, and the other are shut [out]. The one are enjoying the entertainment of the wedding, where the other came and had the door shut, and cry, "Lord, Lord, open to us," and that in vain, receiving no other answer from the bridegroom but, "Verily I say unto you, I know you not" [Matt. 25:12].

And therefore, from this parable I would raise these two general observations or propositions:

I. *That the visible church of Christ is made up of true and false Christians.*

II. *Those two sorts of Christians do in many things agree, and yet in many other things do greatly differ.*

I. The visible church of Christ is made up of true and false Christians. There is a mystical and invisible church of Christ that is only of true saints; 'tis this church, is the spouse of Christ. This is she that is the bride, with reference to which Christ in the context is called the bridegroom. This is that church that Christ loved and gave himself for, that he might sanctify {her}.

And there is a visible church of Christ in the world. This is that outward church, made up of those [who] have the profession and outward appearance of Christians.

This is that church of Christ in which the external public Christian worship, and the ordinary officers [and] ordinances of Christian worship, are upheld.

And this is of larger extent than the other. In this are contained not only true Christians, but many that are not Christians indeed, but only in appearance.

This is signified in the parable we are upon, of the two sorts of virgins that went forth to meet the bridegroom.

The same is signified in the following parable, beginning with the 14th verse, in which the visible church is compared to a company of servants to whom their master commits his good, in which company are two sorts of servants: the one faithful, and the other unfaithful [Matt. 25:14–30].

The same is represented in the latter part of the chapter, in the description of the day of judgment, where the visible church seems to be compared to a shepherd's flock, wherein are two different kinds of creatures: the one sheep, and the other goats [Matt. 25:25–36].

The same is represented in the 13th chapter of Matthew, by the wheat and the tares that both grow together in one field.

The same is represented in the words of John the Baptist, [in the] 3rd [chapter] of Matthew, [v.] 12, where the visible church is compared to a [threshing] floor, in which both wheat and chaff lie together.

And again, the same is represented by the Apostle in II Tim. 2:20, where the visible church is compared to a great house in which there are various sorts of vessels, some of gold and silver, and others of wood and earth; and some to honor, and others to dishonor.

So that this is abundantly held forth to us, not only in the parable of the ten virgins, but elsewhere, that the visible church of Christ is made of those two sorts, viz., true and false Christians.

First. 'Tis evermore so with respect to the universal visible church. That is, if we take the visible church of Christ, in all parts of it through the world, 'tis always so, in all ages and at all times, that 'tis made up of these two sorts. Here,

1. There never yet has been a time, but that there was a number of true saints in the visible church of Christ. It has been so, ever since God first set up his church in this fallen world. God ever has had, and ever will have, a church.

Satan hath long endeavored to extirpate the church. The dragon hath persecuted the woman, and hath cast water out of his mouth as a flood to destroy her [Rev. 12:15].

And oftentimes, God hath in his providence suffered him to prevail against it, so far as to bring her to the very brink of ruin; but God always hath stood on her side, and han't suffered Satan to swallow her up. Ps. 124:1–3, "If it had not been the Lord who was on our side, many a time may Israel say; If it had not been the Lord who was on our side, when men rose up against us: then they had swallowed us up quick, when their wrath was kindled against us." But the church is built on Christ, that is an immoveable rock, and therefore "the gates of hell never could prevail against it," nor ever shall. Matt. 16:18, "on this rock will I build my church."

Even in the most corrupt times of the church, when there seems to be the greatest appearance of the church's being destroyed, yet God has reserved a number of true worshippers. As it was in the corrupt times in Israel, when Elijah thought that there was none but he of God's worshippers left: God tells him, "Yet I have left me seven thousand in Israel, all the knees which have not bowed unto Baal, and every mouth which hath not kissed him," I Kgs. 19:18.

And so it was in the times of the greatest popish darkness, when all the world seemed to wonder after the beast [Rev. 13:3]. Yet there were always a number that opposed the corruptions and abomination of the church of Rome, and a great number, though they appeared very small in comparison of the rest.

The number of God's sealed ones in that time of great apostasy, while others followed the beast, followed the Lamb wheresoever he went. While others were defiled, these were virgins that were not defiled; where others were corrupted and ruined, these were redeemed from amongst men, as in the beginning of the 14th chapter of Revelation.

God always has a holy seed in his visible church, whereby religion is kept from wholly dying in the world, even in the most degenerate times. Is. 6:13, "But yet in it shall be a tenth, that shall be eaten: as a teil tree, and as an oak, whose substance is in them when they cast [their leaves]: so the holy seed shall be the substance thereof." But,

2. There are ever more false professors with the true. Very commonly, these make the far greater part; and here Christ tells us that though many are called, yet few are chosen, Matt. 20:16. The number of true saints in the visible church, are commonly but a small remnant out of a great multitude. Rom. 9:27, "Though the number of the children of Israel be as the sand of the sea, yet a remnant shall be saved."

Indeed, at sometimes the proportion of true professors to false ones in the visible church, is much greater than others. Sometimes religion is in much more flourishing circumstances in the church than at others, and then the number of true saints is great.

So it was in the primitive times of the gospel. True piety greatly flourished under the preaching of the apostles, and there were multitudes of true saints; and the churches planted by the apostles were in great part real Christians. And so again, in the time of the first Reformation from popery, religion greatly flourished, and there were many true saints. But yet, even in the most flourishing circumstances of the church, there are a great many false Christians with the true; as we know it was in the apostles' times.

Second. 'Tis commonly so in particular churches. 'Tis rarely so in particular societies of visible Christians, where God's ordinances are upheld and the gospel is preached in its purity, but that there are some godly persons, and that, even in places that are very corrupt. There was a Lot even in Sodom; and in Jerusalem of old, when it was exceeding corrupt and the city was so overspread with abomination that it was ripe for destruction, there was a number that sighed and cried. Ezek. 9:4, "and the Lord said unto him, Go through the midst of the city, through the midst of Jerusalem, and set a mark upon the foreheads of the men that sigh and that cry for all the abominations that be done in the midst thereof."

And on the other hand, in the most pure churches, where the doctrines of the gospel are preached in their greatest purity, and delivered in the most powerful and convincing manner, and vital religion is in the most flourishing circumstances, there will be some false professors mixed [in]. Thus there was a Judas even among the twelve disciples that went about Christ as his family of children.

REASONS.

There is a threefold reason may be given of this, or reasons of three kinds: one on the part of false professors that are members of the visible church; and another on the part of true Christians that are members of the mystical church; and another on the part of Christ, the head of the church.

[1.] The first reason, which respects the false members of the church, is the dreadful proneness there naturally is in the heart of man to hypocrisy. We are told, Jer. 17:9, that "the heart is deceitful above all things, and desperately wicked; who can know it?"

Men are naturally exceeding prone to deceive themselves in their opinion they have of themselves, and that from their pride and self-love.

Their pride makes 'em prone to entertain high thoughts of themselves, to look on themselves through a magnifying glass, to give honorable appellations to themselves, to think themselves virtuous and religious. And as they have a high thought of themselves, so they are ready to think God has a high thought of themselves: and hence, those that are indeed no Christians look on themselves as Christians, and profess themselves to be such.

And their self-love makes them exceeding prone to flatter themselves, that they have the necessary qualifications of an happy state. They are very ready to think themselves free from what they heard inevitably exposes them to ruin.

For every man would feign flatter himself that he is not like to be miserable, and he has a great deal of strong prejudice to blend into a thought that he has what is necessary to make him happy.

And hence, many men that hear the threatenings and promises of God's Word, and live in places of light, think themselves Christians, when they ben't Christian, and so make a false profession of Christianity.

And hence it is that false professors do abound everywhere where the light of the gospel comes, as it comes everywhere where the visible church is.

And then there is an exceeding proneness in men naturally, not only to deceive themselves, but to deceive others also. There is a seed or principle of pharisaism in every man, whereby he is prone to do things and to say things, to be seen of men, to make false pretenses and professions to deceive them, and to beget an high opinion of 'em in others.

Men naturally seek the honor that is of man, more than that which is of God, and to regard more how they appear in the eyes of men than in God's eyes. And to be a Christian is credible in the church of God; and this is another reason why false professors do abound in the visible church of Christ.

But besides this, there is a proneness in the heart of man to endeavor to deceive God him[self]. Man naturally is prone to be putting on a mask and disguise, even [when] he comes to appear before God, and to make false pretenses to him. And 'tis exceeding difficult to get men wholly off from a notion of God's being pleased with their fair outside; and many hope for acceptance with God from nothing else but a good outside.

These things are the reason why false professors abound in the church, as to what pertains to such false professors.

2. The second reason I would give of it, is on the part of the true professors of Christianity. And the reason as to what pertains to them, is that they can't search the hearts of others. Those that are indeed members of the mystical body of Christ, they can't look into others' hearts, and certainly determine who are of their society and who are not, so as to refuse to admit or receive any to be of their company, or to partake with them in their external privileges, but only such as are truly godly.

And Christ, in the rules that he has given for the reception of persons into the visible church, has wisely accommodated himself to the nature and state of his people here in this world. He has given 'em no power to search others' hearts, for that he has reserved to himself as his own prerogative. Rev. 2:23, "and all the churches shall know that I am he which searcheth hearts and the reins."

To go to make them judges of other hearts, would be not only to exalt 'em above their natures, but also to enstate 'em in his throne, and to invest 'em with that which belongs in proper to God only.

They are fellow servants, and Christ never committed to them power of judging their fellow servants.

Other men ben't their servants, but Christ and they have no business to judge another man's servant. Rom. 14:4, "Who art thou, that [judgest another man's servant]?"

If they do so, they are not doers of the law, but judges, as the apostle James say, Jas. 4:11.

Therefore, the rule that Christ has given his church to proceed by in admitting others to external privileges with them, is to proceed only by what is visible and external: for 'tis only that that is liable to our observation. As to the heart, that is invisible; that belongs to God to judge of, and not us.

The officers and rulers of the church, they are none of them searchers of men's hearts. And though some of them may be well-skilled in experimental religion and soul concerns, yet Christ has not seen fit to make their private judgment of the state of men's souls, their rule in admission of members into the church of Christ.

For they are but poor, fallible men at best, and if they should reject all that they think ben't truly godly, they may reject many that are truly godly. And therefore, Christ has given to none of his ministers power to separate wheat and tares in this world as judges, lest while they go about to root up the tares, they should root up the wheat also. Therefore, he would have both grow together till the harvest, till he comes as judge to separate them, who alone is equal to the business, Matt. 13:29–30.

So that nothing is left to the church as their rule with respect to admission or exclusion of members, but those things that are visible to the eye of the public, and not those things that appear to the private opinions of men. But such a public visibility won't exclude false professors; hence it comes to pass that false Christians are at all times, and everywhere, mixed with true in the visible church.

3. The last kind of reasons respect Christ,[23] the head of the church, why he so orders the state of the visible church in this world, that many false professors shall be in it. And two reasons may be given of it:

(1) Christ would not anticipate the work of the day of judgment, and do the work of that day, before the time. If Christ should now so order it, that true and false Christians should be precisely distinguished and separated, he therein would do the work of the day of judgment beforehand: for the business of that day, is to make such a separation. But Christ would not anticipate the work of that day.

For everything there is a season, and a time for every business, and purpose [Eccles. 3:1]. But the present time is not the time of judgment; it don't appear in God's sight a proper time.

The present time is a time of probation, and a future time, a time of judgment. To do the work of judgment now, would be to confound a day of probation and a day of judgment together.

There is a certain appointed time for judgment, a day for separating sheep from goats, wheat from chaff. The appointed day shall declare these things. The harvest is the proper time for separating wheat from tares; and therefore Christ says, "Let both grow together then till the harvest," Matt. 13:30.

And therefore Christ himself, while on earth, in acting as the head of the visible church, did not separate true professors from hypocrites, but admitted Judas among the disciples to like external privileges with them—though he knew that he was a devil—because he would not do the work of the day of judgment beforehand.

(2) There are wise ends why Christ so orders the state of the visible church, that many false professors shall be in it. Particularly these two:

23. MS: "Xs."

1. As a means of gathering in the elect. By means of such a state of things, many natural men are in the visible church of Christ, whereby they enjoy external privileges of visible Christians, and are the constant subjects of the means of grace; which proves a means of many of them being afterwards brought savingly home to Christ, and into the invisible church.

And this is a principal means of upholding the church of Christ in the world, from age to age.

If no natural men were in the visible church of Christ, then no natural men would be the adoring subjects of the appointed means of grace, and so wouldn't enjoy those means of their conversion that now they do. But one end of the ordinary dispensation of the ordinances of Christ, is the conversion of sinners.

2. For the rendering of reprobates more inexcusable, and the greater manifestation of divine justice in their condemnation. Wicked men are rendered abundantly the more inexcusable for being members of the visible church, for living under such light, such advantages; and their guilt becomes the greater for their sinning as they do against the light and their profession.

And this, the Scripture teaches us, is one end why 'tis ordered that some men live under means of grace. Isaiah was sent to preach to some in Israel for this end, Is. 6. Christ gives this reason why he preached to the unbelieving, obstinate Jews, Matt. 13:14. And therefore it is said that Christ "is set for the fall and rising again of many in Israel" [Luke 2:34], and that he shall be a precious cornerstone, a sure foundation to sinners [Is. 25:16].[24] So to others he is set for "a stone of stumbling," I Pet. 2:8.

APPLICATION.

I. Hence, we need not wonder when we find it so. Many professors come in.

II. Hence, they do greatly err that go about to make a separation between true and false Christians in the world, as though they had power of discerning and certainly distinguishing between godly and ungodly, and so will venture positively and absolutely to decide concerning[25] the state of others' souls.

---

24. In revising for repreaching, JE deleted this sentence.
25. MS: "concerns."

They do err that will positively determine for persons that they are converted, but more especially they who are positive and peremptory in determining against 'em, being forward to say of one and another that they never were converted, and that they han't a jot of true grace in their hearts.

By such censoriousness, persons do certainly do that which is not agreeable to the state and circumstances of the church in this world. If men in the present state had been endowed with such power, Christ never would have so ordered it, that true and false Christians should evermore be mixed together in the world. Such persons take upon them the part of the judge, and anticipate the work of the day of judgment.

III. If it be so, {that the visible church is made up of true and false Christians}, hence we may assuredly gather that the present state of the church is not its last state. [It will be] succeeded by another {state}. A state of such mixture is a state of confusion, {and cannot last}. Godly and ungodly are most contrary in their natures and state. {They are} as contrary as sheep and wolves. Can it be believed that a shepherd will never separate such, but always will suffer sheep and wolves {to dwell together}? Can it be imagined that a prudent husbandman, however he may suffer wheat and chaff to be together for a while, yet will always sift [them together]?

This is a strong argument for a future state as a day of judgment.

Doubtless, there will come a time when there shall a pure church, {composed of} only saints. Christ's bride shall be pure, "not having spot, or wrinkle, or any such thing" [Eph. 5:27].

IV. If {the visible church is made of true and false Christians}, then let us all look to ourselves, and see to it that we are true Christians.

We have reason to think, from what has been said, that true and false professors are mixed here amongst us, as 'tis all over the visible church {of Christ}.

We live when we hope there are many true Christians, but yet there are wise virgins and foolish mixed {together}. Don't let any of us content ourselves with being accepted in the visible church.

Let us consider what has been said, viz., that one end why it is thus ordered {that the visible church is made of true and false Christians}, is that it may render the state of those that live and die false Christians the more inexcusable.

Both now have been of the visible church. If [you are] a false Christian, better be none at all. Better [to] have been a heathen, {for false Christians are} more inexcusable, [their] guilt [is] greater. "I know thy works, that thou art neither cold not hot" [Rev. 3:15].

False Christians in the visible church, of all mankind, will be those that will be lowest in [hell].

Therefore, let us see to it that we are not of that number.[26]

[DOCTRINE RESUMED.]

Two propositions have been raised from this parable:

I. *That the visible church of Christ is made up of true and false Christians.*

II. *That those do in some things agree, and in others greatly[27] differ.*

Having spoken to the former of these, I come now to the other. And in the

First place, I would take notice how many things wherein true and false Christians agree. And,

1. I would take notice of those things wherein true and false in general agree. And,

2. Wherein they may and do sometimes agree. But,

1. I would take notice of some things wherein true and false Christians do in general agree.

(1) They agree in a profession of Christianity. They all agree in that, that all have lamps, and all are upon the same professed design, viz., to go forth and meet the bridegroom. They are all the professed attendants of the bride, visible guests at the wedding, and all agree in profession of respect to the bridegroom. They go forth to meet the bridegroom, and take lamps in their hands, with that pretense of putting honor and respect upon him.

They all profess to believe the same great and fundamental doctrines of religion: as that there is one God, that Jesus Christ is the Son of God, that there is another world, and an eternal judgment.

26. This point marks the end of the fourth preaching unit and of the second booklet. The next booklet is identified and dated by JE: "No 2, Matt. 25:1–12, Jan. 1737, 8."

27. MS: "great."

They are baptized into the same covenant of grace, and all profess that God is to be feared and loved and honored above all; that sin is to be hated and repented of, and that God should be our main end; and that Christ is to be loved and trusted in and obeyed, and that the things of another world are mainly to be regarded.

They in like manner profess these things, or things that so imply them, in their prayers to God, when they attend in public or private prayers. They in like manner profess to God that [he] is an infinitely great and glorious, and just and merciful God, and that they are poor, sinful, unworthy creatures; unworthy of the least of God's mercies, and deserving of his eternal wrath.

They in like manner profess that they have no righteousness of their own to recommend them to God, and that they can come to God only through Christ, that he is the only Savior of mankind.

They in like manner in their prayers profess thankfulness to God for the mercies he bestows upon them, and dependence on him for the mercies that they stand in need of.

(2) They all of them attend the same external duties and ordinances of religion. This is another thing implied in their all having lamps, and all going forth to meet the bridegroom. True Christians and false, they all use the same Bible as their rule of faith and practice. They keep the same sabbaths; they in like manner attend on the ordinances of God's house; they attend on the same appointed duties of public worship.

They all appear to join in the public prayers, and in singing God's praises. False Christians, they come before God as his people, come and sit before him as his people, and hear his Word, as they do, Ezek. 33:31.

(3) They are of the same company or visible society. The wise virgins and foolish, they were one company; they went forth together to meet the bridegroom. So the wheat and tares, they both grow together till the harvests.

They are both admitted before the day of judgment, are mixed together in the same flock.

Judas was reckoned with the twelve apostles. He was one of the company that constantly attended Christ, and were with him as his children.

They are wont to worship God as one religious society, and to join one with another in it. They are wont to stand together to put up their requests and petitions to God, all with one voice, having one person to be the mouth of the whole congregation.

They sit and sing God's praises together. They sing the same words as it were with one voice.

They sit together to hear God's Word. They come together as one holy society or family to the Lord's Table.

They sit together to see Christ's body broken and blood poured out, as it is symbolically represented, and they eat and drink together.

And so they converse together, and associate themselves one with another, as those that are of the same Christian society.

(4) They agree in the hopes that they entertain hope of future blessedness. The foolish virgins went forth with the same hopes with the wise; they all hoped to meet the bridegroom, and to be found ready when he came, and to be welcomed by him. All hoped to enter in with him into the marriage. The foolish virgins, as well as the wise, hoped to be joyful guests at the marriage feast. So true Christians and false agree, in that they hope to go to heaven: that is the professed design of all, to get heaven. They hope, when death comes, to be found ready, to have their souls conveyed into the glorious presence of God, and into the arms of Christ's eternal love.

They hope to be welcomed to glory by Christ, and by saints and angels above. They hope, all of them, at the day of judgment, when Christ appears coming in the clouds of heaven, to lift up their heads and with joy behold the sight; they all hope then to be caught up in the clouds, to meet the Lord in the air, and leave the wicked behind in horror and amazement.

Though they think many will then be in amazing circumstances, yet they hope not to be some of them.

They hope that when Christ comes to separate the righteous from the wicked, they shall be set at the right; and that when the sentence comes to be pronounced, they shall have the blessed sentence pronounced on them: "Come, ye blessed [of my Father, inherit the kingdom prepared for you from the foundation of the world," Matt. 25:24].

(5) False Christians agree with true ones in this, that they seek heaven. They not only hope for it, but do various things in order to it. So the foolish virgins, they sought the favor of the bridegroom, and to be admitted in with him into the marriage for that; and they took their

lamps and went forth to meet the bridegroom, in like manner as the wise did.

So false Christians very commonly do seek heaven; they attend on various ordinances, and perform many duties, in hope of getting heaven by it. We read that Herod, when he heard John [the] Baptist preach, did many things, Mark 6:20. So Christ tells us that many "seek to enter in" at the strait gate, that "shall not be able," Luke 13:24.[28]

These things, true Christians and false in general agree on. I proceed now, in the

2. [Second] place, to mention some things that they may and do sometimes agree in. And these are of two kinds:

(1) Either those that they may agree in through resemblances or appearances of godliness in false Christians. And,

(2) Through the infirmities and failings of true Christians.

[(1)] So I would mention some things wherein true Christians and false [may agree through resemblances or appearances of godliness].

1. A false Christian may make profession of special experience of a work of grace in their hearts, as well as true Christians. He may not only make such a profession of Christianity as visible Christians in general do, in professing their assent to the fundamental doctrine of the gospel, and in either explicitly or implicitly owning their baptismal covenant; but they may pretend that they have had experience of a special word of God's Spirit in their hearts, opening their eyes to see spiritual and divine things, and in renewing their hearts and drawing them to God and Christ. They may tell of those things that they call great spiritual discoveries, and wherein they think they have had special communion with God.

Yea, they may make pretenses of eminent experiences. So did some of the Galatians to the apostle Paul, that yet he afterward was afraid of. Gal. 4:15, "Where is the blessedness that ye spake of?"

2. False Christians may not only make an high profession of religion, but may indeed have many religious affections. They may have

---

28. Portions of this sermon booklet are made from a discarded prayer bid, which reads:

> Leut. Stebbins being Sick he desires the prayers of the Congregation that God would heal again if it be his will and determined to fit him for his pleasure. The Children they also desire Prayers for he is Dangerously Sick.

religious affections of sorrow; as had Saul, when he lift up his voice and wept at the thoughts of his own unworthy behavior, and acknowledged that David was more righteous. I Sam. 24:16–17, "And it came to pass, when David had made an end of speaking these words unto Saul, that Saul said, Is this thy voice, my son David? And Saul lifted up his voice, and wept. And he said to David, Thou art more righteous than I: for thou hast rewarded me good, whereas I have rewarded thee evil." And so had Judas when he condemned himself, and said, "I have sinned, in that I have betrayed the innocent blood," Matt. 27:4.

They may have great affections of gratitude for God's mercies. As the Israelites had at the Red Sea, of whom we read, Ps. 106:12, that "they sang his praise." Natural men's hearts are capable of affections of gratitude towards God, as well as towards men, for kindness received. We read of Saul's being mightily affected with gratitude to David for sparing his life, when he had opportunity to have slain [him]. He expresses himself very gratefully [on] that occasion; I Sam. 24:18–19, "And thou hast showed this day how that thou hast dealt well with me: forasmuch as when the Lord had delivered me into thine hand, thou killedst me not. For if a man find his enemy, will he let him go well away? wherefore the Lord reward thee good for that thou hast done unto me this day."

So the Galatians, that the Apostle seemed afterwards to doubt of, were mightily affected with gratitude to the apostle Paul for the good that they supposed that he had been the instrument of to their souls. Gal. 4:15, "for I bear you record, that, if it had been possible, you would have plucked out your own eyes, and have given them to me."

Persons may be much affected in reading or hearing of the great things Christ did and suffered for men, and yet be false Christians. The thoughts of the great suffering and abuses Christ underwent, may work upon man's nature, as hearing any other very tragical story. And it may work on man's natural principle of gratitude, when they hear how that Christ did this from love to sinners.

False Christians may be affected in the hearing of the gospel preached. They may love to hear the Word preached; the preaching may be very pleasant to them. So it was to the Jews of old. Ezek. 33:32,[29] "And, lo, thou art unto them as a very lovely song of one that hath a pleasant voice, and can play well on an instrument: for they hear thy words, but they do them not." It may be joyful to them, as it is to the stony-ground

29. MS: "33:31."

hearers [Matt. 13:1–23]. They may be lifted and quite carried away with admiration of it, as some of Christ's enemies were at his preaching. They said, John 7:46, "Never man spake as this man." They may seem to feel very pleasantly while the Word is preached, as the Galatians did when they said, What a blessedness is it [Gal. 4:15]. They may have an affection of zeal, as Jehu had, who yet was not of a perfect and upright heart, II Kgs. 10:18.

They may have affections of praise. They may feel in themselves a disposition to praise God and cry out in God's praises, as the Jews did to Christ when he made his last entry into Jerusalem: the whole multitude seemed to be greatly affected and moved, and their hearts were lifted up, insomuch that they cut down branches of palm trees and strewed them on the way, and strewed their garments in the way where Christ was to come, as if they thought he was so great, that the ground was not worthy that the beast that he rode upon should tread on it. And they cried out with a loud voice, "Hosanna to the son of David: Blessed is he that cometh in the name of the Lord; Hosanna in the highest" [Matt. 21:9].

False Christians may be very much affected with some great and extraordinary work of God, and their hearts may be lifted up with it, and they may seem to have a disposition to praise God for it, as the Jews had, when they see the wonderful miracles that Christ wrought. Mark 2:12, "And immediately he arose, took up the bed, and went forth before them all; insomuch that they were all amazed, and glorified God, saying, We never saw it on this fashion." The same is expressed in Luke [5:]26, "And they were all amazed, and they glorified God, and were filled with fear, saying, We have seen strange things today."

3. False Christians may agree with true Christians in that, that in many things they may be very strict and exact in their walk. In this respect, foolish virgins may have lamps as well as the wise virgins, and their lamps may in some respects shine very bright.

They may be very exact in their dealings with their neighbors, and to rules of justice, and in other moral duties: as the Pharisee blessed God that he was no extortioner, unjust, nor adulterer [Luke 18:11]; and as the young rich man that came to Christ, whom he directed to keep the commandments, and had the commandment of the second table mentioned to him, said with great freedom, "All these have I kept from my youth up" [Matt. 19:20]. And as the apostle Paul says of himself before his conversion, that "touching the righteousness which was of the law," he was "blameless," Philip. 3:6; and says, in Acts 26:5, "that after the most straitest sect" of their religion, he "lived a Pharisee."

False Christians may be very exact in their attendance on the ordinances of religion, as the Pharisees were exceeding exact in their observance of the ordinances and institutions of the law of Moses; as particularly, so strict were they in observing the law that instituted tithe, that they paid the tithe of all the herbs that they had in their gardens. They "tithed mint and anise and cummin" [Matt. 23:23]. A false Christian may abound in religious performances, as the Pharisees made many and long prayers, and were very much insisting they fasted twice a week.

4. False Christians may have a strong and confident hope of their good estate. They may naturally hope that they shall get heaven when they die, as visible Christians in general do; but they may look upon themselves as being already entitled to that blessedness, yea, and they have a strong confidence of it.

That they are in a good estate may be a point settled with 'em, a thing that they have long concluded upon, and don't call into question; and when they go before God in their prayers, it may be with that notion, and may apply themselves to God as some of his children, and may suppose it in all their talk with others. All may go upon that supposition, that they are converted men, and those whose state is safe.

So it was with the Pharisees. They did not question their being in favor with God: when they came before God in prayer, they went on that supposition, and thanked God for it, Luke 18:11. And so they went upon that supposition in their talk with men. The Prophet seems to have respect to them in that [place], Is. 65:5, "which say, Stand by thyself, come not near to me; for I am holier than thou."

5. They, as well as true Christians, may be received into the charity and good opinion of those that are true Christians. There is no appearance in this parable as though the wise virgins did not receive the foolish ones to their charity, till the midnight cry came; till then, there seemed to be no visible distinction between 'em. All were together; they went together in one company. It don't appear that the wise virgins were jealous of 'em, or suspected 'em not to be of their number, or did not think 'em as good as themselves.

So it oftentimes is that false Christians are well received among true Christians. They have lamps as well as themselves, and that is all that is visible to them; as to the inside of their vessels, that is hid from 'em, they can't see whether they have any oil or no.

They are oftentimes well accounted of by the godly; from what they hear and say what they see in them, they don't call their sincerity into question. The godly have their love and affections knit to them under that supposition, that they are some of Christ's.

And they associate themselves with 'em under that notion, as the wise virgins associated themselves with the foolish, and went forth all together. They may, time after time, talk with them about spiritual things, under that notion that they are some that are savingly acquainted with these things.

[IMPROVEMENT.]

[I shall] conclude by making improvement of what has been said, in some inferences.

I. If it be so, that true Christians and false do agree in so many things, then hence we may learn how unfit we are to be men's judges. For if it be as we have said, we learn that it must be an very difficult thing [to] distinguish between true and false professors, and too difficult for those that can't see the hearts of men. It is impossible for those certainly to do it, that can't look into men.

Men have nothing else to judge by, but what is visible; but, by what has been said, we may see that false Christians may agree with true in all those things that are visible to the world, or that are visible to their neighbors and those that are about 'em. The foolish virgins agreed with the wise in their lamps. We have no account of any difference between their lamps and the wise virgins', but the lamps of the one shone and gave light, as those of the others. That which the difference between them lay in, was in the emptiness of the inside of their vessels, which was hid from sight.

This should be a warning to us, not to be too forward as to presume in judging the state of others' souls. We may see many hopeful appearances of godliness in others, which may oblige our charity, but there is no sufficient ground for us to pass sentence on men as if we were judges.

No qualifications that men can have, make 'em fit to be judges of others. In this matter, being wise men don't do it. A being holy and experienced men don't do it. The wise virgins were experienced persons, but there is no appearance in the parable of their judging or finding out their foolish companions, till the midnight cry came.

II. If it be so, that true Christians and false may agree in so many things, hence we may learn what care and strictness everyone should use with himself, with respect to the grounds of his own hope. The being upon a right and sure foundation for eternity, is a matter of the greatest possible concern and importance. 'Tis a dreadful thing to build wrong; a man had better not have been born, than to settle and continue on a wrong foundation. Persons should use exceeding care concerning the ground of their hope, these two ways:

First. They should use great care in first settling on hope of a good estate. We should proceed with the utmost caution in this matter; otherwise a man, that moment that he settles it with himself that he is in a good estate, he may eternally undo himself, and as effectually as he would have killed his body, if he had that moment run a sword through his own throat.

Second. They should from time to time be very strict in examining the grounds of their hope, even after they have ventured to settling. They should be searching their foundation over and over again, and that because, by reason of their having so many things that are common both to false Christians and true, many persons build wrong. "The heart is deceitful above all things" [Jer. 17:9]. The Apostle exhorts all Christians to that duty of examining their state. II Cor. 13:5, "Examine yourselves, whether ye be in the faith."

III. Hence we learn what things we should not rest in as evidences of our being true Christians, viz., none of those things wherein false Christians and true may agree:

Not on a profession of Christianity, though that profession may be orthodox and sound.

Not in an attendance on the same external ordinance and duties that God's people attend.

Not in being admitted into the same society, and belonging to the same church, or sitting at the same Lord's Table with them; not in that we are seeking future blessedness in the use of appointed means.

Not in any common religious affections; not in that, that we have affections of sorrow for sin, and have heart-melting, and can shed tears about our own unworthiness.

Not in that we have some kind of affections of gratitude to God for particular remarkable mercies we have had, or for God's great mercy in giving his Son to die for sinners.

Not in that we have found ourselves disposed to shed tears sometimes when we have been reading in the Bible, or have heard the Word preached.

Not in that we have sometimes felt well in hearing the Word preached, and it has been a lovely song to us.

Not in that we have found our hearts lifted up with admiration of sermons that we have heard, and have been ready in the time of it to say, What a blessedness is it.

Not in that we have been affected when we have heard or read about Christ's sufferings, and love to sinners in it.

Not merely in that, that we have felt within ourselves a disposition to praise God, as the children of Israel sang his praises at the Red Sea.

Not in that merely, that we have found our hearts much moved and lifted up by what we have beheld of some great and extraordinary work of God's that has been wrought amongst us, like the Jews who glorified God when they saw Christ's miracles saying, "We have seen strange things today," and, "We never saw it on this fashion" [Luke 5:26, Mark 2:12].

Not in that, that we find we have a spirit of zeal against some sorts of wickedness.

Not in that, that we are very strict and exact in many things in our external walk and behavior.

Not in that, that we are strict in many moral rules and religious ordinances, or abundant in some religious duties.

Not in that, that we have found ourselves lifted up with joy, and have had heretofore a strong confidence that our state was good.

Nor in that, that we have been received into the charity and good opinion of God's people, and have been, without scruple, accepted as some of them: not in any one, or in all of these together.

But let us, before we conclude ourselves to be godly, see to it that we have something beyond all these things, something or other that is beyond all that wherein true Christians and false agree.

All these things are signified by the lamps that were common both to the wise and foolish virgins; they are none of them certain signs of that oil by which the wise virgins were distinguished. Let us seek those things that are distinguishing, and see to it that we have 'em, before we conclude ourselves to be in a good estate. Matt. 5:20, "except your righteousness shall exceed the righteousness of the scribes and Pharisees, ye shall in no case [enter into the kingdom of heaven]."[30]

[DOCTRINE RESUMED.]

[The text we are upon is] Matt. 25:1–12, especially vv. 5–7, "[While the bridegroom tarried, they all slumbered and slept. And at midnight there was a cry made, Behold, the bridegroom cometh; go ye out to meet him. Then all those virgins arose, and trimmed their lamps]."

Two general *Propositions:*

I. *The visible church is made up of true and false Christians.*

II. *That those do in some things agree, and in others they greatly differ.*

[*First.*]And it was proposed to show how that, in many things, true and false Christians agree.

1. True and false Christians in general agree.

2. Wherein they may and sometimes do agree.

Two kinds of these works [were] observed, either:

[(1)] Those things true and false Christians may agree in, through the resemblances or appearances of godliness in Christians; and,

(2) Through the infirmities and failings of true Christians.

A third thing might have been mentioned, viz., those things they agree in through that self-love that is common to all.

Having already spoken to the former of these, I come to the latter, viz.,

(2) To show wherein true Christians and false may agree through the infirmities and failings of true Christians.

And under this head, there are six things may be observed from those three verses that have been now read:

1. That there is abundance of corruption in the hearts of true Christians as well as others.

2. True Christians may sometimes, in many respects, agree with others in the corrupt frames that they are in.

3. [They may agree,] in some respects, in the ill acts they commit, [the] ways they walk in.

---

30. This point marks the end of the fifth preaching unit and of the third booklet. The next booklet is designated "No. 3" by JE, and a notation by another hand gives the date, "1737–38."

4. That in a time of decay of religion amongst a professing people, 'tis commonly so that all, both wise virgins and foolish, slumber and sleep.

5. That one great reason of both wise virgins and foolish slumbering and sleeping as they do, is the bridegroom's tarrying.

6. When true Christians slumber and sleep, the midnight cry is like to be unexpected[31] to them, as well as the foolish.

Here, the

1. [First] thing, is that there is abundance of corruption in the hearts of true Christians as well as others.

Here, several particulars may be observed under this head:

a. There is a body and fountain of sin in the hearts of the godly, as well as others. There is not only some small remains of corruption in them, as there may be a gleaning after an harvest, but there is a body of sin and death, so as exceedingly to defile the nature. And therefore the Apostle, who was not only a true Christian, but one of the most eminent Christians that ever was in the world, cries out, "O wretched man that I am! who shall deliver me from the body of this death?," Rom. 7:24.

Instead of being but small remains of corruption, there is but a little grace. Corruption is done away no further than grace prevails. As it is with a place that has heretofore been filled with perfect darkness: darkness is done away no further than light prevails. But in the hearts of the godly, there is but a small beam of light, and therefore a great deal of remaining darkness.

b. The corruption that is in the hearts of the godly, so far as it prevails, is of as hateful a nature as that which is in the hearts of wicked men. Though the godly are, by the grace of God, made better than wicked, yet 'tis not because their corruptions are any better than the corruptions of wicked men. The corruption that there is in the heart of a godly man, according to what there is of it, is as opposite to God, as contrary to his nature, and as much of an enemy to him, as the corruption [in the heart of a wicked man]. Corruption in them tends as much, according to the degree of its prevalency, to contempt of God and hatred of God, and disobedience to his commands and rebellion against his authority, and ingratitude for his mercy, as in any persons whatsoever.

'Tis as hellish in its nature. Sin, wherever it is, is the image of the devil, whether it be in a godly man or a wicked man.

31. MS: "unexpecting."

Thus pride in the godly, is as hateful as pride in a wicked man. And so [the same] may be said of covetousness and sensuality and malice: those things are as hateful in the godly as in the wicked. In their nature, though not in degree, they are as hateful to God, and as worthy of the hatred of all men.

The hearts of men may be made better by infusing a principle contrary to corruption. But the corruption of their hearts never can be made better; it can't be changed. Neither is there nothing to be done towards any amendment with respect to it, but by destroying of it.

Sin is of so bad a nature, that it never can be mended, for it is infinitely evil. As 'tis with God, 'tis impossible he should be made worse, because he is infinitely good. So 'tis with sin against God, which is infinitely evil: it can't be mended or made better.

The corruption that is in the hearts of the godly, is of as hateful a nature as that which [is] in the hearts of wicked men in its nature, and more hateful in its circumstances. Sin is nowhere so hateful to God as in his own child. That which a man abhors and loathes, he will abhor nowhere so much as nearest to him; defilement is nowhere so hateful, as 'tis in some precious jewel or choice vessel. The more God loves his saints, and the more precious they are to him, the more hateful to God is sin, and in them.

c. There are the seeds of all the same kinds of sin in the godly, that there is in natural men. The elect, they bring the principle of as many lusts into the world with 'em as others, and not one lust is totally rooted out in conversion.

So that a godly man has in his heart as many natural principles of corruption remaining in him, as a natural man has. A natural man has a seed of 'em against God in his heart, and so has a godly man. A natural man {has a} principle of other sin, and so {has a godly man} of contempt of the gospel of Jesus Christ. And so there are principles of pride, of self-righteousness, of sensuality, of envy, of malice and revenge in the hearts of the godly, as there is in the hearts of natural men. And indeed, there is no one sin that men commit, but that a godly man has that in them that tends to it.

Yea, a godly man has that sin and corruption in him that, in its own nature, tends to the commission of the sin against the Holy Ghost. And the reason why godly men never commit that sin, is not because they han't that corruption in their hearts that tends to it, or that exposes 'em to it; but only because God's faithfulness to his own covenant promises will preserve them from it.

d. There is a principle of love to sin, and oftentimes the exercise of such a principle, in the heart of a godly man. It is a mistake if any imagine that there is no love to sin in a godly man.

Indeed, the godly do differ from natural men in this, that they have a spirit to hate sin, and that as sin, or as against God. But yet they have a contrary spirit in 'em at the same time, and their spirit of love to sin may [be], and is very often, in exercise.

There is no man so holy upon earth, but that at sometimes feels the workings of love to these and those sinful acts or ways.

There is two contrary principles struggling one with another in the heart of a godly man,[32] like Jacob and Esau in Rebecca's womb. There is no impossibility or contradiction in this; indeed, it would be a contradiction to suppose that a godly man should both love and hate sin in the same act, but not that he should have contrary principles inclining to both, which at different times may be in exercise.

As long as a principle of sin remains, [it] is impossible but that there should remain a principle of love to sin: for surely every lust loves itself. 'Tis of necessity that a lust should love its own object. To suppose that there is a lust in the hearts of the godly, and yet no love to the sin lusted after, is a contradiction.

If there was no love to sin in a godly man, there would be no sin, for love to sin can't be rooted out till sin itself is: for a principle of sin consists in the inclination of the heart. The lusts of the heart, and the sin of the heart, are the same thing; and where there is an inclination of heart, there is a love of heart.

If a godly man did [not] at all love sin, then he would not at all desire, or in the least incline, to commit sin. And if he did not at all, at any time, ever incline to commit sin, he would have no sin in his heart.

Root out all sinful inclinations out of the heart, and you root out all sin out of the heart. Indeed, there are these two ways where a godly man don't love sin:

(a) He don't love sin with a love of settled esteem, i.e., sin is not that which he statedly entertains a good opinion and value for, as wicked men. Wicked men esteem the ways of sin: they place happiness in 'em; they have a settled and established value for the objects of their lusts.

32. MS: "men."

But it is not so with a good [man]: he has no established, good opinion of sin, but on the contrary, he looks upon [it as] vile and abominable, that which debases and dishonors his nature, that which is worthy to be abhorred and detested. He looks upon it as the wound and disease of his nature, and as the great calamity of his soul. This is the settled opinion and esteem that a godly man has of sin; as the Apostle cries out, "O wretched man that I am!"

(b) A godly man don't love sin by a stated choice of it. The stated and established choice of the soul of a godly man, is not of sin, or any of the ways of sin, but of God and the ways of holiness.

In his settled choice, he renounces sin universally. He renounces every one of the ways of sin.

The heart of a godly [man], in its ordinary election, fully forsakes sin and cleaves to holiness. Ps. 119:30, "I have chosen the way of truth, thy judgments have I laid before me."

But yet, in these two ways a godly man may find a love to sin, may at times love sin with [a] love of desire:

a. He may find stirrings of desires after sin, or after the objects of his lusts. If they were not the objects of his desires, they could not be the objects of his lusts: for that which a man feels no desires of, surely he don't lust after. David, when he lusted after Bathsheba, he desired to commit adultery with her.

b. They may have delight in sin. As they may desire the object of lust before 'tis obtained, so they may delight in it when obtained. The same principle that will cause one, will cause the other also.

The sin that lust inclines[33] to is, and must be, that which in its own nature is pleasing and gratifying to that lust. Otherwise, the lust would not go out after it, and the lust of the heart and the corrupt nature may take delight in it.

Every nature delights in what is agreeable to it. But sin is agreeable to that corrupt nature that is in the godly.

Thus is that verified, Gal. 5:17, "The spirit lusteth against the flesh and the flesh against the spirit, so that ye cannot do the things that ye want."

e. The corruption that is in the hearts of the godly, has its foundation in the same thing as in the hearts of natural men, viz., ignorance

---

33. MS: "inclined."

of God. There is a great deal of corruption in the heart of a godly man, because there is a great deal of blindness and ignorance of God.

There is some true knowledge of God, but 'tis but little. The godly in this [world] see but very darkly; 'tis but a little portion that is known of God. The light that shines in their hearts, is but a light that shines in a dark place, where there is a great deal more blindness than light.

The knowledge that a godly man has of God in this world is so small, that it is compared to the knowledge of a child, I Cor. 13:11. Through the smallness of the degree of spiritual light and knowledge, it comes to pass[34] oftentimes that the sense that the godly have of God's perfections, is distinctly sensible only in some particulars. There are some spiritual things that they have had no distinct spiritual discovery of. Some hope they have had at times a sensible view of the excellency of God's grace or faith, fullness or holiness, but that may be a difficulty with 'em, that they are afraid that they never had sight of his majesty and greatness. Many [a] Christian's doubt about their state arises from such defects; they have had sensible and distinct views but of some things. If they had as much of a sight of others as they have of those, they should not be afraid.

Thus true Christians and false agree, in that there is abundance of corruption in the heart of one, as well as the other.

2. True Christians may sometimes, in many respects, agree with others in the corrupt frames that they are [in]. As the godly have a great deal of corruption, and but little holiness, so they may be in very corrupt frames through the exercise of that corruption.

Grace being small, it [is] sometimes covered and hid, like a coal or spark buried up in ashes, or a jewel buried in rubbish, or a star hid in a cloud. As the wise virgins slumbered and slept, so grace in them may be as it were asleep for a considerable time.[35]

Godly men may be in very stupid and senseless frames. They may be in a senseless frame as to any spiritual or gracious sense of things in their hearts, having little or no sense of Christ's excellency, or of [his] love to sinners, or of God's mercy to them. [They may have] no sense of that beauty and holiness of spiritual things.

They may be in frames wherein their hearts may be like a stone. They may sit unaffected under the most affecting dispensations of God's

---

34. MS: "pass that."

35. JE deletes: "The corruptions take the advantage of this, and may put forth themselves. Corruption in the heart of the saints may be in strong and vigorous exercise."

Word, and when the most affecting things are set before them; as when they are hearing of the wonderful and glorious things that God has done for sinful men by Christ, or when they see those things represented and held forth in the Lord's Supper.

They may be very senseless[36] and stupid, as being void of a sense of the importance of spiritual things. They may be in such frames, that they may greatly stand in need of awakenings as well as natural men. A godly man may very much need awakening preaching; they may need to have the law set home upon their consciences, to make 'em more sensible of the infinite importance of spiritual things, and the dreadful nature of sin and the vanity of the world. This senselessness is doubtless one thing meant by the wise virgins' slumbering and sleeping. For when men are asleep, they are senseless; their senses are then locked up.

A godly man[37] may be in a careless frame, wherein he don't keep up his watch; which is another thing included in the wise virgins' slumbering and sleeping. Sleeping and watching are true contraries.

The disciples were in such a frame that night that Christ was betrayed. Christ directed 'em to watch and pray, lest they should fall into temptation. But they did not keep up their watch, but fell asleep time after time; and through their unwatchfulness, were not prepared for the temptation that came upon 'em when Christ was apprehended, and so were easily overcome by it, and all forsook him and fled.

A godly man may be in a very slothful frame, very much indisposed to duties of religion, indisposed to any diligent reading of the Scripture, or meditation, or to the duty of secret prayer, that may be a great backwardness to duty. Thus the spouse was in a very slothful frame, and backward to duty, when she slept; but her heart waked, and her beloved stood at the door, Cant. 5:2–3.

Godly men may be in a worldly frame, and in a proud frame, as David was when he numbered the people, and as Hezekiah was. [Godly men may be] in a very unbelieving frame, as the disciples were when Christ upbraided them of their unbelief. And they may otherwise be in very ill frames, and may have very evil workings of heart.

And from the godly's being in such ill frames, two things may come to pass:

36. MS: "as."
37. MS: "men."

a. It may be many times so, that what seems most sensibly to influence 'em in religion, may be natural principles. When they read and pray, and when they avoid these and those acts of sin, that which much more sensibly influences them than anything else, may be natural conscience and self-love, much more sensibly than love to God: for godly men are often moved by such principles. So Job mentions his fear of destruction from God as what restrained him from sin. Job 31:23, "[For] destruction from God [was a terror to me]."

And when grace is not in exercise, they are influenced mainly by those: for grace influences no farther than it is in exercise.

b. A godly man may for a time feel no otherwise, to his own sense, than when before he was converted. He may for a time, while grace is asleep, seem to have no more spiritual view or sense of things than before his conversion, and to be for the present as stupid and senseless.

Thus true Christians may agree with false in their frame of heart.

3. True Christians may in some respects agree [with wicked men], in the evil acts they are guilty of, and in the ill ways they walk in.

a. True Christians may fall into such transgressions, as we have many instances that make it evident in the Scripture. And,

b. True Christians, being blinded by some lust or prevailing corruption, may sometimes walk in evil ways. They may continue in ways that don't become a Christian, and that are very displeasing and offensive to God; tending much to the dishonor of religion and the wounding of their own souls, and sometimes to the procuring many of God's frowns and judgments in the world. So Solomon greatly sinned and wounded himself by his multiplying wives, and tolerating and countenancing their idolatry. And so Peter, even after his denying his Lord and repenting, was said in a way greatly to be blamed in countenancing the Jews in their superstition and uncharitableness towards the gentiles, for which the apostle Paul sharply rebuked him [Gal. 2:11].

APPLICATION.

I would make some improvement of what has been said, before I proceed to the consideration of other particulars. And I would improve it in a twofold warning: one with respect to our censure of others, and another with regards to persons' judgment of themselves.

First. If it be so, that it may be with true Christians in so many respects as it is with false, through infirmities [and] failing, then this should be a warning to us, not to be too forward to[38] cast others out of our charity, for those things that we may see amiss in them.

Those things may be sufficient for a person to judge all of his own state, that mayn't be sufficient for others so to judge; because a person himself can better determine the nature of his own acts and the principles, whence they proceed, than others can. He may know how far he sins against light in it, and what conviction he goes against. Others can't tell those things, because they see only the outside as it were of the act; what is internal is hid from them.

Second. If it be as we have heard, that true Christians may agree with others in these things that have been mentioned, then persons ought not to determine against them, because they find such things in themselves.

Not because {you} find an appearance of so little grace, and such abundance of corruption, [and not] because the things you see in you are of so lustful and vile a nature. Godly persons are sometimes greatly affrighted with this, {and sometimes} so bad, they scarcely don't express it.

[Not because they find] such kinds of sin and corruption, that they never imagined were in the heart of the godly, [such as] self-righteousness, [or] atheism. {Or because they find such kind of sin and corruption that they} never imagined, {such as} malice and revenge, [or] love to sin. If you don't love it with {a love of settled} esteem, {by a stated} choice, {you should not determine against yourself; nor} that you find so much blindness to spiritual things, some things that others speak of you don't know that you ever saw, some things of great importance.

[DOCTRINE RESUMED.]

Of the two general *Propositions* that were observed from this parable, that which we were last upon was the second, viz., that true {and false Christians} in some things agree, {and in others they greatly differ}.

We have hitherto insisted {on those things} wherein they agree. And having observed what things they agree in {in the resemblance or} appearances of godliness, we were last in those wherein they agree through the failings and infirmities of true {and false Christians}, and observed these six things from the verse that has been read and the two following verses:

38. MS: "into."

1. [That there is] abundance of corruption in the hearts {of true Christians}, as well as others.

2. {True Christians} agree with others, in many respects, in corrupt frames.

3. {They may agree in the} sins they commit, and ways they walk in.

4. That in a time of decay of religion among a professing people, 'tis commonly so that both true {Christians} and false do slumber and sleep.

5. One great reason of both {wise virgins and foolish slumbering and sleeping as they do}, is the bridegroom tarrying.

6. When true Christians are found slumbering and sleeping by the midnight cry, 'tis both to be unexpected and surprising to them, as well as others.

Having already spoken to the three first of these, I now come to the

4. [Fourth,] that in a time of decay of religion among a professing people, {'tis commonly so that both true Christians and false do slumber and sleep}.

The company of ten virgins, may either be taken to represent the whole visible church of Christ throughout the whole world, or a particular society or professing people of God.

The virgins that went out to {meet the bridegroom}, are represented as a society or one company that were together, that walked together and conversed together.

This society doubtless represents a society of visible Christians, or a professing people of God.

And, as here we see, ['tis represented] that they all slumbered and slept together. When the foolish virgins slept, the wise slept with them; so among a professing people, when it is a time of the decay of religion, this decay don't appear in one sort alone. It is not so, that when the ungodly grow senseless and unawakened and vicious, that the godly do generally remain as lively in religion, as when it was a time of awakening among the ungodly.

And on the other hand, it is not so, that when it is a generally dull time with the godly among a professing people, that it is a time of great concern and awakening with the ungodly.

The time when the ten virgins first set out with their lamps to meet the bridegroom, may represent to us the time of the flourishing of religion among a professing people. Then, the ten virgins were far from being asleep; they all seemed to be engaged in what they were about, to go out and meet the bridegroom, and enter in with him into the marriage [feast].

But the alterations there was among them afterwards, when they began to grow drowsy and fall asleep, may represent the times that commonly follow remarkable outpourings of the Spirit of God, viz., times of deadness in religion, and the prevailing of sin.

Christ, in this part of this parable, doubtless means to teach us the same things as he teaches the disciples in the foregoing chapter, at the 12th verse: "and because iniquity shall abound, the love of many shall wax cold." Christ is there speaking how it would be amongst his professing people before his coming, and so it[39] is in this parable.

When iniquity abounds, and it is a time of general decay of religion, the love of many waxes cold, the temporary love of false Christians waxes cold, i.e., totally ceases. Though they seemed to have their affections much warmed for a while, and when they heard the Word, even with joy received it; yet their goodness proves as the "morning cloud, and the early dew that passeth away" [Hos. 13:3]. And the love of true Christians in a sense waxes cold; as it ceases, its liveliness and the exercises of it do greatly fail, though it don't totally cease in their hearts, as it does in false Christians.

I would, first, briefly explain what is meant by true Christians and false all slumbering and sleeping in a time of the decay of religion; [and] second, give reasons.

a. I would {briefly explain what is meant by true Christians and false all slumbering and sleeping in a time of the decay of religion}.

There are especially two things to be observed in sleep, as in a state of slumber: viz., a failing of sense, and a failing of action.

(a) There is cessation of sense. So in a time of decay of religion amongst a professing people, it is a time of [insensibility]. The ungodly are insensible, and the godly.

The insensibility that there [is] in sleep, does consist in forgetting what is past, and in being insensible of what is present, and inconsiderate of what is to come.

Those that are asleep, forget what is past; in a time of slumber, a man may be said to forget himself. So it is among a professing people, in a time of general decay of religion, [both with a] natural man [and a]

39. MS: "it."

godly man. So the children of Israel in the wilderness soon forgot God's works, Ps. 78:11.

[They are] insensible of what is present. Thus it was with Ephraim. Hos. 7:9, "Strangers have devoured his strength, and he knoweth it not: yea, gray hairs are here and there upon him, yet he knoweth not."

[They are] unmindful of what is future. So it was foretold it should be in Israel in times of their degeneracy, in Moses' prophetical song. Deut. 32:29, "O that they were wise, that they understood this, that they would consider their latter end!"

(b) In a state of slumber, persons cease from action. So in a time of the decay of religion amongst professing people, all, both {true and false Christians}, may be said to slumber and sleep, as they in a great measure cease from their activity in matters of religion.

Natural men cease from a diligent seeking salvation. They cease to strive to enter at the strait gate, {and cease to} call earnestly on God, and return to a way of slothfulness. "Slothfulness casteth into a deep sleep" [Prov. 19:15].[40]

[The] godly, they also fall into a state of slumber. In this respect, they cease from gracious action. Grace ceases to act on them as it used to do, and they don't abound in those fruits of grace, those acts of a holy life; and their diligence in a great measure ceases. And as activity in religion ceases, sinful action prevails more and more; [the] natural man returns. And the godly, as the exercises of grace cease,[41] they cease from their care and watchfulness and diligence.

Many ill things will be going forward amongst a people {that slumber and sleep}, and ten to one but the godly will have a hand with them. So when the children of Israel in the wilderness {corrupted themselves}, Aaron had a hand [Ex. 32]. So when a spirit of superstition and uncharitableness prevailed amongst the Jewish Christians, so that they would not eat with the gentiles, some of the apostles, Peter and Barnabas, were carried away with their dissimulation, Gal. 2:11–13.

[a.] I now proceed to give the *Reasons* why it is thus amongst a professing people, why {true Christians and false all slumber and sleep in a time of the decay of religion}.

And there are these two reasons I would give of it:

---

40. This is a conjectural scriptural reference for where JE draws a dash in the MS.
41. MS: "cease and."

(a) The declension of the one, do naturally tend to promote the declension of the other. As when religion flourishes, the religion of one tends to promote the religion of the other. What the godly see of the awakening {of natural men influences them}, and what natural men see [of the awakening of the godly influences them].

So on the contrary, in a decline of religion, the declension, when natural men see, {it influences them}.

This tends to take off convictions {of religion}, and what the godly see of the deadness and loose and sinful behavior of natural men tends to deaden the hearts of the godly.

Though it be sad that it should be so, yet good men are liable to be affected by the bad examples of evil: for they are evil men. Yet it may be, some of them are[42] persons that excel in knowledge and ability, and are men of influence, or they may be newly related to 'em, or upon other accounts may be near and dear to 'em, and so may have great influence to draw away their hearts, as Solomon's wives; and some of them, though wicked indeed, may be those that the godly have had an high opinion of.

All, both good and bad, are liable to be greatly stumbled, and to have their souls much wounded by the falling away of those that have before made a special profession of religion, and are hypocrites. And the time of the decay of a religion, is a time when the religion of such professors is wont utterly to fail, and they are wont to fall away.

(b) The Spirit of God in withdrawing from all, both {true and false Christians} together, treats men in a way agreeable to their union in society. Professing Christians, both real and counterfeit, are united together in this world in one body and society; and being so, they are looked upon and treated of God in every respect as one.

By this means it comes, they are in some sorts partakers of one another's guilt; and when many persons in a society become corrupt, and carry themselves ill, the society becomes guilty as a society in the sight of God, and so punished as a society. When corruption very much prevails amongst a great number, 'tis a sign that others[43] don't as they ought improve the advantage they have, as united with them in society to restrain them, and oppose their declensions and corruptions.

If they did, God would succeed their endeavors. If many godly amongst a people are lively in religion, God won't suffer the ungodly to

42. MS: "of."
43. MS: "others that."

remain stupid, but will succeed their endeavors and answer their several prayers, and will pour out his Spirit on the society they belong to, and their presence will bring down the divine blessing.

So that by virtue of this union together in one society, they become partakers in one another's sins, and so God deals with 'em accordingly, and makes 'em partakers in each other's judgments. And when he withdraws his Spirit from one, he does so also from the other.

APPLICATION.

[*Use* I.] I would apply this Doctrine, in an *Use of Examination* to ourselves, and the present circumstances of this place. Let this Doctrine put us upon examining ourselves, and that in two respects:

First. Let everyone examine himself, in particular, whether he is not slumbering and sleeping at this day. Are we asleep or awake?

It has been a time wherein religion has been flourishing; and if it should be asked whether or no the town in general ben't in a backslidden state, and it is now a time of the great decay of religion in comparison of what has been heretofore, the question would be easy to all. But if it should be asked particular persons, whether they han't a great share in this declension, whether they themselves han't much declined, and whether they han't had a considerable hand in the declension of others, {the question would be} more difficult. But yet, it is probable many would look on this as [an] easy question, and would be free to acknowledge that {the town in the general is in a backslidden state}, and it may be speak on it with a smiling countenance. And therefore,

Second. Examine wherein you are guilty of declining and backsliding. This would be more difficult {a question}. Many [would be] ready to own {they have declined and backslidden} in general; yet if you should examine them as to particulars, would be found very insensible and backward to own themselves guilty in those particulars wherein they are chiefly guilty. [They are] ready to acknowledge [themselves guilty] in those things that they may, with least dishonor or shame to themselves. [They are ready to] acknowledge [they are] very much declined in general, [but] not much to their dishonor. Others will own this; they don't seem to make themselves worse than others {in acknowledging their guilt}. Yea, they may think that to acknowledge this will be to their honor, rather than their shame. They may account that 'tis the part of a Christian, and will be looked upon so by those that hear them, when they seem ready to complain of the hardness of their hearts, and say, "O, we are poor creatures, {we are} so dead and dull, {we have} base hearts, {we have great} reason to humble {ourselves}."

This is credible, fashionable sort of talk. Men don't appear to be looked upon the worse for such talk, but the better, and therefore are ready to acknowledge thus.

But there are many particulars wherein they are chiefly guilty. Thus, if you should ask 'em whether {they are guilty in any particular sins}, you would offend, and it may [be] get their displeasure. As for instance, if you should tell 'em of particulars wherein they have shown a bad spirit, [or] carried themselves very unbecoming Christians.

[They are] ready to confess those things that they think are to be laid chiefly to God, [such as] withdrawing of light. And it may be they will say that they are sensible that 'tis their fault, because this is account-ed the part of a Christian.

But yet it may be [they] are very backward to think ill of them-selves in these and those particulars, wherein they are indeed mainly guilty, and represent particulars of their own voluntary conduct as {not blameworthy}. But let me entreat persons to be strict and thorough with themselves.

'Tis most necessary we should be {strict and thorough with our-selves}. We should have a particular knowledge of our own disease. Therefore, to assist you in this matter, I would propose two or three questions to be answered to your own conscience:

1. Han't you had a share in those things, that have been to the dis-credit of the profession of this town abroad in the country? You can't but be sensible that there have been things that are to the discredit {of this town}. Recollect what you have heard, and consider what you have reason to think those things are.[44]

And [consider] whether those things han't really been amiss. Christianity, when its virtues are truly excited and its rules truly prac-ticed, is lovely in the eyes of the world, [and] of good report. Rom. 14:[17–]18, "For the kingdom of God is not meat and drink; but righ-teousness, and peace, and joy in the Holy Ghost. For he that in these

---

44. See the sermon *City on a Hill* (WJE 19:537–59) in which JE recounts how reports of the revivals in and around Northampton were ridiculed, reports to which JE would have been very sensitive in early 1738, since a revised edition of *A Faithful Narrative* was being prepared for publication.

things serveth Christ is approved of God, and acceptable with men."
[He] alone will glorify our heavenly Father.

2. Examine particular frames and practices, and inquire whether
or no you han't found by experience [that they] have greatly hindered
religion in you. [Inquire whether you have] not been lively {in religion},
not had a sense {of the importance of religion, have been} indisposed
to duty, {or been} exceeding dull and backward, {and what} darkness
followed.

It may be you thought it was right. You could justify yourselves.

3. [Examine] whether or no you don't begin to do and allow of
things that you was afraid to do, when under convictions.

4. [Examine] whether or no you don't begin to do and plead for
things you condemned, when you was in far better frames than you are
in now. Don't those things begin to be practiced, that were disallowed
by you and people in general in the time? Don't you begin now to plead,
and say, "I can't see any hurt in this or that"? At that time when you
was, as you thought, newly converted, and when you was most lively in
{things of religion}, you disallowed and avoided, and agreed with others
in judging them things to be avoided, and that you thought it was commendable to avoid.

Don't you now begin to say concerning some things, that then you
thought you ought to do and made no objection against, that now you
can't see any need of it? [You] don't think [yourself] obliged {now} to
be so much in religion, {or} to be so strict, {or} to attend such and such
things.

And [don't you begin] to say, {you} can't see what hurt {there is} in
such and such liberties, {such} practices in company, going to taverns,
[being] out very late a-nights in companies of young people, absenting
from family prayers, taking liberties in talk bordering on lasciviousness,
[and] singing rude songs?

And in liberties in acting as well as talking in company: neglecting
to attend private religious meetings, [and in] going abroad sabbath-day
nights, and lecture days.

You did approve of a strict observance of these things; {at one time,}
you thought they was right. {You thought it your} duty, {and} you fell in
without objection; {you} was convinced in your mind.[45]

45. JE deletes: "I won't stand now particularly to determine what things are lawful,
and what not."

Why do you begin to think and say otherwise now?

If you say that you think you was in an error then, and that you think you see better now, {then} I won't pretend particularly to determine what things are lawful and what not, but only[46] would put some things to you, for you to answer to yourself.

What cause is it likely that it should arise from, that you then, in a time when the Spirit of God was greatly poured out, and God was present in an extraordinary manner to teach men their duty, and incline 'em to it, and you yourself was more influenced by the Spirit of God by far than you are now—you thought {these things were right}—but now when it is a dead time, religion comparatively neglected, God is withdrawn {and} now corruptions begin to pour forth, and you yourself with worse frames, not so religiously disposed as you was then, you think {you was in error}? Can it be rationally thought that the people in the town in general, should be more likely to have right notions {of things than you}?

Or do you think that you in particular are less likely to think right, {and} without being blinded by your lusts, when your heart is dead {and} cold?

Set reason to work, and now be persuaded a little to hear the voice of reason. Can you think that if the Spirit of God should now be poured out again in a remarkable manner as before, {that} people would not in general think those same things would not be avoided, {and that} such things would not be generally commended [and] approved of all, {such} as avoiding going to and fro needlessly after public worship? And if you yourself now should have the Spirit of God come powerfully on you, [would you approve of the things you approve of now]?

A Christian, as he would be devoted to Christ's glory, ought to avoid not only those things that are unlawful in themselves and absolutely considered, but also those things that, they have reason to think, tend to lead to the hurt of religion in their issue and events.

The reason is exceeding plain. A prudent person would do so in his own concern for his own interest. He would not only avoid {things that are unlawful in themselves}. And why should not the lovers of God do so for his glory? Let us consider how we would do by an earthly friend, that we entirely loved.

46. MS: "only you."

When it is proposed to you to do this or that, and you are tempted to allow of this or that practice, don't say with yourself, "It's not in its own nature unlawful; I can't [see] any hurt in the thing itself." It becomes a lover of God to ask himself a further question than that: {Will it lead to the hurt of religion}? It don't become dear friends to deal with one another with such a sort of exactness as that, to allow one another no more than what is in its own nature most strictly due {to another}. This way of managing don't argue a very entire friendship.

Good friends are watchful against what does but remotely tend to each other's hurt and dishonor.

And again, let it be considered whether we han't reason to think that strictness in these and those things, at and before the late {revival of religion}, which now begin to be neglected, was not evidently smiled upon [by] God {at that time}, such as the avoiding making lecture days.

Use II. Let us rouse out of sleep. Let every one wherein, on examination, he finds himself [asleep, awake]. Let natural men [rouse themselves].

Don't let us listen to carnal reasonings, which are but the dreams of those that slumber and sleep.

Let us set about it in good earnest. Stir up ourselves, and stir up one another.

Let the first step of amendment be in our walk. Let us avoid those {things that are carnal}. And then, let again the next step be in our talk.

No people on earth have such great obligation and loud calls to be awake in religion, {and not to be in} such a frame {of slumber and sleep}. God has lately smitten us.[47] Let it not be to be said of us, as of those that [are] in a drunken sleep, Prov. 23:35, "They have stricken me; [. . .] they have beaten [me], and I felt it not."

[Use] III. [To] those that are awake, take care; don't fall asleep.

[Use] IV. Let those few that are awake again do their utmost, that others may be waked up that are sleeping around them.

---

47. JE could be referring to a number of recent events. Later in the sermon, he mentions "adult persons that have lately gone into eternity," implying an epidemic or an unusually high mortality rate. Also, according to excerpts from Deacon Ebenezer Hunt's Diary, recorded by Sylvester Judd (MS, Forbes Library), the wheat harvest of 1737 was very poor, "being Killed by the hard winter and a long flood in the spring, & something of a blast added thereto. We are threatened with a scarcity, but God favored us with a pretty good Indian harvest." JE could also be referring to the fall of the gallery in the church on March 13, 1737.

You, if awake, see that which they don't {see. You} see the lamentable circumstances they are in.

Use endeavors, by example, [and by] prudent counsels and reproofs.

[Awake others] by earnest prayers.

Let wakeful Christians amongst us, those that are [roused] with united strength and grace, try if they can't call down the influences of the Spirit of God to waken others, as well as more thoroughly to rouse themselves. [There is] great encouragement for your fervent prayers. If the prayers of the saints have, in time past, shut up and opened heaven, to cause showers of rain to cease or be poured out, much more {can they call down the influence of the Holy Spirit}. James, last [chapter, vv.] 16–18: "The effectual fervent prayer of a righteous man availeth much. Elias was a man subject to like passions as we are, and he prayed earnestly that it might not rain: and it rained not on the earth by the space of three years and six months. And he prayed again, and the heaven gave rain, and the earth brought forth her fruit."[48]

[DOCTRINE RESUMED.]

[We are upon] the parable of the ten virgins, in the beginning of Matt. 25, especially vv. 5–7.

In speaking of those things wherein true Christians and false may agree through the infirmities and failings of true Christians, there were these six things observed from these three verses:

1. Abundance of corruption.

2. Frames.

3. Acts and ways.

4. In a time of decay of religion.

5. That one great reason of both true Christians' and false slumbering and sleeping, is Christ's tarrying.

6. When true Christians slumber and sleep, the midnight cry is like to be unexpected and surprising to them, as well as others.

Having spoken to the four first of these, I come now to the

5. [Fifth thing, wherein true and false Christians may agree,] viz., {that one great reason of both wise and foolish virgins slumbering and sleeping as they do, is the bridegroom's tarrying}. The virgins, when they first set [out], expected soon {to meet the bridegroom}. But {the

---

48. The sixth preaching unit ends here.

bridegroom tarried, and they grew} weary of waiting; {and as} it was late in the night, [their] natural inclination was to sleep. {They} began to doubt whether he would come.

Here it must be remembered, that by false Christians, as by the foolish virgins, is meant all that live under the light of the gospel and attend its ordinances, and pretend to be Christians or the followers of Christ, that are not sincere and real Christians, but are indeed natural men.

So that all that belong to Christian assemblies, are either true Christians or false. Those among us that are in a Christless, graceless condition are false Christians. They are some of the foolish virgins, spoken of in this parable; they all hope to enter in with the bridegroom into the marriage.

This tarrying of Christ, is especially with respect to a twofold coming:

a. With respect to his coming at the day of judgment. One great reason why the visible church of Christ does so slumber and sleep as it doth, is that [it] is so long before the great day comes.

The doctrine of the day of judgment, in which men are taught that Christ will come with glory, majesty and mighty power on the clouds of heaven to judge the quick and dead, and that all, both small and great, must stand before him to give an account, is a very awful and awakening doctrine, tending very much to rouse both saints and sinners, and excite to watchfulness and diligence that they may be ready for such a day.

But this doctrine has been preached in the world now for many ages, but men see nothing of the accomplishment of it; and many that hear of it are the less moved by it, because they look upon [it] as at a great distance. They hear that there are many things yet to be accomplished in the world before the day of judgment, and they never expect to see it while they live, nor till a great while after they are dead.

Hence, the visible church of Christ in the world is in a more drowsy condition. It is not generally expected throughout the Christian world that Christ would quickly and suddenly appear. It is not likely that there would be that carelessness and deadness in religion that now there [is]. It would doubtless greatly change the face of things in the church of Christ; men's minds would be otherwise engaged than they are now, and their practice would be far otherwise.

And we are taught in the Scripture that, near the end of the world, it shall be an exceeding dead time as to religion, and a time wherein wickedness shall dreadfully prevail; a time of the great prevailing of idolatry and a spirit of atheism. Luke 18:8, "when the Son of man cometh, shall he find faith on the earth?" And the one great reason of it will be, Christ's staying so long before he comes to judgment. Many shall make also of it as an argument, that Christ is an imposter, and that there will never be any such thing as a day of judgment, and that there is no truth in religion. II Pet. 3:[3–]4, "Knowing this first, that there shall come in the last days scoffers, walking after their own lusts, and saying, Where is the promise of his coming? for since the fathers fell asleep, all things continue as they were from the beginning of the creation." And that it will then be a time of exceeding prevailing of a spirit of negligence and carelessness about the things of religion, and a time when men's hearts shall be wholly swallowed up in the cares and pleasures of the world, and giving themselves up to all manner of licentiousness. Luke 17:26, etc., "And as it was in the days of Noe, so shall it be also in the days of the Son of man. They did eat, they drank, they married wives, they were given in marriage, until the day that Noah entered into the ark, and the flood came, and destroyed them all. Likewise also as it was in the days of Lot; they did eat, they drank, they bought, they sold, they planted, they builded."

And the Scripture teaches us, that then it shall be a time wherein many professors of religion will apostatize, and fall away. Christ is speaking of that time in Matt. 24:12, "because iniquity shall abound, the love of many shall wax cold." And we are also taught, that then it shall be a time of great persecution in the church of God, wherein Christ's nominal servants shall beat their fellow servants; and the reason given of this, and of their licentiousness and sensuality, is Christ's delaying his coming, Matt. 24:48–49.

And it is this time of great degeneracy that shall be a little before Christ's coming to judgment, that [he] has a more especial respect to in this parable, when he says, "while the bridegroom tarried, they all slumbered and slept"; intimating that that time will be a time of general drowsiness amongst all sorts, good and bad, so that when Christ does really come to judgment, he shall as it were find the whole world in a midnight sleep not expecting his coming, and neither good nor bad in an actual preparedness for it.

b. This tarrying of Christ, is with respect to his coming by death. This is not to be here excluded; for what the day of judgment is with respect to the world in general, that is the day of death to a particular person. What that is to the visible church, this is to every visible Christian. As Christ comes at the day of judgment to call all the world to an account, so he comes by death to call a particular soul to an account.

His tarrying with respect to this coming of his, is one great reason why both true Christians and false slumber and sleep as they do.

Death is awful in itself, as the dissolution of the human frame, and a final leaving this world, and a separation of soul and body; but 'tis a much greater thing, considered with respect to [the] change it makes in the circumstances of the soul, and as an inlet into eternity, and a summons before God's awful judgment seat.

And the consideration of it, and true sense of it, would tend greatly to awaken and quicken both true Christians and false. But one great reason why it has none of this effect, is because it tarries and don't yet come, and so is beheld and looked on as at a distance.[49]

Christ's tarrying with respect to his coming in these respects, has influence on both good and bad, to be an occasion of their slumbering and sleeping, in the following ways:

(a) It seems the less real that Christ will come. Things that are at a distance and not yet seen, are ready to appear to us as if they were not real things, but to look like dreams or fables.

The day of judgment is the less realized amongst men, because it is that which we have heard of from our infancy and never have yet [seen]; and 'tis that which has been preached to the world age after age, but never has yet been accomplished.

So 'tis a difficult thing to realize death, for though we all rationally know that we must die—not only the Word of God but universal experience teaching it—yet death being that which we have often heard of, and never yet have been the subjects of, or known anything about by experience, and looking on it as nothing very nigh, 'tis hard to have a realizing view and sense of our own mortality, and to have imposed upon us as a thing wherein that we must die.

---

49. JE deletes: "One great reason why such as these slumber and sleep, and remain careless, and senseless, is Christ's tarrying with respect to his coming by death and judgment."

Death and the grave, and especially the eternal judgment that follows death, when we think of it with application to ourselves, is ready to be covered with a kind of mist; so that they look as things very distant, and scarcely appear as things real.

Ungodly men, because they han't been yet called to an account by the Judge, and that eternal punishment they have heard so often of is not already come upon 'em, are ready to think it never will come.

They have often heard the threatenings of God's awful displeasure against such as they, and have been told how angry God is with them; but they see no tokens of God's anger, they feel nothing of it. Things go on smooth and well with 'em, year after year; God keeps silence; all things are still and quiet. Hence, they don't realize it, that God is so angry with them as they have heard.

They have heard often of the dreadful misery of hell, and how that they that were in such a condition as they, were every day in danger of it; but yet it don't count. They don't find that they are disturbed or molested in their ways, but let alone. Hence they {are lead to} call it in question, whether there be any such thing as hell. Ps. 10:6, "He hath said in his heart, I shall not be moved: for I shall never be in adversity." Ps. 50:21, "These things hast thou done, and I kept silence; thou thoughtest that I was altogether such an one as thyself: but I will reprove thee, and set them in order before thine eyes."

And the godly, as they have remains of a spirit of unbelief, so this spirit in them nourishes itself from the delay of Christ's coming.

Spiritual and eternal things sometimes appear as real and certain things to 'em, and they have a lively sense of their reality; and when they have, they are not asleep.

But when they slumber and sleep, unbelief prevails. At such times, they don't realize as they should do, how that they must stand before the judgment seat of God. If they did, it would have a great tendency to rouse 'em out of their slumber, to make 'em more watchful, and put 'em upon diligence to prepare to give account of themselves to God. The reward that Christ has promised his disciples for their diligence in his service, appears less real to them in their sleepy frames, for its being looked on as at a distance.

(b) Things at a distance are less affecting than things that are looked upon as very nigh, and that, though they are judged to be as certain. The carnal, unbelieving hearts of natural men, and the carnal part in the hearts of the godly, are ready to put Christ's coming at a great distance because he is not come yet.

We are all exceeding prone to that, to look on death and judgment as remote things. It looks remote to persons when they are young, i.e., remote from themselves, though it don't seem to them to be remote from others. When young persons look on those that are old, death looks very nigh to them; but yet, when they come to be old, still death don't look nigh, still there is the old disposition works, viz., to keep death at a distance.

And things that are looked upon as distant, don't affect and move persons as things that are beheld nigh at hand, though they are not indeed of the less importance: much as things that we view at a great distance in the air, look little in comparison of what they do when nigh. The further they are removed, the less and less they look, till at last they vanish out of sight, though our reason tells us that they are as[50] big as when we were near 'em.

And thus, by putting judgment and punishment at a distance, wicked men encourage and embolden themselves in sin. Eccles. 8:11, "Because sentence against an evil work is not executed speedily, therefore the heart of the sons of men is fully set in them to do evil." Amos 6:3–6, "Ye that put far away the evil day, and cause the seat of violence to come near; that lie upon beds of ivory, and stretch themselves upon their couches, and eat the lambs out of the flock, and the calves out of the midst of the stall; that chant to the sound of the viol, and invent to themselves instruments of music, like David; that drink wine in bowls, and anoint themselves with the chief ointments: but they are not grieved for the affliction of Joseph."

And so the godly themselves, through their infirmities and carnality, and in their slumbering frames, are not so much moved by the promises of future rewards for their looking on 'em as at a distance, and so are not so engaged in pressing towards 'em.

Through their infirmity, [they] are in this like children, who will be much more moved by the promise of an immediate reward, than one to [be] bestowed many days hence.

(c) From Christ's tarrying, they are ready to look on their present things as of long continuance, and so to set their hearts on them.

50. MS: "are."

Christ[51] hitherto tarrying and delaying his coming, they are ready to put his coming at a distance; and the more distant Christ's coming appears, of the longer continuance will the things of this world appear, and so of the greater[52] value and importance will they appear: and this proves a temptation to 'em, to set their hearts on things of the world, and so to be lulled asleep with them, having the heart ever charged with the cares and pleasures and vanity of this life.

If Christ's coming was apprehended to be very nigh, either by death or the last judgment, men would not think it worth their while to be much concerned about these things, being that they must so soon have forever done with them. But Christ deferring his coming, they are ready to treat these things as if they were everlasting things.

And setting their hearts much on them, they very much engross the affections and concerns of the mind, and have stupefying influence on the soul, to make it dead to the things of religion and involve it[53] in a great deal of sin: for the Apostle has taught us that the love of the things of this world, is the root of all evil, I Tim. 6:10.

Men, by this means being inordinately engaged after the pursuits and honors of the world, become covetous and proud and contentious and envious; and pursuing after pleasures, they become licentious and very sensual. This exceedingly stupefies the heart.

The godly, when they are in their slumbering frames, they look on their future inheritance as at a distance, and so don't think so much of that; but their present possessions they are ready to think of long continuance, and so are ready to have their hearts taken up with them, which involves 'em in many snares.

(d) And lastly, this is a temptation to 'em, to delay and put off a preparation for Christ's coming till hereafter. They have lived hitherto, and Christ is not come yet; and they are ready to hope for time enough hereafter.

Thus natural men {delay, and} put off getting an interest in Christ, and the godly are ready to delay to stir up themselves to get into an actual preparedness; hope to be in better frames before they die; would not have death come and find 'em in such frames as they are in now. We may suppose that both the wise virgins and foolish, when they began to

51. MS: "Xs."
52. MS: "great."
53. MS: "in."

give way to a sleepy disposition, hoped that they should wake up again time enough before the bridegroom should come.

They had waited so long, and he had not come, that they began to think it would be a long time before he came, and thought they might have a convenient time to sleep, and yet be ready when he actually came. Thus foolish virgins put off buying oil {for their lamps, like} natural men seeking grace {who delay and put off seeking}.

Hypocrites, and those that have false hopes of their state, delay that thorough examination of their state, {even} as [the] foolish virgins delayed trimming their lamps {before the coming of the bridegroom}.

If those that have false hopes expected soon to appear before him whose eyes are as a flame of fire, they would not rest in those things that they now do: {they} could not be quiet and easy in such sorts of signs and evidence as now they are; they would not think themselves so safe as to dare to go to sleep. The godly would not so neglect themselves: they would be more thorough to obtain sensible and clear experiences and lively evidences of their good estate, and so seek after assurance; they would not put off trimming their lamps till hereafter, but would do it daily, as continually expecting the bridegroom.

APPLICATION.

The *Use* that I would make of what has been said under this head, is to warn both godly and ungodly against so ill an improvement of the bridegroom's tarrying. And to enforce this warning, I would offer some things to your consideration.

First. Consider that you will at last see that this is a foolish improvement of Christ's tarrying. There is nothing got by giving way to the inclination of the flesh, to slumber and sleep while the bridegroom tarries. Many thousands and millions have lost their souls by it.

The foolish virgins, if they had not spent the time in sleep, but on the contrary, had been watchful and had gone in season to buy oil, and had kept awake to keep their lamps burning, might have been ready, {might have} escaped that misery, {and might have} had the same privilege with the rest {of the virgins}. And what losers the godly will be by it, will be seen more fully under the next head of discourse.[54]

---

54. See below, pt. 6, p. 112.

By this slumbering and sleeping while the bridegroom tarries, you will but make a work of repentance.

Second. Consider that now Christ's coming may seem distant to you, yet when the time comes and you look back, it won't seem distant from the present times. The time of Christ's coming often seems very distant when persons look forward, before it is come, but never when it looks back, after it is come. Then the time it will appear as it is: but a very short time.

Then you will see the truth of what Christ has said concerning his own coming. Rev. 22:20,[55] "He that testifieth these things saith, Surely I come quickly." And also of what the apostles have said, Philip. 3:5, "The Lord is at hand"; Jas. 5:9, "The judge standeth before the door."

Then, when you come to look back on the time past, between that and the present, how short will it appear: even as, as it were, a dream, a tale that is told, a moment, a mere nothing, a spate that is slipped away before you was aware. Then will you see that time to be so short, that you will be convinced that you had no time to sleep in [it]. Then will you see what need there was, that all of it should be spent in the most watchful diligence; then will you be as it were between time and eternity; and then will the whole of time that has passed with you, before Christ's coming, appear as nothing.

Third. Consider that you don't know how soon the bridegroom will come. 'Tis an unreasonable way of arguing that the corrupt, carnal hearts of men fall into, that because they have often heard of Christ's coming, and been warned to [be] prepared for it, and that notwithstanding he is not come yet, and that therefore his coming is at a distance. It in no wise follows. It is an inference that corruption, and not reason, draws from such premises.

You know not but that the bridegroom is now just at the door, while you are slumbering, and many of [you] without a drop of oil in your vessels, and your lamps totally gone out. Many have argued, as you now do, that because the bridegroom has tarried before, that therefore he will tarry yet a great deal longer, and so have given themselves time to go to sleep; and, contrary to their expectation, the midnight cry has been presently heard. Before they have slept any long time, they have been waked up again with that solemn cry, and see that it was so indeed.

55. MS cites ch. 21.

Surely the proper and most rational improvement that you can make of this uncertainty of the time of Christ's coming, is to be found always waking and always ready. This is the improvement Christ makes of it, in the conclusion of this parable. Matt. 25:13, "Watch, therefore, for ye know neither the day nor the hour wherein the Son of man cometh." And the same he often makes of it elsewhere, as [the] 42nd verse of [the] preceding chapter: "watch therefore, for ye know not what hour your Lord doth come."

Fourth. This improvement of the bridegroom's tarrying, is a most ungrateful improvement, in that Christ hitherto has tarried, to give us opportunity to be the better prepared for his coming.

'Tis an instance of his great mercy and longsuffering to sinners, that he han't yet come to judge them, but has been waiting to be gracious, giving them a space to repent in, giving 'em opportunity to go and buy oil, that so when he comes they may enter in with him {into the wedding feast}. II Pet. 3:9–10, "The Lord is not slack concerning his promise, as some men count slackness; but is longsuffering to us-ward, not willing that any should perish, but that all should come to repentance. But the day of the Lord will come as a thief in the night; in the which the heavens shall pass away with a great noise, and the elements shall melt with fervent heat, the earth also and the works that are therein shall be burned up." Sinners, therefore, in making such an improvement of Christ's tarrying hitherto, are[56] very ungrateful, as well as very foolish; when Christ stays to give 'em opportunity to prepare, and they, instead of that, improve it to be more and more unprepared.

And so when the godly make this improvement {of the bridegroom's tarrying}, they are guilty of great ingratitude to Christ: for hereby he gives 'em opportunity to be better prepared. Though they have some preparedness for his coming, yet by his tarrying they have opportunity to get in much better preparation for it, to get more grace, more oil, and to meet the bridegroom with a brighter lamp, and so to have more abundant entrance administered to them with the bridegroom into the marriage.

Let both sinners and saints amongst [us] be both warned from these things, to rouse out of their slumber. There are many of you that are here present, of both sorts, that are now asleep. All that you have

56. MS: "is."

heard hitherto from this subject has not waked you, but you still go on slumbering.

If you knew that the bridegroom was to come tomorrow, would it not rouse you? Would you not in many respects carry yourself very differently from what you now do?

Then consider, that you know not but that it will be on the morrow, yea, and this very night. You that are Christless souls and unawakened, and sleeping on the brink of hell, going on in ways of sin: consider that you know not but that this night your soul shall be required of you.

Christ may come by an apoplexy, or some such disease, and you may suddenly drop down dead, as many others have done; or you may die in your beds, and your sleep that you sleep this night may be your last sleep out of which you shall never wake, but in hell. Yea, I would put it to you further, whether if you knew that Christ would come to call you to his judgment seat this year, you would live as you now do. {Would you live} so careless, {would you live} so negligent and slothful, {so} worldly {and} carnal, {if you knew}? Why, then, consider how likely it is, that there are some of you with whom it will be thus.

Did those adult persons that have lately gone into eternity, did they know of it, or had they any notice of it long aforehand? What more signs had they of Christ's coming by night, with respect to them, than you have with respect to you?

There is a next that is to follow, a next of the adult persons that are now present: that is to go to his grave.

He or she sits here somewhere amongst us; we know not where to look for him, we know not in what seat or pew. But God knows him by name: he sees the spot where he or she sits; he knows how it is with him, whether he [is] a true Christian or false one; he sees whether he be awake or asleep; he knows the frame of mind that he is in now at this present time, and what he thinks while he is hearing this discourse.

It may be he is one of those that is in a careless, slothful way, neglecting his soul. It may be he is one that has of late lived in some evil way. It may be he is one that has lived in some secret sin, filthy, forbidden pleasures, and gratifying some lust time after time in the dark, or very lately has so done: and it may be, notwithstanding a special profession of religion.

Very probably, if that person knew how soon Christ would come and call him to an account, he would be far from living as he now does.

Matt. 24:43, "Know this, that if the goodman of the house had known in what watch the thief would come, he would have watched, and would not have suffered his house to be broken up."

Let us, everyone, seriously consider these things, and that the Lord would give all wisdom to make a good improvement of 'em.[57]

[DOCTRINE RESUMED.]

In speaking of those things wherein true Christians and false may agree, through the infirmities and failings of true Christians, six things were observed from these three verses [vv. 5–7], five of which have been already spoken to. There remains now only the

6. [Sixth,] and last, viz., that when true Christians slumber and sleep, the cry of the bridegroom's coming is like to be unexpected and surprising to them, as well as others.

It is a cry at midnight to one as well as to the other. It is a sudden cry that wakes both out of sleep, and it was to both as a cry that wakes persons out of sleep at midnight [is] used to be, viz., surprising.

In speaking to this head, I would, first, particularly take notice what is implied in the expression of a "cry at midnight," by which it appears that 'tis something surprising; and then, in the second place, show how it is a surprising cry to slumbering saints as well as sinners.

a. I would particularly take notice what seems to be denoted by it being a "cry at midnight," by which it appears to be that which is surprising. And particularly, two things are to be observed:

(a) That it is not only a voice or speech, but a "cry" that is made; which signifies a loud and earnest voice, as occasioned by something of very great concern and importance.

The word is always used in Scripture.[58] There are several sorts of cries: there is a cry of lamentation, such as was in Egypt at midnight also, when there was not an house wherein there was not one dead [Ex. 12]; and there is a cry of supplication; and there is a cry of complaint. So the cry of the sins of Sodom is said to be "very great," Gen. 18:20; and so the cry of the children of Israel in Egypt, is said to "come up to God," Ex. 2:23.

---

57. The sixth preaching unit ends here; JE repeats the text, "Especially vs 5. 6. 7," before resuming.

58. JE deletes: "for a voice that is very earnest, as of something very moving and affecting, and of great concern."

And there is a cry of warning and alarm, as when fire breaks out, or when a people are suddenly beset by an enemy.

But each of these sorts of cries intimates something of great concern and importance, and in a very earnest expression of it.

So is this cry that we have an account of in this parable: "Behold, the bridegroom cometh, go ye out to meet him." It is a voice of warning and alarm, a loud and earnest voice, giving notice of something to the ten virgins of the utmost concern to them, and worthy greatly to move them.

(b) 'tis a "cry at midnight." Of which several things may be noted:

a. 'Tis a cry in a still time. The middle of the night is commonly a still, dead time, wherein there are not those noises that are in the daytime; a time wherein man and beast are still and motionless, all things retired, and all locked up in sleep.

A cry, therefore, is the more surprising at such a time, because it is a time wherein noise is most unusual and most unexpected. It is a great deal more moving and affecting, than at another time. A little noise will be taken notice of in the dead of night, that would not be at all taken notice of at another time.

Those noises that are usual, and that persons are not moved at in the daytime, if heard at midnight, would strike with great impression on the mind, and waken the attention. But especially is a great and earnest cry surprising at such a time.

This cry, spoken of in this parable, is in a still time; before it, there was no noise. It comes suddenly, it comes all at once. There was no noise before, that was a forerunner of it, to give warning of its approach; no resemblance of any such thing.

The cry comes, when it is a still time in men's own consciences, when conscience han't been much in warning of 'em. They have thought but little about anything of that nature; they have lately had no alarms of conscience to disturb them, or make them uneasy.

It comes when things are all quiet, when persons had been very much let alone. The cry of ministers has not been heard. If they have cried, their cry han't reached their hearts and consciences, so as to make it any other than a still time there.

It comes often at a time when God has let 'em much alone—he han't called of late by the motions of his Spirit, but all has been still and quiet—and at a time when such a cry was not thought of; and if it had been thought [of], would have appeared a more remote thing at that time, than at any time. Who would all at once expect such a cry at a time when all was so still and quiet, and everything appeared so far distant from anything of that nature?

b. Midnight is a time wherein persons commonly have divested themselves of all cares.

In the daytime, persons' minds are commonly full of one care and another; there are many concerns that they are busied about. Inconveniences and difficulties and dangers of one kind or another are then thought of, and the mind is exercised about 'em; and persons are contriving how to obtain this and that good that is needed, or to avoid this or that evil that they are exposed to: and those cares may hold in the evening.

But midnight is commonly a time when persons have laid aside all those things. They have thrown by all care and business, and composed themselves to sleep.

And therefore, such a loud, important and earnest cry, calling for their utmost concern and attention, coming suddenly upon 'em, will be the more surprising[59] [than] in the daytime, when the mind was devoted to care and business. The news of something that required care would not be so shocking: for then the mind was as it were ready-prepared for care, the loins more ready-girt. But at midnight all is relaxed, the loins ungirt, and the clothes put off; a sudden and great alarm at this time finds a man unprepared for it, and so is surprising to him.

c. Midnight is a time of darkness, and most remote from light. It is a season wherein there is none of the light of the sun, and is [most] remote of any time of night from it, long after the sun has set and the evening's twilight has vanished away, and long before the sun rising [and] the appearance of the dawning of the morning.

So this cry is made when it is a time of darkness with the ten virgins, or with visible Christians; when the ungodly are furthest from common enlightenings and convictions of spiritual and eternal things.

And [it] sometimes comes at times wherein true Christians are furthest from clear divine light, from a lively sense and clear apprehension of spiritual things. It comes when they are in dark frames, when

---

59. JE deletes: "Their minds being divested of all care, will be the less guarded against [it]. And such an earnest cry about that which is of so great concern calling immediately for their utmost care, will strike the mind with deeper impression."

their understandings are darkened through the deceitfulness of sin, and when they are furthest from knowing the light of hope, or having the evidences of their good estate clear and bright, and furthest from having the comfortable, sweet light of God's countenance: and therefore it comes at a time when it is surprising to them.

d. Midnight is a season wherein persons are commonly in their deepest sleep, wherein they are not only asleep, but in their soundest sleep. And therefore 'tis a season when they have most of all forgot themselves, and [are] furthest from any care or thought; and is a time when to be suddenly waked out of sleep with a loud earnest and important cry, will be most surprising to them.

e. Midnight is a time wherein things of that nature, that is declared by this cry, are wont least to be expected. The cry declares, "Behold, the bridegroom cometh." Midnight, at the dead of the night, is a time wherein it is very unusual for persons to travel to and fro. It is not a time for traveling, but a time for rest; and it being very late in the night, the ten virgins for that reason did not expect the bridegroom, it being past the time when any such thing was usual, and that they thought they might safely venture to go to sleep. And being therefore so much unexpected, it was so much the more surprising.

f. Midnight is commonly a time wherein persons are least disposed or prepared for action, or to enter on any important business. They are then least disposed to action, because they are dull and drowsy; it is a time when it is very much against the disposition to be disturbed, or to bestir themselves. They love then to keep their beds, and fold their heads to sleep.

When the cry was heard, "Behold, the bridegroom cometh," it was a time when the ten virgins were not in a good disposition to bestir themselves to go out to meet the bridegroom.

And midnight is a time when persons are least prepared suddenly to engage in business, or to go forth on any important design. Then the body is relaxed, and is most void of activity and strength, and the clothes are put off, and they ben't ready to answer any sudden important cry to call 'em forth immediately, and without delay. They must stay first to put on their garments, which they need to have well about them in order to any great undertaking. And therefore 'tis said, Rev. 16:15, "Behold, I come as a thief. Blessed is he that watcheth, and keepeth his garments, lest he walk naked, and they see his shame"; i.e., blessed is he that keeps awake and keeps his garments on, that he may have 'em ready against Jesus come.

Persons, when they go to sleep in the night, are wont to put off their garments from 'em, whereas they that watch are wont to keep their clothes on. Because Christ will come as a thief, suddenly and without warning, they that are then asleep with their clothes off, will be surprised, and must not stay to put their clothes on: they go forth immediately, for when Christ comes, there will be no waiting on persons.

And it will be well for them that are found watching and with their clothes [on]: they will be ready to go forth, and may go forth with honor. But those that are found asleep, with their clothes off, must not stay to dress then, but must go forth naked as they be, and so will appear and be exposed, to their shame.

So we are often told that he will come as a thief in the night, i.e., suddenly and without warning, when he is least expected, and men are least prepared for him. I Thess. 5:2–3, "For ye yourselves know perfectly that the day of the Lord so cometh as a thief in the night." II Pet. 3:10, "But the day of the Lord will come as a thief in the night." So Matt. 24:43–44, and Rev. 3:3.

A thief chooses to come at such a time as when he is least expected, that they mayn't be prepared to apprehend or resist him. He chooses a time when he thinks the inhabitants are in the deepest, soundest sleep, that he may steal the more securely.

I come now, in the

b. [Second] place, to show how it is like to be a surprising cry, both to sinners and slumbering saints.

(a) It will be so to sinners. It will be an amazing cry to them. So the first notice of Christ's coming at the last judgment will be, and so will Christ's coming by death to judge them in particular be.

Very often the news of approaching death is exceeding surprising and amazing to them; it fills them with dreadful horror. But if, through a stupid senselessness or a false hope, death don't amaze them beforehand, yet when they come actually and immediately to be summoned into [the] presence of the Judge, their souls will be filled with amazement.

They that would not regard the loud calls and invitations of Christ, not regard Wisdom's cries, that we read of, Prov. 8:3–4, "She crieth at the gates, at the entry of the city, at the coming in at the doors. Unto you, O men, I call; and my voice is to the sons of man," [and would not regard] the cry of ministers when they cried aloud or called earnestly upon [them]: then they shall regard this cry. It will strike them with more terror than the handwriting on the wall did Belshazzar, which cause the joints of his loins to be loosed, and his knees to smite one against another [Dan. 5].

That cry that shall be made to them, shall be answered with a cry from them when they hear it; they shall lift up a loud and bitter and most dolorous cry, and shall weep and wail, and gnash their teeth. How still a time soever it has been in their consciences before, though all has been as still within them as the dead of the night, now their consciences shall of a sudden be alarmed. It will be a midnight cry to them, as they shall be found in utter spiritual darkness and blindness, and a total ignorance of God and spiritual things.

They will have reason to be surprised and amazed by this cry, who will be in an utter unpreparedness. They will be found asleep, in a dead sleep, dead in trespasses and sins. They will be found naked, and therefore must come forth naked as they are.

And this cry commonly comes upon wicked men while they are flattering themselves in their own eyes, and while they are not only in a sleep, but in a pleasing dream of long-continued tranquility and prosperity. I Thess. 5:3, "For when they shall say, Peace and safety, then sudden destruction cometh upon them, as pain on a woman with child, and they shall not escape."

So this cry came upon the rich man that we read of, Luke 12:16, etc. "And he spake a parable unto them, saying, The ground of a certain rich man brought forth plentifully: and he thought within himself, saying, What shall I do, because I have no room where to bestow my fruits? And he said, This will I do: I will pull down my barns, and build greater; and there will I bestow all my fruits and my goods. And I will say to my soul, Soul, thou hast much goods laid up for many years; take thine ease, eat, drink, and be merry. But God said unto him, Thou fool, this night thy soul shall be required of thee: then whose shall those things be, which thou hast provided? So is he that layeth up treasure for himself, and is not rich toward God."

So Zophar represents the destruction of wicked men, as coming when in their prosperity. Job 20:22–23, "In the fullness of his sufficiency he shall be in straits: every hand of the wicked shall come upon him.

When he is about to fill his belly, God shall cast the fury of his wrath upon him, and shall rain it upon him while he is eating."

And Job represents the suddenness of the wicked man's destruction by a very lively metaphor. Ch. 27:20, "Terrors take hold on him as waters, a tempest stealeth him away in the night." Terrors {are represented} as waters, like a mighty flood coming suddenly on upon him, surrounding him, that he can't fly from it, and soon overwhelming him, or coming pouring down upon him, like a mighty fall of waters that there is no resisting.[60]

[The] tempest stealeth {him away in the night; it} comes as a thief. [It is] suddenly and unexpectedly gone with him before they have time to flee or get out of the way, as those that watch privily to steal any person to carry away {come suddenly}, or as a wild beast lurks privily to steal his prey [and comes] suddenly upon him.

And his being carried away by a [tempest] denotes the terribleness, as well as suddenness, of his destruction. And then it telleth in the next words: "The east wind carrieth him away, and he departeth: and as a storm hurleth him out of his place" [Job 27:21]. It is to be noted that this is spoken of as being in the night, as the midnight cry is in the parable we are upon. So Elihu represents their trouble and destruction, as coming upon 'em at midnight. Ch. 34:20, "In a moment shall they die, and the people shall be troubled at midnight, and pass away: and the mighty shall be taken away without hand."

(b) This cry is also like to be surprising to slumbering saints. Though they won't be liable to that terrible amazement that the wicked will be, yet if they are found slumbering and sleeping, it would be a midnight cry to them as well as the ungodly: and therefore, as we have already shown, an unexpected cry.

It is a mistake in any to think that those that are converted can't be surprised by the news of approaching death. If they are in dark, dull and carnal frames, that may be surprising and terrifying to them, as well as others.

That cry, "Behold, the bridegroom comes, go ye out to meet him," may wake [saints] out of sleep in a surprise, and that for three reasons:

---

60. See "Images of Divine Things" no. 27, in *Works of Jonathan Edwards, 11, Typological Writings*, edited by Wallace E. Anderson and Mason I. Lowance, Jr., with David Watters (New Haven: Yale University Press, 1993), 58.

a. If it comes upon them while slumbering and sleeping, it comes upon them unawares. {Even saints,} in such frames, don't consider it and meditate on it as they ought to do. Death and eternity ben't so familiar to them at such times; {they are} very much unacquainted with them.

If they conversed much with them in their thoughts, they would not be strangers, {and the midnight cry would be} no surprise {to the saints}.

At such times, their thoughts are taken up about other matters, {about} worldly vanities, and so death and judgment are strangers to 'em, {and they are} put into confusion at their approach.

And therefore Christ warns his disciples against these things. Luke 21:34–35, "take heed to yourselves, lest at any time your hearts be over-charged with surfeiting, and drunkenness, and cares of this life, and *so* that day come upon you unawares. For as a snare shall it come on all them that dwell on the face of the whole earth."

b. When they are found slumbering and {sleeping}, they ben't found in a disposition fitted for it. They ben't in a good disposition and frame of mind to receive it, and to do what the cry calls upon 'em to do, {viz.,} to go forth to meet the bridegroom.

{They are in a} dark frame, [a] sluggish frame, {and a} carnal frame. Such sinners are very far from being fitted for leaving all this world, and going into an eternal world, and going to appear before the judgment seat of God.

[They are] like a man as he is at midnight: loins ungirt, {his} garments not about him, {his} body relaxed. {Their} being so unfitted, it puts them into an hurry and confusion.

c. When the saints are slumbering, they commonly don't know that they han't an habitual preparedness for that cry. As they are far from an actual preparedness, so they han't at such times clear evidences of a fundamental preparedness. Grace [is] not in exercise {in them}, and so not the evidence of it. {Their} minds [are] exceedingly clouded with corruption; they have their evidences very dim. {This is} signified by the lamps of the wise virgins burning dim: {they} arose and trimmed their lamps, {so that they did} not go out totally, as the foolish virgins' did; {they burned} but very dim. And hence, no wonder that they are surprised.

['Tis] dreadful to have that matter doubtful.

['Tis] dreadful to have a suspicion remaining in the time of that solemn cry, {and} to have immediately to go forth to meet the bridegroom is a great thing.

APPLICATION.

Use I of *Instruction.*

First. Hence, 'tis no certain sign that persons ben't converted, that they are afraid of death.

Second. If we see persons under fear and darkness on a deathbed, this is not sufficient for us to conclude 'em natural men.

The improvement we should make of it, is to take warning.

Use II may be of *Awakening* to those that are asleep in their sins.

Consider how dreadful that amazement will be.

First. How many things there will be to contribute to it. The greatness of that which the cry declares, [the] greatness of its importance to you, [is of] immediate concern. [It] respects your whole interest, [the] welfare of body and soul, to eternity. {When you go} to meet a great Judge, [you will be] immediately before a Being of infinite majesty, holiness and justice. [Consider] your exceeding unpreparedness {for eternity: whether your nature} ben't unchanged, {the} dreadful reigning corruption {in your heart, the} sins you have committed, [the] calls slighted {and} opportunities lost, mercies alienated, {your sins} all unpardoned, {and with} no Savior.

Second. Your terror and surprise [will be] without remedy. [There will be] no avoiding {the judgment}, no hindering [it, though you] cry to the mountains.

The things that now quiet you, [will be] no remedy then. [There will be no] worldly enjoyments. [You will only have] false hopes, no friends, [and] no time given you. Time and opportunity will be at an end.

Third. Your amazement that you will have then, will be but the beginning of your amazement. Often wicked persons are in great amazement on their deathbeds. {But this is} but a beginning, {and} light in comparison. Sometimes [they] have such fear on [a] deathbed, as makes 'em tremble and groan and cry out; {they} go from this [world] groaning and crying to {God for mercy. But this is} but a light thing, in comparison of what will be at the day of judgment.

That terror and amazement that is then begun, will last to all eternity, but only in an immensely great degree.

[*Use*] III. Let the saints be hence exhorted not to slumber and sleep {before the midnight cry}.

Let those that are asleep, [awake]. Let others that are now awake, {remain awake}. You have heard what you will be exposed to by it.

[There will be] no security from it if you give way to a slumbering spirit, {if you are} slothful, {or} worldly, {or} unwatchful. [You will only be] saved as by fire, as when a man is waked at midnight with his house on fire, [and he is] scarcely saved.

Don't think [there is] no danger of this, because [you are] converted.

Here, consider three things:

First. What pity it is, that such persons as you hope you are, should needlessly expose themselves to a surprise as this; those that are in such a blessed condition, that God has done so much for, and that [have] such a foundation laid for their comfort and rejoicing at such great expense, and by such a wonderful work of God as he hath wrought in their redemption. What pity [it is], that such persons as those for whom comfort has been purchased at such a price, should deprive themselves of comfort, and hide the foundation of their joy from themselves, and so expose themselves to fears and terrors.

Second. How especially undesirable is fear and surprise at such a time as when that cry is heard, "Behold, the bridegroom cometh," or when they come to be in a deathbed, and seem to be leaving the world to go into eternity.

Doubts and fears [are] undesirable at any time, but especially at such a time. [For] then, above all times in the world, will the saints need to have clear evidences {of their preparedness, and of the} light of God's countenance.

['Tis] undesirable on two accounts:

1. Doubts and fears {on a deathbed} will be more terrible at such a time, than any other. Then [will be] a most important season, a season wherein great work [is] to be done. {'Tis a} great thing to die, {for} then it will be a juncture wherein all things with respect to the eternal state immediately to be determined {will be resolved}. Then [will be] a most important change.

When the saints come to die, they will especially need clear evidences {of preparedness. 'Tis} probably enough to do to grapple with the distemper {on a deathbed}. Death is terrible to nature, destroying {the frame of the body, before} leaving all the world.

2. Because surprise will be very unsuitable and improper for saints on such an occasion. ['Tis a] proper occasion of rejoicing to be saints {waiting to hear the midnight cry}, then called to meet the bridegroom. {'Tis an improper occasion for} sorrow and distress, not proper for a wedding. {'Tis} not a suitable frame to meet a bridegroom in, who is coming on a joyful occasion.

Children of the bride chamber should not mourn while the bridegroom is with them, or on the news of his coming to be with them.

It becomes a saint to long for the coming of his Lord, and to say, as Rev. 22:20, "Even so, come Lord Jesus," and to love his appearing. This is mentioned as [a] character of the saints. II Tim. 4:8, "[Henceforth there is laid up for me a crown of righteousness, which the Lord, the righteous judge, shall give me at that day: and not to me only, but unto all them also that love his appearing]."

Surely it becomes [saints] especially to love it, when nearest.

Let these things be effectual with you, to move all that have this hope in them, to stir up themselves and to take heed that, let Christ come when he will, he mayn't find 'em slumbering, {but} watching with their garments {on, with their} loins girt, {being} diligent[61] and laboring in all their duty, watching and fighting against all sin, and fervent in spirit, serving the Lord.[62]

[DOCTRINE RESUMED.]

[The text we are upon is] Matt. 25:1–12, especially at this time, vv. 7–11: "Then all those virgins arose, and trimmed their lamps. And the foolish said unto the wise, Give us of your oil; for our lamps are gone out. But the wise answered, saying, Not so; lest there be not enough for us and you: but go ye rather to them that sell, and buy for yourselves. And while they went to buy, the bridegroom came; and they that were ready went in with him to the marriage: and the door was shut. Afterward came also the other virgins, saying, Lord, Lord, open to us."

You may remember, {I proposed} two general *Propositions*:[63]

61. At this point, near the end of the fourth booklet, is a sermon outline on Eph. 3:8 (no. 453a); WJEO 52.

62. Here ends the seventh preaching unit and the fourth booklet. The next booklet has "No. 4. Feb. 1737, 8," written in another hand on the first page.

63. A shorthand notation by JE states that he preached this a second time from Luke 13:24–28.

{I. *The visible church is made up of true and false Christians.*

II. *That those do in some things agree, and in others they greatly differ.*}

And under this second proposition it was proposed, first, to consider what things true Christians and false agree in. And I have already observed what things they do agree in in this world, under several heads that have been spoken to.

[3.] I come now to consider what they will agree in, in another [world], or after the midnight cries. 'Tis observable in that parable, that there are some things that the wise virgins and foolish agree in, after they hear the midnight cry. In the general, they will then [be] of a mind about many things, wherein before they greatly differed.

The midnight cry will, in very many respects, make a great difference between true Christians and false.

It will, above all things that ever were, make the difference between 'em to appear. Those that appeared very much alike, and could not be distinguished before, will appear in that great difference immediately after the midnight cry is heard.

And that cry will separate 'em one from another; though till then they have been of one company, yet after that they shall be so [that] no more tares and wheat shall no more grow together then, but shall [be] set at a vast difference one from the other, and have a great gulf fixed between 'em.

But though the midnight cry will make such an apparent difference, and set such a wide distance between one and the other, yet in some respects it will be effectual to bring 'em together. It will have a wonderful effect, to make 'em agree in their judgment and sense of things.

In this world, the godly and ungodly exceedingly differ in their judgments. They are as wide as the east is from the west, in their sense of things of a spiritual and eternal nature; and the ungodly can't be brought to think about those things as the godly, by all that can be done.

But the midnight cry will bring 'em to be of a mind; it will be more effectual to bring even the ungodly to be of the same mind with the godly, than all the sermons that ever they heard preached, and all the books that ever they have read, or all the counsels [and] reproofs that they have had from the godly.

It will be more effectual to give 'em the same judgment of things that the godly have, than if the godly had spent their whole lives in reasoning and disputing with them.

There is a much greater agreement in opinion in another world, than there is in this world. There never yet has been seen in this world such an agreement in judgment, as there will be seen when the last trumpet comes to sound.

Now the world is exceedingly rent with differences of opinion, and endless disputes and altercations, that han't served to bring 'em together, but rather in many things to make the breach wider.

But when that cry is heard, and that trumpet sounds, it will put an end to all those disputes, and bring all to be of a mind, more than all the sermons that have been preached, and disputes that have been heard, and books that have been written, from the beginning of the world.

(1) Show in what respects they will be of a mind.

(2) How this will appear.

[(1) Show in what respects they will be of a mind.]

1. Then the[64] ungodly will agree with the godly in the conviction that they have of the truth of divine and eternal things.

In this they greatly differed in this world. The godly were convinced of the reality of divine things, but the ungodly were not. Many of them in the present state do openly deny many of the fundamental articles of religion, and others doubt of them; and none are soundly and thoroughly convinced of the reality and certainty of divine things.

But in another world, they will be convinced. Then, all the ungodly will believe the same great doctrines that the godly believed in this world. They will then be convinced of the being of a God, and that he is an almighty God, and an infinitely holy and just and sin-hating God. Then they will be convinced that the Scriptures are the Word of God, and that Christ is the Son of God, and the only Savior of the world. Then they will be convinced that there is another world, that there is an heaven of eternal rewards, and an hell of everlasting punishment.

If they before have been heterodox in their opinions, the midnight cry will bring 'em to, and they will thenceforward be orthodox. Those great doctrines of religion that are most mysterious and above our

64. MS: "they."

comprehension, and that they have therefore stumbled at and rejected, they will now be convinced of the truth of.

Those many objections that they formerly made against this and the other divine truth, will now all be quashed, and all their wranglings and carnal reasonings will be struck dead at once.

Then they will be convinced of the justice of God in the damnation of sinners, which before was that which they were so full of objections against. At the day of judgment, the ungodly will be convinced of the justice of God as well as the godly, for God will then manifest and make known his justice to the whole world; and therefore that day is called "the day of the revelation of the righteous justice of God," Rom. 2:5.

2. They will agree in their sense of the value and importance of things. This is held forth very plainly in this parable by the behavior of the ten virgins, both wise and foolish, after the midnight cry is heard. This is a thing that they greatly differ in in this world. Ungodly men ordinarily have quite other notions about the importance of things than the godly have; they have very different notions about the importance of temporal things. The godly are [those] that God has taught the vanity of the world. The spirit of a natural man is to set his heart on those worldly things, and treat them as if they were things of the greatest importance. How hard a thing is it to persuade them that those things are vain, and of little worth: but let what will be said to them, unless God is pleased to teach 'em by the powerful influences of his Spirit, they will still pursue after those things, as if they were the only things. They will make gods of them, and treat 'em as if they were to continue forever.

But hereafter, the ungodly will agree with the godly in their notions of the vanity [of] those things. They will see that all that which is said in the Scripture, and which they have been taught in the preaching of the Word, about the vanity of the world, is true. All the wealth, pleasures and glory of this world, will then appear as nothing in their eyes.

They will see that the things that they have formerly set their hearts upon have not profited 'em, and will be convinced that they were fools for pursuing of them as they did.

And they will agree with the godly then, in their sense of the infinite importance of eternal things.

The godly in this world are taught of God that those things are the greatest things, and therefore they treat them accordingly. And in another world, the ungodly will be of the same mind. They were often told of the vast importance of those things before: they were told that salvation was the one thing needful, and that it would not profit them if they should gain the whole world and lose their own souls [Matt. 16:26]; and [they] had these things proved, from the nature and endless duration of these things, in the plainest and fullest manner, but all did not convince them: but now they will be convinced.

They often heard what a dreadful a thing it was to sin against an infinitely great, omniscient and holy God, but yet were not made sensible of it, but notwithstanding made light of sin and sinned boldly. But now they will see that it was as they heard.

They were told before how dreadful a thing it was to be under guilt, and often heard it declared to 'em, how amazing and unbearable the wrath of an infinite Being was, but had not an abiding sense of it; and many of them no sense at all, but heard things without being moved by [them].

The godly, they were made in some measure sensible of it, and hereafter the ungodly will agree with them in it. They will need no more than they will have, to make 'em sensible what unspeakably dreadful things the guilt of sin and the wrath of God are.

They will then agree with the godly in a sense of the great worth of the grace of God in the heart. They will then see that that oil that the godly have in their vessels, is the best treasure.

The foolish virgins manifest their sense of this, when the midnight cry is heard, by begging oil of the wise—"Give us of your oil," say they—and by going in a great hurry to buy some.

They were not sensible of the value of it before. They did not beg of the wise any of their oil till now, nor did they go to them that sold to buy, though they had so much opportunity.

They were easy and quiet without it, but the midnight cry convinces them. Now they are sensible that 'tis worth the buying.

They might have bought before, in season, but they loved their money too well. They were not willing to part with their lusts and with their worldly enjoyments for it; they could not be brought to it, to sell all for Christ. When it was proposed to them to sell all that they had, that they might have this durable treasure, they refused, like the young men that [we] have account of, Matt. 19:21.

But now, what would they not give for oil? Now they are in haste to buy; they make no objection of the dearness of the commodity. Now they see that 'tis worthy that they should sell all for it; now they would willingly give all the world, yea, and ten thousand worlds for it, if they could obtain it. Their cry used to be, "Who will show us any temporal good? What shall we eat, what shall we drink, wherewithal shall we be clothed? How shall we be rich, how shall we get up in the world? How shall we gratify our sensual appetites?" But now it is, "How shall we obtain a little of this precious oil?" One drop of this now will appear to 'em more worth, ten thousand times, than all the riches and grandeur and pleasures that the whole world can afford.

Now they will be sensible of the infinite importance of an interest in Christ, which [they] so neglected to seek after before, though so much exhorted to it.

Now the ungodly will agree with the godly, in a sense of the preciousness of time. Before, they were not sensible of it, and therefore squandered it away, and worse than lost it.

They will be sensible then what a precious season and opportunity they have had, and how precious those means of grace were that they enjoyed, those sabbaths, those sermons, those sacraments that they have had.

Both wise virgins and foolish will then agree in their sense of the value of a bright lamp, and clear evidences of their good estate, when Christ comes. And therefore we see, that when the midnight cry is heard, they both arise, and trim their lamps.

The wise virgins, they arise and trim their lamps, found to be but dimly burning when they rise awakened out of sleep; and the foolish virgins, they also fell to trimming their lamps, though they were quite gone out.

Also, what does it signify to go to trimming a lamp to make it burn, after it is totally gone out? But the foolish virgins, they act like persons in a dreadful amazement.[65] They were terrified to hear the midnight cry, and awake, and see their lamps gone out; and therefore they fell to trimming of 'em, to make 'em burn. As a man in a dreadful fright will try to do things that are impossible to be done: a drowning man will catch at a rotten twig, that, if he exercised reason, he would know could not save him.

The ungodly will then be made sensible, as well as the godly, of the dreadfulness of a false hope.

65. MS: "it."

Those that have had such a hope, and have made a false profession and show of godliness in the world, and have been received for saints, will then be made fully sensible how little worth the religion and hope of an hypocrite is, that thus fails and turns into disappointment and confusion.

They will then see how little worth that reputation they have had for godly had been; how little it has availed 'em to be looked upon converted and received as such in the world, when they shall have their mask taken off, and shall be stripped of their painted garb and shall walk naked, and all shall see what they be, to their eternal shame and contempt.

Thus both true Christians and false will agree in the esteem they have of the privileges that the godly are then admitted to, in being acknowledged and received by Christ, as some of his.

The foolish virgins are sensible of the great worth of the privilege that the wise are admitted to, in being admitted in with the bridegroom into the marriage.

This they manifest by their coming as they do afterwards, and so earnestly seeking the same privilege, coming and standing at the door, {saying,} "Lord, Lord, open to us."

Three particulars may be observed under this head before I proceed to the next thing proposed.

a. That the ungodly will then universally be brought to such a sense of the value of things. Not one will remain unconvinced, even the most stupid and senseless and sottish sinners. They will then have their eyes opened, those that now are the basest, vainest persons, that such as never spend a serious thought. There are some now in the world that make a mere scoff at those great things; but they, as well as others, shall be fully convinced as well as others.

b. Those godly that were found slumbering and sleeping by the midnight cry, will then have a new sense of those things awakened. The godly, in their slumbering frames, do often in a great measure forget those things; they lose that lively sense they have had of the vanity of the world, and the vast importance of spiritual and eternal things. But this midnight cry will thoroughly bring 'em to. The wise virgins, when the midnight cry is heard, manifest that sense they have of the great worth of a preparedness for the bridegroom's coming, by arising, and trimming their lamps. They show their sense of the great worth of an interest in Christ, by their so carefully seeking clear evidences of it at that time.

And they also show their sense of the infinite worth and value of God's grace in the heart, by their unwillingness to part with any for the supply of others. When the foolish {virgins ask them for oil}, they make answer, "Not so, lest there be not enough for us and you: but go ye rather to them that sell, and buy for yourselves." They are choice of their oil at such a time as this.

They manifest their sense of the excellency of the privilege of those that shall be received by the bridegroom, by the speedily going forth to meet {the bridegroom}, and by their joyfully entering {into the wedding with him}.

c. The godly will all be made more sensible of the importance of things, when that time comes, than ever they were before. Though they have been convinced in some measure of the infinite {importance of eternal things}, yet there is still in them a great deal of blindness and senselessness, and there is a great deal of a spirit remaining to idolize worldly things. They still think too highly of temporal enjoyments, and accordingly are guilty of a great deal of worldliness.

But hereafter they will see their folly in it, when they shall see, as they have never seen before, that this world is nothing, and that eternal things are the great things, and the only things, needful.

I come now [to show],

4.[66] How it will hereafter appear that natural men will thus, in their judgment and sense of things, agree with the godly. And it will appear in three things:

(1) In their wishes of being in the state of the godly, and envying their happiness. They shall see the blessedness of the saints, {as the rich man in hell} saw Abraham afar off, Luke 16:23; [they shall] see many come from the east and the west, and north [and south], Luke 13:29; at day of judgment [they] will see [the godly on Christ's right hand].

Then how will they wish that they were in their circumstances, which is taught us in the foolish virgins' begging of the wise some of their oil, representing to 'em their own necessitous circumstances, in that their lamps were gone out. How moving is their argument they make use of: they are in dreadful necessity, for the bridegroom is coming, and they have not a drop of oil, and their lamps are gone quite out. What shall they do, if the wise virgins won't give 'em some of their oil?

66. MS: "II."

When that time is come, spoken of in Luke 17:34–36, "when two shall be in one bed; the one shall be taken, and the other left; when two women shall be grinding at a mill; and the one shall be taken and the other left; and, two men shall be in the field, the one shall be taken, and the other left": how wistly may we suppose he that is left will look after him that is taken? The ungodly will feign hang by the skirts of their godly friends and acquaintance, if that might be allowed.

O, how happy will they appear in their eyes, at that day when God arises to shake terribly the earth, and the heavens and the earth being on fire, are ready to be dissolved, and when they see the amazing deluge of God's wrath coming: I say, how happy will those appear in their eyes that are then safe with Christ, at the[67] right hand of Christ, acknowledged of him, protected by him, and made much of as his jewels, when they shall have no friend to appear on their side.

(2) They would then be ready to seek it, and do their utmost to obtain it, if they could have any hope that it would be to any purpose. This is signified in the parable by their going to buy oil after they heard the midnight cry: now they ben't backward to buy oil, to do whatever they can to obtain it, when it is too late, but they neglected it before.

Wicked men are exhorted in this world to be seasonable and thorough in using means for their salvation; to lay aside other concerns so far as they hinder this; to apply themselves to their utmost to strive to enter in at the strait gate; and not to stick at difficulties that are in the way, not to begrutch the self-denial that was necessary.

But all was in vain. How very negligent are many of their souls, notwithstanding all those counsels. How little is the pains that they are willing to be at; how little the self-denial they can be willing to bring themselves to; how little of the world's enjoyments are they willing to part with for heaven.

But when the midnight cry comes, then they are brought to a disposition to take pains to deny themselves, or do or suffer anything for salvation, if it would be to any purpose.

Now to spend twenty or thirty years in a painful, constant, laborious [suffering], appears a dreadful thing to 'em, and they cannot comply with it. But how little a thing will this appear hereafter to do for their salvation; it will look nothing in their eyes. If they might have the opportunity again, how readily would they comply with it.

67. MS: "his."

Now they stick at little, slight suffering; but then they would be ready to run through fire and waters, if that would do.

When they [are] exhorted to buy oil now, the great objection is that it is too dear; they keep making an objection of [it], that it costs too much pain, too much inconvenience, too much crossing their inclination.

But when the foolish virgins go to buy oil after the midnight cry, they make no objection against the price. They would give anything if they could but obtain.

Then they would not be backward to pray for mercy, if that would do any good. Now they are very backward to this. They have so little sense of the importance of it, that they can't be brought so much as to ask for it, or at least not in any consistent and earnest manner. They are now counseled to cry for wisdom, and lift up [their voice], but ben't willing.

But then they won't be unwilling for it; then, if they could have any hope, O! how earnestly would they cry, and how constantly and perseveringly! See how the foolish virgins cry, in the 11th verse of this parable, "Lord, Lord, open to us." And so it is elsewhere represented. Ch. 7:22, "Many will say to me in that day, Lord, Lord, have we not prophesied in thy name? and in thy name have cast out devils? and in thy name done many wonderful works?" Luke 13:25–26, "When once the master of the house is risen up, and hath shut to the door, and ye begin to stand without, and to knock at the door, saying, Lord, Lord, open unto us; and he shall answer and say unto you, I know you not whence ye are: Then shall ye begin to say, We have eaten and drunk in thy presence, and thou hast taught in our streets."

Time was when Christ cried earnestly to them, and they would not regard him, so far were they from being brought to be willing earnestly to cry to him. They had other things to mind.[68]

(3) Another way that their sense of the great importance of {things, when that time comes, will be manifest}, will be their bitter bewailing and lamenting their loss of them.

When they see themselves shut out, and see that 'tis in vain to cry, "Lord, lord open to us," then will they weep and wail, and gnash their teeth. Luke 13:28, "When ye shall see Abraham, and Isaac, and Jacob, and all the prophets, in the kingdom of God, and you yourselves thrust

68. In revising for repreaching, JE inserted a cross-reference: "last Papers 2d Page +." However, no corresponding mark can be found; it is possible these "papers" were temporary additions for when he repreached portions of this series.

out." And Matt. 8:11–12, "And I say unto you, That many shall come from the east and west, and shall sit down with Abraham, and Isaac, and Jacob, in the kingdom of heaven. But the children of the kingdom shall be cast out into outer darkness: there shall be weeping and gnashing of teeth." So is it said of the man that had not on a wedding garment, and so was cast out and deprived of the joy and entertainments of the wedding. Matt. 22:12–13, "And he saith unto him, Friend, how camest thou in hither not having a wedding garment? And he was speechless. Then said the king to the servants, Bind him hand and foot, and take him away, and cast him into outer darkness, there shall be weeping and gnashing of teeth."[69]

APPLICATION.

Use I may be of *Instruction* in two *Inferences*.

First. Hence we learn that the midnight cry will cause a great change in ungodly men. If in so many things it will bring 'em to be of the same mind with the godly, this must be a very great change: for they are exceeding far from it in this world. [There was a] great change in the foolish virgins. There won't only be a great change in their bodies by death, as the frames of that will be dissolved—a great change in their persons, as soul and body, that were before united, will be separated; and a great change in their state and circumstances, as they will be taken forever from all things in this world, and will have their abode in another, exceeding different world—but there will be a very great change in their souls.

---

69. The eighth preaching unit ends here. JE begins the next with a recapitulation of his arguments thus far:

> Matt. 25:1–12, especially verses 7–11.
>
> Having before considered what things true Christians and false will agree in in this world, we were last upon the consideration of those things wherein they will agree in in another, from this proposition, viz. that after the midnight cry, godly and ungodly will both be of one mind about many things, concerning which they before greatly differed.
>
> 3. That the ungodly would then agree with the godly, in the conviction they have of the truth of divine things.
>
> 4. They will agree in the sense they have of the value and importance of things, which it has been showed, [(1)] will appear in their wishing to be in the state of the godly; (2) in their readiness to seek take pains and deny [themselves]; (3) By their bewailing and lamenting their loss of them, or the opportunity of their obtaining them.

Then, those that were senseless and secure and asleep in sin, will be effectually awakened, never to be insensible anymore. Those that before were unconvinced, will be now thoroughly convinced.

Though there will be no change of nature or principle in natural men in another [world], but they will have the same wicked hearts that they now have, and without the least jot of goodness, and their wickedness shall then be without those restraints that it is now under, and so shall rage to a more dreadful degree; yet there will be an exceeding great change in them.

They will now be thoroughly concerned, so convinced of the truth and importance of the spiritual and eternal things, as never to doubt anymore. They will now be convinced of the justice of God, though not with any humiliation of heart. They will now be convinced of the truth and certainty of the gospel, though not by any sight or sense of the glory and excellency of it.

And they will be changed, in many respects, in their judgment and sense of almost everything. All the things of this world will then look quite otherwise to them than now they do, and all the things of another world will look exceeding differently to them from what they now do. Time and eternity will seem far otherwise than now they do. They will have quite other thoughts of the ways of sin, and the ways of holiness. They will have other thoughts of the means of grace. They will have quite other thoughts of worldly riches and honor and pleasures. They will have other thoughts of death and judgment, heaven and hell. They will have other thoughts of God than they used to have: of his greatness, [his] holiness, [his] justice. [They will have quite other thoughts] of the Scripture [then they used to have, and] of good men and wicked men. None of these things hereafter will appear in any measure to them as they do: they will have an exceeding different sense of them.

What different thoughts of things had the rich man in hell, from what he had when he was upon the earth: [what] other thoughts of Lazarus; [what] other thoughts of the enjoyments of this life, and of time and eternity. When he was upon earth, he "was clothed in purple and fine linen, and fared sumptuously every day"; {but he} now entreats that Lazarus might be sent "to dip the tip of his finger in water, and cool my tongue" [Luke 16:19–26].

So that all men must be changed. There must be a great change made in the souls of all men. Those whose souls ben't savingly changed in this world, they shall be the subjects of such a change, as we have now heard of, in another world. Then, wicked men's eyes, which have been close shut all their lifetime, shall be opened. As we are told of the rich man in hell, he lift up his eyes; as 'tis said of a mole, that he never opens his eyes till he is dead: so may it be said of wicked men.[70]

When we come to see the day of judgment, as we all shall see it, then we shall see a great change made in all men from what once they were. Then shall we see a great change made in the most senseless and sottish men. We shall see a great change made in those who gave themselves up to mirth and luxury. Then we shall see a great change made in wicked kings, and other great men, that now look upon themselves above religion, or look upon religion as a thing too mean for their regard. And then we shall see a great change made in hypocrites, and those that have entertained a false profession: a greater change than ever was made in 'em in this world, by that which they called their conversion.

Second. Hence we may learn what occasion wicked men in another world will have to think of the sermons they have heard in this world, and that, because they will then have their judgment and sense of those things, that they were told of in those sermons, so changed.

They will then be greatly convinced of the truth of which they heard in those sermons, wherein they were told that their surety was an infinitely great and dreadful, holy and sin-revenging God, and how angry this God was with wicked men, and how dreadful his anger was; and were told that this world was vain and worthless, and that there was another world, a world of eternal happiness or misery that would come in a little time; and that very shortly they must appear before the holy judgment seat to give an account, who they would find a holy and just judge, that will by no means clear the guilty; and were told that time was precious, and that it was great folly for them to neglect to improve, and that an interest in Christ was the one thing needful.

Many in this world think but little of the sermons they hear, wherein they are told such things; it goes in at one ear, as it were, and out t'other. They sit and hear it, but little do they regard; they go away, and scarce ever think any more of it. Yea, many of them hear with such a regardless frame of spirit, that they can but scarcely be said to hear in the time. They spend great part of the time in thinking of other things. And thus it is that they treat sermons, time after time.

70. On moles, see "Images of Divine Things" no. 179, WJE 11:118.

And if they may be said to think of what they hear in the time of it, that is all the time they allow for their thoughts to be exercised about it. When they are gone from the house of God, they are gone from the house of God; their thoughts are otherwise employed. All the week long they are taken up about worldly and vain objects, and not in meditating on the things they heard on the sabbath.

But how little soever they think of what they hear in sermons now, yet in another world they will have occasion to think much of them, for their minds will be altered about 'em. They will then be so convinced of the truth and importance of 'em, as will engage their thoughts about 'em. And they won't have worldly enticements and pursuits.

They will doubtless then remember a great deal more of sermons than they do now. Passages that they heard in sermons will then come to mind, such and such sentences that the minister spoke, such expositions as he used on such or such occasion: things that they had forgot before, and had not thought of for many years, and it may [be] never thought of 'em since they first heard 'em. The conviction that they will receive of things in another world, will make 'em revive in their memories. They will come fresh to mind then, as if they were spoken but an hour ago.

Men in hell will think much of the warnings that they had; they will doubtless come fresh to their minds. And the things that now, when they are heard from the pulpit, make very little impression, and when they are thought of afterward, 'tis in a very regardless manner; in another world, they won't be thought of in a regardless manner: then they will come to mind with great and strong impression.[71]

Then will the poor, miserable soul think with itself, "O, how was I at such and such a time told of these things, that I now see to be true! How often was I told of this midnight cry! How was I at such a time warned of this judgment, and told of these and those circumstances of it! How was I told of this hell! What expressions did my minister use in the pulpit at such a time to set forth the state of the damned, and what arguments did he use with me to improve my time! How true was the word that he said at such a time! How are his words verified, and what just cause was there for all that he said in such a sermon, that then I was unconvinced of!"

The wicked in another world will doubtless be full of such reflections as these, about sermons that they have heard in their lifetime.[72]

71. In revising for repreaching, JE drew brackets at either end of this paragraph.

72. In revising for repreaching, JE added: "Prov. 5:11, 'And thou mourn at the last.'"

There will be nothing like the conviction wicked men will have in hell to make 'em remember sermons; it will have a wonderful effect this way. It will doubtless make many men that died and went to hell when they were old, think of sermons that they heard in their youth, and will bring to remembrance particular warnings, particular expressions that they heard from the pulpit, many of them; and won't only bring 'em to their memory, but fasten 'em in their memory, and will cause that they never shall forget 'em. Now wicked men soon forget all that they hear in the most solemn awakening discourses; a little time wears 'em out of their memories. But when they come to be raised in their memories in another world, a whole eternity won't wear 'em out; they will never forget 'em anymore.

Now they won't take pains to remember what they hear, but then, they won't be able to forget 'em. Gladly would they forget 'em, if they could, but they won't be able to 'rase 'em out of their memories.

Let wicked, careless hearers consider those things, those that have not been wont to regard what they hear. Consider that you shall regard 'em, whether you will or no, first or last. You that won't be careful to remember the warnings that are given you, you will remember 'em; if you han't that conviction of their truth and importance now, that tends to fasten 'em in your memories, you shall have it in another world.

And possibly this sermon may be hereafter thought of in hell by some that now hear it, and some that now do but little regard it, and will soon forget in this world. The torments of hell may revive it in their memories.

Use II may be of *Exhortation.*

First. Be exhorted seriously to examine your present thoughts, and the ways that you allow yourself in, and consider whether it be likely that they are agreeable to that judgment you shall make of things in another world. You have heard what an exceeding great change will hereafter be made in the sense and judgment of wicked men; therefore, seriously consider what kind of judgment you are like to make hereafter of yourself, of your present thoughts and ways.

Is there nothing that you now commonly do, no particular way that you have of gratifying your own inclinations, or managing and conducting yourself in the course of your life; no way of dealing with your neighbor; no way of behaving yourself in your families, that may be said to be your way, and a thing that you commonly do and allow, but what you can rationally judge you shall think well of, and justify yourself in another world?

Be entreated to be serious in this matter, and critically to try your ways in secret, and in your families, and towards your neighbors, towards your superiors, and towards your inferiors and your equals.

Labor as it were to realize the midnight cry to yourself, and to think with yourself what affect it will be likely to have upon your judgments and thought, and sense of things, if it should come this night.

And labor in your meditations to set yourself as it were in another world, and so to look back from thence to this world, and to the different parts of your present life, and think with yourself how things will be likely to appear to you then.

Now, it may be, you have various reasonings in your own heart about your own ways. You reason with yourself thus and thus to quiet your own conscience; you have such and such arguments to prove that such a thing that you do is no hurt, and that you do no other than well in them; you have these and those examples for what you do and allow.

Examine all those reasonings and excuses, whether they are such as are likely to appear sound and substantial in another world, or whether or no when you come there, they won't all vanish away like shadows.

Examine those excuses you have for those omissions that you live in: if you live in the omissions of secret prayer, or at least do often omit it, or omit giving in a way of charity to those that need.

You now have probably something that you justify yourself with: but inquire, whether your excuses are such as you are like to hold in another world. There are many excuses that men have for these and those ways that they hold a long time, and are fast in them; there is no reasoning them out of 'em; yea, they hold 'em till they grow old, and to their dying day: and yet are forced to let 'em a-go at last, when they come into another world. They are swept away at one shake, like a spider's web with a besom.[73] Let persons thus examine what they have to say for their heats of spirit that they get into time after time, and their behavior by which [they] manifest it. Let persons thus examine what they have to say for their speaking evil one of another, and running out one against another by their own and their neighbor's firesides.

And let our young people examine whether they shall, in another world, justify their absenting themselves from time to time from family

73. A broom.

prayer, and their taking those liberties in company that they know by experience tend to stir up lust, and that they can't but rationally judge have been the very things that have led to many gross acts of uncleanness, and that their being customary have been one principal occasion of so many instances of fornication in the country.

It may be now you laugh at it when you hear those things condemned, but consider whether or no [it] to be likely that then you shall think the condemnation of 'em to be laughed at.

Consider whether or no the way that you are in and allow, ben't that that the most eminent and holy persons do generally condemn. If it be so, certainly what you have heard may well lead you to doubt of the lawfulness of it: for you have now heard that all will hereafter agree with godly men in their thoughts and judgments of things.[74]

Second. Labor that you may now be established in such a judgment and sense of things as you shall have hereafter, such that you may now be convinced of those truths that you shall be convinced of then, and you may now set such a value on things as you will then, that you may entertain such thoughts of the things of this world.

You may exercise your own reason, and consider with yourself what thoughts it will be likely you shall have, of the improvement of time; [what thoughts you shall have] of what is the wisest and best course; [of what is of] the most important interest; of [the] worth of sermons, sabbaths and sacraments. If you ben't very atheistically inclined, you can't be much at a loss about [it]. If you inquire at the mouth of reason, that will soon tell you. And when you have heard what that says concerning your future thoughts of things, let it be your earnest endeavor that you may, as far as possible, now have the same thoughts and the same sense of things impressed upon you.

Here, consider for *Motive*:

1. You have all reason to think that the judgment you will then make of things, will be the true judgment. Then, you will be in circumstances wherein you see things in a true light. Then, those worldly enjoyments and objects of your lusts, that now blind and infatuate you, will be forever taken away from you. Then, you will no more remain senseless and stupid.

74. In revising for repreaching, JE wrote the reference, "see last Papers." However, no passage corresponding to this reference can be found (see also above, p. 131, n. 68).

Then, you will be no longer able to blind the eyes or stop the mouth of conscience. Its eyes will then be fully opened, and it will be strong, and there will be no stopping its mouth; its voice will be heard aloud. If you till then have gone endeavoring to stop its mouth, yet then it will roar as a lion out of the forest.

Then you will see what is true. Those things that are now unseen things, will then be seen things. Those things that are now future things, will be then present things.

Then your judgment will be true, for then you will find by experience what is true; what is now known only by hearing of them, as at a distance, will then be known by present experience. Things that are durable and everlasting, will then be present. Therefore, the judgment and estimate you will then make of the truth and importance of things, will doubtless be a right judgment.

2. The judgment that you will make of things after the midnight cry will be your last judgment, if you continue in sin till then. You will then change your judgment, and that change will be the last change that ever you will make in your judgment of those things that pertain to your state in this world and the other.

You will never change back again, though you will have such a long space of consideration, even a whole eternity. You will forever be confirmed in the judgment that you will then make; it will be impossible for you ever to change your judgment of the vast import of eternal things then.

3. Consider, that if you don't come to judge right of things now, the change that will be made in your judgment hereafter, will be of no advantage to you. What advantage will it [be] of [to] you then to be convinced of the truth {of those things}? Your concern in those things then will be unalterable. What advantage {will it be to you, then to be convinced} of the vanity of the world? Whether you are convinced of it or no, you never can have any more concern with it. What advantage {will it be, then to be convinced} of the preciousness of the soul, {or of the} worth of an interest in Christ, [or of the] preciousness of time?

It will be of no advantage then to be brought to a disposition to be willing to seek, {or} to take pains, {or to} cry earnestly for mercy.

Third. If you ben't brought to judge of things as they be in this world, your being brought to it in another world will only be to aggravate your misery. It will then do you no good; it will only be a torment to you to see that there is a God, {and the} soul so precious. Consideration of these things will be forever tormenting to you. [They will] make you your own tormenter, cause tormenting thoughts and reflections on your own folly in neglecting {your soul's interest}, when you had so good an opportunity {to seek it}, when warned.

Fourth. Consider of what great benefit it may be of to you, if you frame right judgments of things now. Though hereafter it will be in vain, yet if you are convinced now, it will not be in vain. Then, it will be too late, but it is not too late now.[75] Whoever thou art, whether young or old, whether a little or a great sinner, it is not too late for you to change your judgment, and come to yourself.

Now God is not inexorable, as he will be hereafter, but is ready to hear prayers. He don't now say "to the seed of Jacob: Seek me in vain" [Is. 45:19]. Now, he that is hereafter to be your judge, is ready to become your Savior.

Now you have the price in your hands; the talents that your Lord has committed to you, ben't yet taken from you. Now God says to you, as in Is. 1:18, "Come now, and let us reason together, saith the Lord: though your sins be as scarlet, they shall be as white as snow; though they be red like crimson, they shall be as wool." Now precious time is yet continued; now you have opportunity to go and buy oil. Therefore, labor now to act according to such an estimate as you shall hereafter make of things.

Fifth. Consider what advantages you are now under to frame a right judgment of things. 'Tis not because wicked men have no advantages to come to a true judgment of things now, that so many of them ben't convinced till the midnight cry, or at least such as you art that live under the gospel. 'Tis not because you han't been convinced long ago. God has plainly told you what is true, and you have had most convincing arguments set before you to convince you, hundreds of times. You have had, and now have, abundant evidence set before you of the worthlessness of the things[76] of this world, and the vast importance of those of the next. How plainly have you been told now [of] those things that may well convince you? Therefore, if you are not convinced, it can be owing to

75. In revising for repreaching, JE drew a pick-up line here.

76. The fifth booklet ends here, while the final page of the current preaching unit is the first page of the next booklet. At the beginning of the next booklet, JE wrote: "Math 25. 1 —— 12 . see next P." His shorthand notations at the beginning of the next booklet indicate that it was "preached the second time."

nothing but your sottishness. Let these things therefore sink down into your hearts: apply your heart unto wisdom now. And now labor to make such a judgment as you may pass in hereafter, and shall never have occasion to condemn; and now act as hereafter you shall wish you had acted.

O, how great and precious a gift [is this wisdom] in this world! Ask it of God, and cry earnestly to him for it who gives liberally, and upbraids not [Jas. 1:5].

And learn of the wise virgins; be ready to hearken at all times to their counsels. For remember that hereafter, you will be of the same mind with them.

And search the Scriptures. Hear what God says, and hearken to all his instructions and counsels. For in the Word of God you may certainly find those very things declared, that you will believe, and be convinced of in another world.[77]

[DOCTRINE RESUMED.]

The second general *Proposition* that was observed from this parable was that {true and false Christians do in some things agree, and in others they greatly differ}.

We have already considered wherein they agree. I come now, in the *Second* place, to consider wherein they differ. And those things wherein they differ, may be referred to these three heads:

1. [Their] radical difference consists [in that, that] the one have oil in their vessels, and the other have none.

2. There appears a great difference between them, in those things that are the consequence of this radical difference.

3. They greatly differ in their general character, that is manifest from the consideration of both the foregoing.[78]

But in the

[1.] First place, their most essential difference lies in that, that the one have oil in their vessels, and the others have none. It has been already shown how they agree, in that both have lamps. It has been shown how they agree in their profession of Christianity, and in attending the

---

77. This point marks the end of the ninth preaching unit.

78. A second shorthand notation by JE indicates that he preached part of this sermon a second time.

same external duties of religion, and being of the same visible society, and in that they both seek and hope to go to heaven.

And [it has been shown] that false Christians, as well as true, may make profession of experience of a work of conversion, and may indeed have many religious affections.

They may have great religious affections of sorrow, and may have great affections of gratitude, and may be much affected in reading and hearing of the great things that Christ did and suffered, and may be affected in hearing the gospel preached, and may love to hear the Word preached; it may be pleasant to them, yea, they may be lifted up and carried away with admiration of sermons that they hear.

They may have an affection of zeal against sin and error. They may have affections of praise, may have a disposition to praise God, and may be very much affected with some great and extraordinary work of God that they see, and their hearts may be lifted up with it.

And [they] may in many things be exceeding strict and exact, and may have a strong hope and confidence of their good estate, and may be received into the charity and good opinion of those that are true Christians.

Thus, they may agree in their lamps. But let 'em agree never so much in these respects, let the foolish virgins have never so flaming lamps, yet herein there will forever remain a great difference in this respect, viz., that true Christians have oil in their vessels, whereas false Christians have none.

The difference between true Christians and false is not gradual. It don't consist in that, that false Christians have but little oil in their vessels, and true Christians have a great deal; but in that, that true Christians have oil and false have none. Not the least drop of oil is there in the vessels of the foolish virgins.

This OIL in the vessels of true Christians may be thus described:[79]

'Tis a spiritual and abiding principle in their hearts, that may be said to be a new nature in their souls, consisting in the Christian spirit that they are of.

---

79. JE deletes: "an abiding principle in the heart, that may be said to be a new nature in the soul, consisting in the Christian and gracious spirit that they are of." On oil as a type of grace, see the list of "Scriptures" in "Images of Divine Things," nos. 17 and 30, WJE 11:132, 133.

Whatever profession false Christians may make, and whatever affections they may have, and whatever strong and confident hope they may entertain, this is what they have none of.

This principle, this nature and this spirit, that has now been spoken of, is the proper fullness of the soul, whereby it partakes of Christ's fullness. But souls or vessels of false Christians have none of this fullness, but are empty, and their hearts hollow.

This is as it were the substance by which God's wheat differs from chaff. There seems to reference to this in Is. 6:13, "But yet in it shall be a tenth, and it shall return, and be eaten as a teil tree, and as an oak whose substance is in them when they cast their leaves, so the holy seed shall be the substance thereof." By this, true Christians differ from false, as a sound tree differs from one that is hollow and rotten.

This is that seed that remaineth in them, that are born of God. This is that "good thing" that is in God's people "towards the Lord God of Israel." I Kgs. 14:13, "In him only of all the house of Jeroboam is found some good thing towards the Lord God of Israel."

This is that "one thing needful" that Christ speaks of, Luke 10:42. This is that substance and weight and purity, wherein silver and gold differ from shining dross; and this is the substance and a sweetness, wherein fruit differs from flowers and leaves.

This is that root in themselves, wherein the seed growing in good ground differs from that which grows up in stony ground, Matt. 13:21. This is the "good treasure in the heart," spoken of, Matt. 12:35.

But this great difference between true and false Christians may be more fully and clearly explained, by considering distinctly the several things contained in it. And therefore [I will] show:

3. (1) [It is a] principle in [the] heart.

4. (2) [This is a] spiritual principle [in the heart].

5. (3) [It is an] abiding [principle].

6. (4) [It is a] new nature [in the soul].

7. (5) [It consists in the Christian] spirit they are of.

(1) It is a principle in the heart. The vessel that this oil is contained in, is the heart. The main and most essential difference between true Christians and false, is inward, in the hidden man of the heart, and don't consist in anything external.

Nor does it consist in any natural knowledge that true Christians have got in their heads more than others, but in the excellent principle they have in their hearts. Man looks on the entire appearance, but God looks on the heart; that is what he especially requires. Prov. 23:26, "My son, give me thine heart." True Christians do give their hearts to God; they have their hearts drawn. The change that is wrought in a true Christian, is no superficial thing; it consists in no flashy affections that make transient impressions only: but what is wrought and experienced in the soul of a true Christian is inward, and digs and reaches the bottom of his heart.

Whatever strong impressions false Christians may have made upon their imagination, and however greatly their affections may be moved, so as to cause tears or great joy and admiration, and a high conceit of themselves, yet their hearts ben't reached. Their impressions don't come to the bottom of their hearts, nor do their affections come from thence: they leave the heart as it was.

'Tis a great gospel privilege and blessing to have a change of heart, to have the stony heart taken away, and an heart of flesh given. Ezek. 11:19, "And I will give them one heart, and I will put a new spirit within you, and I will take the stony heart out of the flesh, and will give them an heart of flesh."

(2) This is a spiritual principle in the heart. There may be moral principles in men that are not spiritual principles. A man may be of a just principle, and he may be of a generous principle, he may be of a neighborly principle, and not be of a spiritual principle.

The epithet of "spiritual" is often used in the New Testament as distinguishing of true Christian grace from all that appearance of value that may be in unregenerate men. Gal. 6:1, "Ye which are spiritual, restore such a man in the spirit of meekness." Col. 1:19, "Hath filled us with all wisdom, and spiritual understanding." Rom. 8:6, "To be spiritually minded is life and peace."

Here, some may be ready to

Inquire, What is meant, when it is said that this principle is spiritual? We have often heard the term, but what is the import of the expression, and how is that which is truly spiritual nature, distinguished from that which is merely moral? I answer,

1. This principle is not called "spiritual," chiefly because the seat of it is in the soul or spirit of a man, and not in his body. A great many other

things have their seat in the soul, and there only, that ben't spiritual, in the sense of the New Testament. So is the understanding or knowledge of a natural man; it has its seat as much in the soul, as the understanding of a godly man. But yet we find spiritual understanding distinguished from their understanding. All men's idea or thoughts are seated in the soul, or in that part of man which is a spirit, and not in the body; but yet, all ben't spiritual. Nor,

2. Is it called "spirit," because it is conversant about those things that are immaterial and not corporeal. So are many things in natural men. Natural men may have reasonings about the nature of the soul, and about the nature of other spiritual beings. They may have a great deal of knowledge, not only about natural bodies, but also about the nature of spirit. But yet these reasonings and this knowledge, mayn't be spiritual, in the language of the New Testament. But,

3. Affirmatively, this principle is termed "spirit" because of the original and principle of it, viz., the Spirit of God.

'Tis hence the term is derived, as it is used in the New Testament. The word "spirit" has not respect to the spirit of man, that is the seat of what is spiritual, nor with respect to spiritual substance, that is the object of God; but with respect to the Spirit of God, that is the author, original and principle of it.

Thus Christians are termed "spiritual" persons, because they are born of the Spirit, and have the Spirit of God dwelling in them; and things are called "spiritual" because they relate to the Spirit of God. As is evident by I Cor. 2:13–14, "Which things also we speak, not in the words which man's wisdom teacheth, but which the Holy Ghost teacheth; comparing spiritual things with spiritual. But the natural man receiveth not the things of the Spirit of God: for they are foolishness unto him: neither can he know them, because they are spiritually discerned."

Here the Apostle explains himself, that by "spiritual things," he means things of the Spirit of God, and things which the Holy Ghost teacheth.

So Eph. 5:18–19, "be ye filled with the Spirit; speaking to yourselves in psalms and hymns and spiritual songs, singing and making melody in your heart to the Lord." The songs are called spiritual, as proceeding from the Spirit they are filled with. So Rom. 8:6, "to be carnally minded is death; but to be spiritually minded is life and peace." Here, to be "carnally minded," is opposed to being carnally or fleshly minded. And now, let this be compared with the next verse but two: "but ye are not in the flesh, but in the spirit, if so be the Spirit of God dwell in you." Here you see that that which is spiritual, is opposed to carnal or fleshly, as it related to the Spirit of God.

And so it is that that principle, which is in the hearts of the godly, is a spiritual principle, viz., as the Spirit of God is the source of it, and as it is of the nature of that Spirit. Which probably is one reason why it is compared to oil in the parable we are upon.

Oil is the most common and useful type of the Spirit of God of any in the Scripture.[80] So was the oil with which the priests and other persons and things were anointed: anointing them with oil, signified sanctifying them with the Spirit of God. So Christ is said to be anointed with oil, as he had the Spirit of God poured out upon him. [Ps.] 89:20, "I have found David my servant, and with my holy oil have I anointed." Ps. 45:7, "Thou lovest righteousness, and hatest wickedness: therefore God, thy God, hath anointed thee with the oil of gladness above thy fellows."[81]

So all true Christians are said to receive an anointing, as they have the grace of the Spirit of God in their hearts. I John 3:27, "But the anointing which ye have received of him abideth in you, and ye need not that any man teach you. But as the same anointing teacheth you all things, and is truth and is no lie, and even as it hath taught you ye shall abide in him."

So here this principle in the heart is called "oil" in the parable—doubtless the same as {the} oil in [the] candlesticks, Zech. 4:2–3—because 'tis a spiritual principle. And it is so, in three respects:

a. 'Tis a principle that is not from nature, but is wrought in the heart wholly by the Spirit of God. That which [is] spiritual is supernatural, or above nature; and therefore, we find what is spiritual, and what is not, set in contradistinction, the one to the other, in Scripture. I Cor. [2:]14–15, "the natural man receiveth not the things of the Spirit of God: for they are foolishness unto him: neither can he know them, because they are spiritually discerned. But he that is spiritual judgeth all things."

80. On oil as a type of the Holy Ghost, see "Discourse on the Trinity," in *The Works of Jonathan Edwards, 21, Writings on the Trinity, Grace and Faith*, edited by Sang H. Lee (New Haven: Yale University Press, 2003), 21:157–58, and the ordination sermon, *Sons of Oil, Heavenly Lights*, in WJE 25:257–74.

81. MS: "because spirit not by measure."

So that this principle in the heart that we are speaking of, is no principle that is naturally there, and so is distinguished from those ingenuous dispositions of nature, that some have more than others. Some, by their natural disposition and constitution, are more disposed to some moral virtues than others, but such principles are not spiritual.

This that is in the hearts of the godly, which they are distinguished [by], is nothing that arises from the working of natural principles, such as self-love, natural fear, natural gratitude, [or] natural admiration of something extraordinary, as the affections of false Christians do.

Nor is it wrought in the heart by any natural power or strength of their own reason, or any of their natural faculties, or by the strength of their endeavors, or from the natural strength of others.

So that this principle is distinguished from all moral principles, that come merely by a sober and virtuous education.

But it is of His infusing. Hence the apostle John says, godly persons "are not born of blood, nor of the will of the flesh, nor of the will of man, but of God," John 1:13. They have "received an unction from the holy One," I John 2:20.

Nor is it only from the operation of the Spirit, as assisting and working on men's natural principles, such as their self-love and natural conscience; but it is from the Spirit infusing a new and divine principle. 'Tis not only a natural principle, stirred up and set to work by God's Spirit, as men's natural conscience is stirred up by the Spirit under legal awakenings and convictions: but 'tis from the creating power of the Spirit of God, giving a new heart, infusing a new principle; a principle quite above natural self-love, natural fear and natural gratitude, natural conscience; something heavenly, something of God. Herein, this differs from common illuminations, superior to all that is born of the flesh.

The principle itself, as well as the exercise of it, is from the Spirit of God by the new birth; as is evident by its being represented as a seed implanted in the heart in the new birth, I John 3:9.

This is a principle of spiritual life and action that is from Christ, and is the same with that living water that Christ speaks of, John 4:14.

b. 'Tis a spiritual principle, not only as 'tis at first infused by the Spirit of God, but it is continually from the Spirit of God, dwelling as a spring of life in the soul. It is at first immediately from the Spirit of God, and 'tis always immediately from the Spirit; 'tis always from something above nature.

Much as the water that is in the stream continually is coming from the fountain, and if the communication with the fountain should be cut off, the stream would immediately fail. And as the light is from the sun, not only at the sun's first rising, but it is immediately from the sun all the day long whenever it shines, and if at any time a cloud intervenes to hide the sun, the shining ceases.

The Spirit of God dwells in the hearts of the saints, as we are told that they are "the temples of the Holy Ghost" [I Cor. 6:19].

When once the Spirit of God is given to work this divine principle, the same always abides there. John 14:16, "And I will pray the Father, and he shall give you another Comforter, that he may abide with you for- ever." {And the} latter end of [v.] 17, "but ye know him, for he dwelleth in you," and shall be in you.

And therefore, a true Christian, in having grace dwelling in him, is said to have God dwelling in him. I John 4:16, "He that dwelleth in love dwelleth in God, and God in him."

And God, as he dwells in the hearts of the saints, don't remain there inactive and motionless; and therefore he is said not only to dwell in them, but to walk in them. II Cor. 6:16, "for ye are the temple of the living God; as God hath said, I will dwell in them, and walk in them."

Christ is in them by his Spirit, but he is not in them as one dead, but he lives in them. Gal. 2:20, "I live, yet not I, but Christ liveth in me."

And grace is maintained in the heart of a saint, no otherwise than as life is maintained in the branch of a tree, viz., by sap continually com- ing from the tree; so that if the branch be severed from the stock, it dies.

Herein this principle differs from all that is experienced by natural men. Natural men may have that which is from the Spirit of God. He may have convictions and common illuminations that are from thence, but not as an indwelling spring of life in the soul. The Spirit of God never took up his abode in their hearts, or united himself so to them, as to become a principle of action in them.

They don't feel the Spirit of God acting in them as a full principle of operation in their hearts, as the godly do; and therefore having the spirit of Christ is mentioned in Scripture as that which distinguishes those that are Christ's. Rom. 8:9, "But ye are not in the flesh, but in the Spirit, if so be that the Spirit of God dwell in you. Now if any man have not the Spirit of Christ, he is none of his."

c. This principle is a spiritual principle, as the Spirit of God therein exerts and manifests his own proper nature. 'Tis a spiritual principle, not only as the Spirit of God is the author of it, and the constant spring of it; but as the nature of the Spirit of God appears in the nature of this principle.

This principle, and the Spirit of God, agree in their nature and tendency, and so it is of a spiritual nature.

Hence Christ says, "whatsoever is born of the Spirit is spirit," John 3:6. He don't mean whatsoever is born of the Spirit, is [the] spirit of a man and not his body, but whatsoever is born of the spirit is something of the same nature as that Spirit that it is born of, viz., a spiritual nature, after the same manner as that which is born of corrupt nature is corrupt nature: for "flesh" and "spirit" in the New Testament signify the same as corrupt nature and grace.

As the light that comes from the sun, is[82] of the same nature with that light that is in the sun; and as the water that comes from a fountain, is of the same nature with that which [is] in the fountain; and as the sap that is in a branch, is of that same nature with {that which is in the stock}: so the principle that is in the heart of a saint, is of the same nature with the Spirit of God whence it proceeds.

However, Christians are said to be made partakers of the divine nature, II Pet. 1:4; and they that are filled with grace, are said to be filled with the fullness of God, Eph. 3:19. So far as they are full of grace, they are full of God, because they are full of that which [is] Godlike.

But we know that the nature of the Spirit of God, is an holy nature. Hence 'tis called the Holy Spirit; it is a heavenly spirit, a divine spirit, 'tis a spirit of divine love. Love is especially the nature of the Spirit of God, and therefore 'tis said, "God is love," I John 4:16.

And this is here given as a peculiar mark of the Spirit of God's dwelling in us: "if we dwell in love."

And so in other parts of the epistles. Love's dwelling in us, and the Spirit of God dwelling in us, are put for the same thing. I John 4:12–13, "No man hath seen God at any time. If we love one another, God dwelleth in us, and his love is perfected in us. Hereby know we that we dwell in him, and he in us, because he hath given us of his Spirit." There you see that God's love being perfected in us, in one verse, is expressed by God's Spirit dwelling {in us}, in the next; so in vv. 23–24 of the foregoing

82. MS: "it is."

chapter. So that the principle we are speaking of, is a principle of divine, holy, and heavenly and ardent love.

The Spirit of God is a pure spirit; 'tis a great enemy to spiritual filthiness, and therefore is often compared to fire. Matt. 3:11, "baptized with the Holy Ghost and with fire." [It is] called "the spirit of judgment, and spirit of burning," Is. 4:4. And when poured out at Pentecost.

This also distinguishes this principle from all that natural men experience. The joys and comforts that natural men have, ben't of this spiritual nature. Whatever joys they have, they savor not the things that be of God. They don't perceive the excellency and sweetness, and truth and glory of divine things; they savor cruel things, the things that be of man, and their comforts tend to pride and self-dependence and self-exultation. They don't place their chief happiness in God and holy enjoyments.

And though the Spirit of God may produce effects in natural men, by awakening them and giving them common illuminations; yet he never so operates upon them, as in his operation to communicate himself, or communicate his own nature. He don't exert his own nature as it were in the acts of their faculties, as he does in the hearts of the godly.

When the Sun of righteousness shines upon the soul of the godly man, he communicates his light and heat so to him, that there is as it were a little sun, a living principle of light and heat kindled up in the soul, that is the exact image of the sun that shines upon it.

And so they behold the glory of the Lord, are changed into the same image from glory to glory, as by the Spirit of the Lord.

This glorious sun so touches the heart of a saint with his light and heat, that a divine flame is as it were thereby lit up in the soul, as a candle is lit by touching the fire.

But though the sun, in common illuminations, shines upon the ungodly in a sense, yet 'tis the sunshines upon a dung hill. It communicates nothing of its brightness and sweet influences to it, but is an occasion of its sending forth the greater stench.

So the illuminations of false Christians commonly, through their corruption, are an occasion of pride and self-confidence, and other things in them that are of a corrupt savor.

I come now to the

(3) [Third] thing contained in the description of this oil in their vessels, by which true Christians are distinguished from false, viz., that it is an abiding principle.

It is held forth in this parable that the wise virgins, in that they had oil in their vessels, had something of a more abiding nature than the foolish virgins, had who had nothing but a flame.

They had something that lasted them, and continued while they themselves slumbered and slept, and stood 'em in stead when they awakened again; whereas all that the foolish virgins had, failed, and came to an end in that time.

So that this is one thing, wherein what true Christians have in their hearts, differs from all that false Christians experience. They may feel religious affections working within them, and may have moving impressions and imaginations; but they have no abiding principle.

Because the godly have an abiding spiritual principle in their hearts, therefore they have spiritual experiences not only once, and then meet with [them] no more, but they have such experiences in a course.

They may have some extraordinary experiences at particular times, that they may have but once in many years, and it may be but once in their lifetime; but yet, though there may not be experiences often renewed in the same degree, or just in the same manner and with the same circumstances, yet they will often have other experiences of the same nature and tendency. There will be that which savors of the same, and tends the same way, and is only a lesser degree of the same light and life.

A truly godly man is not once affected and greatly moved with the goodness and love of God, and the grace of Christ in dying for sinners, or some such thing; but there is an abiding sense and savor and relish he has of such things in his heart.

Though he han't it always sensibly. There is not always a sweet sense of divine things in action, yet 'tis apparent that it abides in him in its principle, because on many occasions it is felt.

It is there, and every now [and] then some scripture touches it, and moves it. There is a harmony between the holy Scripture and the gracious soul, which makes one echo to the other.

It is between the Word of God and grace in the soul, as it is between two instruments of music that are set one by another, and set in an exact concord one with the other: if the one sounds, the other will answer it, [and] sound too; if you touch the strings of the one, the strings of the other will answer the stroke, and will move and sound without being touched.

Sometimes this principle in the heart is stirred and moved by what is delivered in the preaching of the Word, and sometimes by a word that is dropped in private conversation. Sometimes 'tis so, that only the mentioning of a single word—as, it may be, the name of God or Christ, or the word "redemption" or "holiness," or the name of some one of the attributes of God or graces of his Spirit—will kindle up the flame.

And so the light shines, more or less, every now and then, though it may be often greatly clouded. There is a sense of the excellency of divine things, a savor and sweet relish of them in a course.

And there is a stated choice of divine things as the most excellent and desirable things of[83] things, wherein the greatest happiness consists.

And there are soul-breathings and appetites after them, not only once or twice, but in a course.

There is a stated adherence of soul to God and Christ as the best good, a stated rest of heart in God and Christ, and delight in them, and a delight in holiness and appetite after it.

In such ways as these, the principle that is in their hearts appears to be an abiding principle. As the apostle John says, "his seed remaineth in him." The seed may indeed be buried up, as a seed is that is sown in the ground, though it be a fruitful soil. But though it [be] buried up, yet it won't lie there dead; it will be working and acting, taking root and shooting forth sprouts. So the same Apostle says the anointing that Christians have, abideth in them, I John 2:27.

Herein true Christians differ greatly from false Christians, who, though things that they meet with may make a great noise and have a great effect in the affections for the present, yet ben't continuing.

The following *Reasons* may be given why what true Christians have is abiding, and the other not so:

a. True Christians only receive a deep, real, living conviction of the truth and excellency of divine things. A false Christian may have that [that] may be very affecting and moving, but it is not attended with a real conviction of soul. Things, though they appear to him in an affecting view, yet don't appear in their evidence, and so coming with that weight, as things of the greatest reality.

---

83. MS: "as."

A man may be greatly affected in reading of a romance, that he at the same time knows is nothing but a fable. Persons have been often-times greatly affected in seeing something acted on a stage play, when they know it was nothing real, and they may be yet more affected when they have some sort of opinion that the thing is true; but they won't come with that weight, and that deep and abiding effect, as when the things are looked upon as certainly true.

Divine things have the weight of real things with the godly. They are convinced of the truth, and they are also convinced of the superlative excellency of them.

A false Christian may have some notion of the wonderfulness of some things we are told of the gospel, and of a sort of goodness in them; but he don't see that they are the most excellent things, as a true Christian does.

There is in the heart of a true Christian a deep conviction of their being the best things of all, the sweetest, tending most to make him happy. He don't only allow it because it is the general voice that it is so, and because he has been taught to say so from his childhood, but is inwardly convinced that it is so; he makes no doubt of it. Hence, he really prefers those things above all.

And this is one reason why what the true Christian has is lasting, and the other not. If a man be greatly affected with an ingenious romance, or some very moving acts on a stage, this affection won't last; it will be very transient, and will soon be gone, because the man don't look upon it real.

And so it will be with all affections that ben't founded on real conviction. But where there is inward, thorough conviction, and things are beheld as real and certain, there the effect will be deep, and it will hold.

When a man is convicted, the effect reaches the very bottom of his heart, and has an abiding consequence.

That such an inward, real conviction of the truth and divine excellency of spiritual things is peculiar to true Christians, is evident from the Scripture, as I John 5:1, "Whosoever believeth that Jesus is the Christ, is born of God"; and ch. 4:15, "Whosoever shall confess that Jesus is the Son of God, God dwelleth in him, and he in God"; and John 17:8, "For I have given unto them the words which thou gavest me, and they have received them, and have known surely that I came out from thee, and they have believed that thou didst send me." I Cor. 2:14, "But the natural man receiveth not the things of the Spirit of God: for they are foolishness unto him, neither can he know them," because they are spiritually discerned.

b. Another reason why what the godly have is more abiding than what false Christians have, is that they embrace religion of free choice. False Christians are not religious of free choice; they don't choose God and Christ, and the ways of holiness, for their own sakes, and of inclination to those things in themselves considered, but always for some by-ends.

Self-love is the highest principle that a false Christian acts from. He is either acted by fear, or from an aim of the praise of men, or from a self-righteous principle, hoping to commend himself to God by his own righteousness, or some way or other, from fame, [or] by respect.

There is some force that is evermore at the bottom; what he does, he don't do freely, of the free inclination of his heart to God and holiness. There is some force that is at the bottom of those affections that he has; and therefore, it is no wonder that his religion don't abide.

What he has, in some way or other, [is] a force against nature, and such religion as that won't hold but a little while. Nature and inclination is more lasting, and will soon prevail over that force.

He that don't follow Christ for his own sake, won't follow him long: for it is found but dull, heavy work to follow him; they will grow weary on't, and will leave him, and follow other things that suit better with their inclinations. But he whose religion is of free choice and inclination, will be likely to hold. He has not an inclination to forsake it; he has no desire of returning back again; his own free inclinations are to go forward, and therefore won't be so exposed to be overpowered by temptations to apostasy.

Why should he leave God and holiness, when he loves God and holiness above all, and places his chief happiness in those things; and if he were left to his own mere inclination without any force or by-end, would chose and incline to cleave to God and holiness?

c. A true Christian embraces God's commands universally, and gives himself up to God without reserve; which a false Christian never does. A true Christian embraces God's commands universally, i.e., he loves all commands; he loves all parts of holiness. Wherever there is any holiness, there he loves it; whatever is well-pleasing to God, he will love it upon that account, though it may be contrary to his carnal inclinations and corporeal interests.

And he chooses all God's commands: and there is that disposition in his heart that is a natural, hearty, real consent to keep and observe all commands, not only the easy but the difficult ones. Ps. 119:6, "Then shall I not be ashamed, when I have respect unto all thy commandments."

False Christians, however they are affected, yet they don't do this. Though their affections may influence them to obey the more easy commands, yet there never was any hearty disposition to comply with the hard and difficult commands; and hence it is that what they have don't abide, but when those hard commands come in the way, then to avoid them, they turn aside to their crooked ways.

False Christians are [like] Saul, of whom we are told that he slew all the Amalekites, but only saved the king, the chief of 'em all, alive. So false Christians may bridle many of their lusts, but there is some lust that is chief with 'em, that is king as it were among them and is dearest to 'em, and has a greater government in their hearts than any of the rest that they save alive.

False Christians, under impressions and affections that they have, may seem to give themselves to God; but they do it but in part, and keep back a great part, as Ananias and Sapphira did part of the law [Acts 5].

That is to say, they never were brought to that temper and disposition towards God, as to be heartily and really disposed, and willing to [be] wholly of God and wholly for God under all difficulties, and in a time of trial to be willing to be for God then, and not themselves.

False Christians don't give themselves to God without reserve, because they reserve such cases as these, viz., that when they can't be for God without suffering much in their own case or interest, at such times and in such instances they ben't willing to be for God, but choose to be for themselves. This is what is meant when it is said that false Christians make reserves: i.e., they reserve cases of difficulty and keep themselves back, and won't let God have their hearts and lives in such cases, though in other cases they may seem willing to give themselves to God. And hence it is that their religion don't hold, but in cases of difficulty they depart from God.

This is what Christ means by counting the cost [Luke 14:28]. Not that every true Christian does really, actually, when he is converted, think of all cases of difficulty that can be in his way (though it is a duty for all to do this, as far as in 'em lies): but the meaning is that a Christian, when he is converted, is brought to such a temper and disposition of heart, that if he should then know and think of every difficulty that is in the way of his duty throughout his life, he would find a hearty spirit to go through with them all, rather [than] to forsake God. And this is the reason that his religion holds.

But false Christians don't think about the costs, and therefore, though they have begun to build, they never finish; they never go through with religion. A true Christian allows no competitor as rival with Christ in his heart; he gives his heart to Christ only, and not part to him and part to another—that is, he has a spirit to give all to Christ.

But false Christians, though they seem to be willing to be Christ's, yet 'tis to be his but in part. They keep a part for mammon, a part for some dear lusts.

A true Christian has but one God, but a false Christian has a great many gods. False Christians are like the Samaritans, that were placed in the land of Israel in the room of the Ten Tribes. They serve the God of Israel, and worship their own gods into the bargain, II Kgs. 17:33.

A false Christian is like Manasseh, of whom we read, II Chron. 33:7, that he set up his carved image, the idol that he had made, in the house of God.

And hence it came to pass that their religion don't hold, but those other gods came in the way and drew away the heart from Christ. Christ has told us we cannot serve God and mammon: [we will] love the one, [and hate the other," Matt. 6:24, Luke 16:13]. But a true Christian gives his whole heart to Christ; and therefore 'tis said, Ps. 119:2, "Blessed are they that keep his testimonies, and seek him with the whole heart."

How often does Christ instruct us, that we must sell all that we have for his sake [Matt. 19:21]. And he that has so done, his religion will abide: for if he has sold all, what has he to draw away his heart from Christ? He has Christ only, that he has chosen. He that allows some rival with Christ, that rival will steal away the heart from him.

d. [Fourth,] and lastly, under this head. That religion which true Christians have in their hearts is lasting, because 'tis a-built on a strong foundation, even on Christ Jesus: and this is the highest reason of all. The foregoing reasons must be taken with this, otherwise, if they were taken alone, they would not be sufficient to account for this principle's being lasting and abiding: but this makes it sure, that it can never utterly fail, and that the gates of hell never can prevail against it.

Herein the experiences of false Christians do greatly differ from those of true Christians. The religious affections of false Christians ben't built on Christ, neither do they respect him as their foundation and end, as the experiences of true Christians do.

Christ, and the free and saving grace of God in him, and that manifestation that God has made of himself in him, is not the ground of their affections. 'Tis not a sight of God, as thus discovering himself in Christ, and in the glorious way of salvation by him, that draws forth their affections. Their comforts that they have, ben't built on Christ; their rejoicing is not a rejoicing in Christ Jesus, but in themselves; their encouragement that they have, is not an apprehension of the free and sovereign grace of God in a glorious, all-sufficient Redeemer, but 'tis some way or other their own righteousness. And this is the more reason that the religion of true Christians is abiding, and the other not. True Christians' {religion} is built on an everlasting Rock, and therefore is itself everlasting.

I come now to the

(4) [Fourth] thing contained in the description of this oil, viz., that 'tis a new nature in the soul. Herein it differs from all that is in false Christians, who, whatever impressions and affections they may [have], they are accompanied with no change of nature, but they pass away and leave the same nature that there was before. But the experiences of true Christians are accompanied with a change of nature, since he that is in Christ is said to be a new creature, II Cor. 5:17. And the principle that is infused into the heart in this work is called "the new man." "Having put off the old man with his deeds, ye have put on the new man," Eph. 4:22–24. These things hold forth a new nature in the soul; and more especially does that representation of conversion, whereby it is called a being "born again."

Every creature receives the nature that it has by its generation: that which is generated of a beast, is of a beastly nature; and he that is generated of corrupt man, has a corrupt nature; and he that is generated of God, has a godlike, a divine, nature: that which "is born of the Spirit is spirit."

So that there is not only a new principle in the heart of true Christians, but that which "is born of the Spirit is spirit."

What anyone's nature is known by:

8. [a.] *The things it tends to;*

9. [b.] *And the things that agree with it;*

10. [c.] *And by the things that it resists and opposes;*

11. [d.] *And by the actions and operations that are natural to him.*

a. Anyone's nature is known by the things it tends to. When we see anything consistently, and from its beginning, seem to have any kind of tendency and inclination, we say that is its nature. So 'tis the nature of a stone to tend downward, [or the] nature of very young plants and animals to grow: we see they constantly tend to these things. {It is the} nature of an infant to suck the breast, [and the] nature of the loadstone to incline to the poles of the earth.

So the new nature appears in its tendencies; and therefore, every godly man, as he has a holy nature, he has in his nature [an] inclination of heart to God and to Christ, and to spiritual objects. He tends to a spiritual happiness; 'tis the natural tendency and inclination of his heart to grow in grace, and to seek holiness.

The nature of any creature is discovered by its appetite. So is the nature of the soul of a saint: it has holy appetites; it hungers and thirsts after righteousness.

b. It appears in the things that it agrees with, and rests in. So the nature of a fish, is discerned by his being suited in the water; [the] nature of plants, is discerned by the soil they grow and flourish in; the nature of the body, is known by the food that suits it.

So is the new nature of a saint discerned the same way. The soul of a saint rests in God and Christ: he has a sweet complacence and acqui-escence in divine things; it has a savor and relish of them, and rejoices in them. He rests in them as his portion, and never is or can be at rest in a state of separation from those things, anymore than Noah's dove could find rest out of the ark.

c. What the nature is manifest by: [viz.,] the thing that it opposes and resists. So the nature of the body resists that which is contrary to it, and if taken into the stomach, will be in a ruffle and struggle till it is thrown out again.

So the nature of the soul is discerned the same way. And it appears that the saints have a holy nature in their souls, because they have a principle there that maintains a struggle against sin. So that the life of a Christian is a life of struggle against sin. Rom. 7:22–23, "I delight in the law of God after the inward man: [but] I see another law in my members, warring against the law of my mind." Gal. 5:17, "The flesh lusteth against the spirit, and the spirit against the flesh, and these two are contrary the one to the other."

Though a saint has much remaining corruption, yet he is not quiet and at rest with it, {but maintains a struggle against it}. Though he may fall into sin and get into ill ways, yet all that while there will not be ease and quietness, but a resistance and struggle.

d. The nature of anything, is discerned by the acts that are natural to it. So the nature of a tree, is discerned by its bearing such a sort of fruit; the nature of fire, is known by its burning fuel. 'Tis the nature of a living body to breath; 'tis the nature of the heart and arteries to beat, by a continual pulsation.

So this way does it appear that the souls of the saints have a new nature: it becomes natural to 'em to put forth holy acts, acts of love, acts of confidence, and acts of obedience. {In true Christians,} these things ben't merely forced against nature, as they are in false Christians, but they are natural and true, though they are greatly hindered by another nature that is against 'em.

In such manifestations of a new nature, true Christians differ from false, [who have] no natural tendency. Though they may have desires {after a new nature, yet they have} no natural desires and appetites. Though [they] may have joy in {holy acts} from newness [and] extraordinariness, or from an apprehension they have of their own interest as concerned in it, yet they have no natural rest and complacency in divine things.

Though [false Christians] may oppose sin out of fear, or for credit, {or some other motive}, yet [they have] no natural struggle against it as uneasy and contrary to the nature of the soul.

Though [they] perform seeming acts of thankfulness when [they think they have] received great mercy, yet 'tis but a sudden gush of affection from some extraordinary mercy, or extraordinary representations of God's goodness. {Though they} may seem to trust {God's commands} and to obey {them}, yet 'tis all a kind of forced business; there is nothing of any proper nature of the soul in these things.

I come now to the

(5) [Fifth,] and last thing, in this description of this principle in the hearts of the saints, viz., that it consists in the Christian spirit that they

are of. A person is according to the spirit that he is of. Christians are of a Christian spirit, as is implied in Luke 9:55, "Ye know not what spirit ye are of." Conversion most essentially consists in that, in the renovation of the spirit that persons are of. As appears by Eph. 4:22–23, "That ye put off the old man, which is corrupt."

Whatever affections and seeming discoveries men may have, they ben't converted, if the spirit that they are of ben't changed, and God has not renewed in them a right spirit. This is that principle that we have been hearing of; this is the oil in the vessel, viz., a Christian spirit. Which is so called especially upon two accounts:

a. Because 'tis a Christ-like spirit. [The] same mind is in the saints, in their measure, that was in Christ Jesus, Philip. 1:5. They are of a spirit like the holy Lamb of God. Now we know that the spirit of Christ was a humble, meek and lowly spirit, a spirit of love, a[84] pliant, submissive and heavenly spirit.

Christians are, in a measure, of the same spirit, because they are in him as his members; and the members must, of necessity, partake of the spirit of the head. Christians must be of the same spirit with Christ, because the grace they have is "a partaking of his fullness, and grace for grace," John 1:16. If one writes exactly after another's copy, we should express that he writes after him. Where it is said, "grace for grace," 'tis meant grace answerable to grace. So we are said to be renewed "after the image" of Christ. Col. 3:10, "And have put on the new man, which is renewed in knowledge after the image of him that created him"; together with vv. 12–13, "Put on therefore, as the elect of God, holy and beloved, bowels of mercies, kindness, humbleness of mind, meekness, longsuffering; forbearing one another, and forgiving one another, if any man have a quarrel against any: even as Christ forgave you, so also do ye." "Beholding as in a glass the glory [of the Lord," II Cor. 3:18]. Christ is "born in the soul," Gal. 4:19.

All is wrought by the Spirit of God, as the Spirit of Christ. And the consequence is, that it works the same temper that was in Christ. We are told what kind of temper this [is that] it works in them. Gal. 5:22, etc., "But the fruit of the Spirit is love, joy, peace, longsuffering, gentleness, goodness, faith, meekness, temperance"; and Eph. 5[:9], "For the fruit of the spirit is in all goodness and righteousness, and truth." Jas. 3:17, "But the wisdom that is from above." And I Cor. 13, at the beginning,

84. MS: "an."

"Though I speak with the tongues of men and of angels, and have not charity, I am become as sounding brass, or a tinkling cymbal."

b. A Christian spirit is such a spirit as the Christian revelation does especially hold forth obligations to.

The Christian revelation declares what condescension {true Christians are obliged to, because of} how Christ abased {himself for them}. This therefore especially obliges to a lowly, humble spirit. {The Christian revelation} reveals, above all things, the dreadful vileness of sin, {as seen} in the death of Christ. {The Christian revelation} reveals a contrite spirit.

[The Christian revelation] reveals the wonderful mercy of God in bearing with our iniquity, forgiving {trespasses}, meekness, longsuffering, forgiving injuries. [It] declares mercy, liberality, [and a] merciful spirit.

[The Christian revelation declares the] marvelous love of God the Father {through the Spirit} of Christ. [It is a spirit of] love and charity. John 13:34–35, "A new commandment I give unto you, That ye love one another; as I have loved you, that ye also love one another. By this shall all men know that ye are my disciples, if ye have love one to another." Now herein true Christians differ from false: for the false Christians may have illumination, {they may have} great joys {and other} things that greatly move [them, but] they don't make this excellent change in the spirit of their minds. {They are} followed with no such amiable, Christlike spirit.

Very commonly [such experiences] make an alteration for the worse in their spirit. [They become] more proud, more assuming, more self-sufficient. A very unlovely spirit seems to be prevalent in, and is dreadfully strengthened and established by, their experiences and hopes and high thoughts they have of themselves. So it was in the Pharisees. O what a difference was there in spirit and temper between those proud and haughty and assuming Pharisees, and the poor, contrite, humble, meek followers of Jesus, that we have an account of [Luke 6:20]. How exceeding different is the temper of 'em from the others. But here, some may be ready to

Inquire, How this may be said to be the spirit that every true Christian is of? For all allow, that there is a great deal of a contrary spirit in {true Christians}; and we often hear that there is but little grace and a great deal of corruption: and how can it properly be said that this is the spirit that they are of, more than the contrary is the spirit that they are of, unless this spirit predominates?

I answer: Though there be abundance of corruption, and more corruption even in the godly, yet this spirit predominates in them, in the following respects:

(a) It predominates in the judgment and esteem of the soul. Grace has got into the throne, as it rules in the understanding and judgment, and highest faculties of the soul, in the esteem of the heart of a godly man.

He is convinced of its excellency, he prizes it above all; and he has a mean opinion of the contrary spirit, and that, not only in others, but in himself. He looks upon [it] as [a] dishonorable and hateful spirit.

Herein differs {the true and false Christian}. An ungodly man never sees, and so is never really convinced of the excellency {of this spirit}. They have a mind void of judgment. {This spirit} don't rule in their esteem; {they} don't really prize it above all.

(b) It predominates in their stated choice of the soul. {The heart} necessarily follows the esteem of the practical understanding. This spirit is chosen. The heart, in its real choice, follows after such a spirit, whereby it may be conformed to Christ.

(c) It predominates with respect to the stated allowance of the soul. Though contrary {to a natural principle, it is} not allowed {to predominate}, any more than a man allows an enemy that he is at war against.

(d) By the grace of God, this spirit is wont finally [to] get the victory, and triumphs over the contrary. If in a day of temptation another spirit seems to prevail, {this spirit is} yet not at rest, {treats temptation} as [a] struggle {to maintain}, and at last, gets the victory. So thus not by [their] own strength, but God's grace, II Cor. 2:14, [they] always triumph in Christ Jesus.

So that, notwithstanding all the remains of a contrary spirit, this may be said to be the spirit that they are of.

It predominating in the forementioned respects, it properly denominates the man. So that every true Christian is in Scripture called one that is "poor in spirit," Matt. 5:3. All true Christians [are] called "the humble." Ps. 34:2, "The humble shall hear thereof, and be glad." [True Christians are] all called merciful men. Is. 57:1, "The righteous perisheth." {True Christians are all called} meek. Is. 11:4, "He shall reprove with equity for the meek and poor of the earth."

Thus I have described that holy principle, that is in the hearts of true Christians: and this is the oil in the vessel. This principle that has been described today, is the great and most essential difference between true and false Christians, wherein they always differ. Let there be what appearances soever of religion in false Christians, they always want this.

Here is the difference between those that have oil, and those that have lamps only.[85]

APPLICATION.

Use I of Instruction.

Hence we may see something of the ground of [the] godly and ungodly being represented in Scripture, as two sorts of persons so vastly different one from the other. This is very discernible throughout the Scripture. Whatever morality and show of piety natural men may have, and whatever infirmities the godly may have, by which there may be, to outward appearance, but little difference; yet the Word of God always speaks of 'em as exceeding different one from another. One are called wheat, and the other tares; [one is] wheat, [the other] the chaff; the one silver and gold and God's jewels, the other dross; the one are called children, the other dogs; one sheep, and the other wolves; one the children of God, the other the children of the devil; one are represented as of the church and the family of God, the other the synagogue of Satan; one the spouse of Christ, the other swine and serpents and vipers. These and other representations of Scripture hold forth a vast difference. That which we have heard of, of the ground of it—viz., that one has that holy oil in their vessels, that spiritual principle in their hearts that we have heard of, and the other have not—this principle is that which is so needful a thing, and so precious, and so great, that having it or being without does indeed make a vast difference in persons in God's account.

Without this, everything in men is hateful to God, even that which makes the most fair and specious show in the eyes of men: for God sees not as man seeth [I Sam. 16:7]. Very often, of those that appear alike in the eyes of men, one appears as a precious jewel, the other as a loathsome serpent in His eyes.

---

85. This point marks the end of the tenth preaching unit and of the sixth booklet. At the beginning of the next booklet, JE wrote: "No. [-] Math 25 . 1 ——- 12 . especially . 3. & 4. vs." In another hand is written: "1738. No. 9."

And though the godly have received but a little of this holy anointing, and have but little of the oil in their hearts, and have abundance of that same hateful corruption that natural men have, yet as this little oil, this small degree of grace, relates to Christ and acts with dependence on him, unites the heart to him who has an infinite fullness of grace, and is infinitely worthy and lovely in God's eyes; so it renders the saints very excellent, precious and honorable ones in his esteem.

So that it is not so much from the degree of this principle in the hearts of the saints, as from its nature and its relation to the beloved Son of God, that it makes so vast a difference in God's account between the godly and the ungodly.

Therefore, the godly have no room left for boasting: the glory belongs all to the Mediator. If they were beheld as they are by themselves, separately from Christ, they also would be vipers in God's eyes.

Use II may be of *Self-Examination.*

Seeing that you have now heard wherein godly and ungodly may agree, and also have heard wherein the great and most essential difference lies, let this put those that have hoped themselves to be godly upon examining themselves, whether or no they have that oil in their vessels that they have heard of. Don't content yourself with that, that you have at such and such a time been very much affected with what you have heard, or read, or thought of; but inquire whether ever you have had that sense of the excellency of God or his attributes, or of Christ and his salvation, that has penetrated your heart and reached the bottom of [it], that has broken it and melted, and drawn it to God.

Have you ever given your heart to God, not by any forced act—being put upon it, to try to give your heart to God out of regard to your own interest: for that is not giving your heart to God—but have you found yourself drawn into such an act, viz., an act giving or yielding your heart up to God or Christ?

Don't[86] content yourself with that, that you have had sorrow, and have had joy and shed a great many tears, but anywise, whether or no you have a new heart put within you. Has the stony heart been taken away, and an heart of flesh given to you?

Principles of nature may work many ways, so as very variously to affect a person. Persons, from the principles of nature, are liable to be

---

86. In revising for repreaching, JE drew a bracket at the beginning of this paragraph.

very variously affected in temporal matters. And so, by the same principles, they may be many ways affected in spiritual matters.

But you must have something that is above nature, something above all that any person has by a good and soft natural temper, or from a tenderness arising from the natural constitution, something above all that the powers of nature can arrive at: that which is above the reach of human learning, or the greatest attainments of those of[87] greatest natural abilities or acquired knowledge, above the reach of all the efforts of human strength, and what no man can impart unto another. It must be a gift from above, something divine wrought in the heart by the power of the divine Spirit; yea, there must be something beyond an assistance of natural principles, that be infusing a new principle and seed from above, that has no foundation in nature, yea, that is contrary to all that was in the heart before.

Don't content yourself with that, that the Spirit of God has been at work with you, and that you have had convictions and illuminations that are from that Spirit. But you must find the holy and heavenly Spirit dwelling in you, and acting as a settled inhabitant in your heart.

With respect to those that are spiritual, the divine Spirit is not as a wayfaring man, that turns aside to tarry but for a night; but he takes their hearts for his everlasting habitation.

Don't content yourself with that, that you have had things heretofore that you could not make yourself, you have had such enlightenings and affections that you can't have again when you will: that might be, and yet you have nothing spiritual. The Spirit of God might assist you, and cause effects in your mind, that you can't cause without his assistance.

But inquire whether or no the Spirit of God has communicated himself to you in his own proper nature. Has he not only affected you, but has he left something behind him that savors of his holy and heavenly nature? Has he so affected your heart, and wrought upon it, that since that your heart is tinged as it were with the sweet savor and odor of that heavenly purity, that heavenly calm and serenity, that sweet divine love, that are the very nature of God's own divine Spirit?

If so, then you have something in you that is spiritual. That is to have a spiritual principle in the heart, viz., to have a principle[88] in the nature of what appears the nature of God's own Spirit.

87. MS: "that of."
88. MS: "that to have a principle."

Don't content yourself with that, that what you had seemed great in the time of it, that it seemed to affect you so as to put nature into a very great ruffle, and so as very much to lift up, and so as to incline you to weep much and to talk much, yea, and to cry out in praise and admiration,[89] and say, "Hosanna," and cry, "O what a blessedness is it": unless you find something abiding, and unless you find a divine sense of things renewed in a degree time after time; unless you find a principle remaining, that though it may sometimes seem to be hid, yet is now and then felt in its powerful supernatural operation—a principle that is touched and moved by that which is divine, and that seems to harmonize and echo to the Word of God—something that makes you, in [an] abiding manner, have a high and exalted esteem of divine [things], and something that in a stated manner makes you choose divine things and divine happiness, consisting in God and holiness, above all things in the world.

Don't conclude that the light that you saw was the daystar rising in your hearts, merely because it seemed to make a great blaze at first. A falling star, that which is nothing but a shining meteor, may make a greater blaze, while it lasts, than the true morning star; but then it suddenly goes out and ends in darkness, and it appears no more. But the true morning star rises time after time; and though it may be often hid by clouds, yet there it is, and it will appear again.

Don't rest in any sort of affection, without a real and deep conviction of the reality and divine excellency of spiritual things.

'Tis one thing to be much affected in hearing of the dying love of Christ, and another thing to be deeply convinced, and to see certainly, that Christ is supremely excellent and lovely.

'Tis one thing to be affected with that, that God has been very good to us and has set his love on us; and another thing to be inwardly convinced, and to see that God is superlatively lovely in himself and worthy to be loved, whether he has loved us or no.

Don't content yourself with that, that you think you are willing to have Christ for your Savior, unless you are willing of free choice, and not forced with threatenings of hell.

Don't content yourself {with that, that} you choose ways of holiness, because you think it is necessary in order to your going to heaven, and so are driven to choose them, if you don't choose it freely, and for

89. MS: "admiranna."

holiness' sake, because holiness is a holy life, is a sweet life, and appears to you to be [a] desirable and lovely life.

And be exceeding strict with yourself in examining whether you do embrace God's commands universally, [and] give yourself to God without reserve. {This is} greatly insisted on by Christ time after time; Christ is often setting it home in the most solemn manner, that unless we fill all {precepts of the law}, unless [we have] a spirit to deny ourselves, [we have not oil in our vessels]. And whatever comforts you have had, inquire what foundation {you have, that you have a spiritual principle}. And don't content yourself with that, that you have had texts of Scripture come to your mind, very comfortable places that seem to come suddenly, and you did[90] not bring 'em by foregoing meditation.[91] If it is so, that is no sign {that you have a spiritual principle}. If you have had scriptures come to your mind, that seem to tell you that you was well on't—suppose that, [Is.] 43:1, "Fear not, I have redeemed thee"; or that, Matt. 9:2, "Be of good cheer, thy sins are forgiven thee"; or that, Jer. 31:3, "I have loved thee with an everlasting love"—that is not the way that we are to know whether we are godly or no, by having a voice or words coming directly to us, as though spoken to us, to tell us that we are so. We have no weapons to judge by any such means, but we are to try ourselves by a rule that is given.

We have no encouragement to expect that God will whisper in the ear, and tell us that our sins are forgiven us; but we are to judge by certain marks and qualifications we find in ourselves, comparing these with the Word of God. We have no rule to conclude from anything else.

Therefore, so far as texts of Scripture are means of working these qualifications in us, so far they are signs of our being godly, and no farther: not as coming directly and immediately to tell, as if they were words spoken out of heaven, to tell us that it [is] thus or thus with you.

You should rather inquire whether you feel in yourself the workings of a new nature. Do you find your heart has a new tendency, new appetites, appetites after holy things?

Don't content yourself {with that, that you} long to experience more, {that you long to be} better satisfied of your good estate. Inquire

---

90. MS: "you they you."

91. Although JE gave this experience some credence in *A Faithful Narrative,* in both *Some Thoughts Concerning the Revival* (WJE 4:432–40) and *Religious Affections* (WJE 2:142–45) he categorizes it as a negative sign.

whether you have new complacencies, a new rest of soul. Is your resting place changed, that whereas formerly you rested in {that that was not a true rest}? And does a new nature appear in a natural struggle? Are there new natural acts?

Don't content yourself {with that, that you} have had what you call discoveries, impressions on your mind, seemed to see Christ, {have} had imagination of something outward, {some} outward form and appearance, of countenance, or shape, or the like. But inquire what spirit you are of, Christ-like or no.

Here, some may be ready to say, "I have experienced things of that nature, that have appeared to me to be of that nature that I have now heard of, at least many of them. What I have experienced has seemed in some measure to work after such a manner, but I am afraid whether or no the devil may not cause such things in my heart to deceive me. We often hear that there are counterfeits of all grace, and we are also told that Satan is transformed into an angel of light. I am therefore sometimes ready to fear whether or no what I experience is not from the devil."

First. Though there may be a resemblance in some things between what the Spirit of God[92] does, and what the devil [does], yet there is vast difference, and the difference mainly lies in those things that have been spoken of. The devil may mimic some of the works of God, but he can't work after such a manner as God doth. We are told that there are no works like his. The holy angels in heaven can't work such works, much less the devils in hell. Though there may be a sort of specious resemblance, yet that resemblance is but a shadow, when you come to examine it and look into it. There is as much difference as there is between light and darkness; yea, as much difference as there is between heaven and hell, as much as between an holy angel and a devil; yea, and a great deal more: for the difference is of the nature of that, that is between the Spirit of God and the devil.

And the difference very much consists in those things that have been mentioned. So that if you find in yourself things of this nature, you have no cause to perplex yourself with any such fears.

Second. The devil can't do anything that amounts to a work of creation. Creation is a work peculiar to God, and is often so spoken of in the Scripture. It is a work too high and great for any creature to accomplish, and that is evident, because any creature, whether he be great or small,

92. MS: "and."

is himself created; and it would be absurd to suppose that one that is created should be able to create: for that would be to ascribe a like power to that whence it received its own being, and all that power it has, which must needs be immensely superior to it.[93]

Hence, he can't give a new heart, he can't infuse a new nature: for this is a work of spiritual creation—Eph. 2:10, "created in Christ Jesus unto good works"—and therefore peculiar to God. A work of spiritual creation is a no less glorious work of divine power than the first creation was; yea, much more so, as is evident by Is. 65:17–18. "For, behold, I create new heavens and a new earth: and the former shall not be remembered, nor come into mind. But be ye glad and rejoice for ever in that which I create: for, behold, I create Jerusalem a rejoicing, and her people a joy." In that the devil can't do anything that amounts to a work of creation, it is evident that he can't infuse any new principle; he can't renew in man a right spirit. All that the devil can do, is to work on man's natural principles. He can't cause any proper supernatural acts in the heart. I would particularly mention two:

1. He can't give a man a spirit to renounce himself for God, a spirit with delight to renounce his own righteousness, and ascribe all the glory of his own salvation to Christ; to delight in the way of salvation by Christ on that account, and look on that as the glory of it, that it exalts God and makes nothing of man.

For this is something above nature. Nature in itself, without something divine in the heart, has no such tendency; its tendency is to exalt self, and depend on self and deify self. And therefore, such a spirit requires a work of creation.

2. He can't give a delight and complacence in all the attributes of God. A natural man may have a kind of delight in some of God's attributes; he may like some things in God very well.

They like very well, for instance, that he should be a good and merciful God. But they never like God just as he is. There is some things in God that he finds fault with.

There are some things in God that tend to work on man's natural principle. The goodness of God, for instance, tends to work on man's self love, and therefore natural man may have a kind of delight in this attribute.

---

93. JE deletes: "And therefore he can't give those things that are above nature, because the giving what is above nature argues a work of creation, or makes a new creature."

But it is a thing above nature for a man to delight in all God's perfection. It is above nature for a man to have complacence in God for his holiness. 'Tis a thing distinguishing of those that are spiritual, to rejoice in God, to admire God, and long after and rest in him as [an] infinite, pure and holy God, as appearing exceeding amiable and beautiful to them on that account.

And so 'tis above nature for man to delight in God for his justice, and for his sovereignty, and his awful majesty. For the sake of those things, natural men are the enemies of God.

Thus, the devil can't do those things, that amount to a work of creation.

Third. The devil can't give those things that are contrary to his own nature. That would be absurd, to suppose that the devil can give what he has not. He can't put that into another's heart that is contrary to all that he has in his own. And particularly, here I would mention two things:

1. The devil can't give a spirit of divine love, a spirit of[94] love to God and love to men. He can't give that principle, whereby the heart goes forth ardently after Christ in abundant desires and delights. He {can't give} that spirit that disposes to forgiveness, forbearance, mercifulness and benevolence, and to do good from an aim above our self-interest.

The devil can't give this, because he han't it. It is as contrary as possible to his nature, for his nature is altogether a spirit of malice and envy and revenge. This is carried in his very name, which is given him in Scripture, as "Satan"; and that which he is compared to, viz., a serpent, Rev. 20:2, "this is the old serpent, the devil"; and his work: "the devil as a raging lion goes about seeking whom he may devour" [1 Pet. 5:8].

2. He can't give a spirit of unfeigned humility. He is especially noted for his pride in Scripture. I Tim. 3:6, "lest being lifted up with pride, he fall into the condemnation of the devil."

A spirit of humiliation is not the spirit of the devil, but the spirit of Christ. "Learn of me, for I am meek" [Matt. 11:29].

[The devil] can't give a spirit to delight to abase self and exalt God, [to] lie at the footstool {of God, to praise} God on the throne, {and} sincerely to say, "Not unto us, O Lord, not unto us, but unto thy name give glory" [Ps. 115:1].

94. MS: "to."

The spirit of the devil is to exalt himself against God. {He} can't give a spirit to have complacence in the sovereignty and supreme dominion of God. The spirit of the devil is to oppose [God].

[He] can't give a broken heart, {a} self-emptying {spirit, a spirit} longing to be more broken for sin.

Thus the devil can't give what he han't, or what is contrary to his own nature.

Fourth. The devil won't cause those things,[95] whose direct tendency is contrary to the interests of his own kingdom. This, both reason and Scripture teaches. Christ refuted the blasphemy of the Pharisees with this argument, when they proposed that he cast out devils by Beelzebub. Matt. 12:25–26, "Every kingdom divided against itself is brought to desolation; and every city or house divided against itself shall not stand: and if Satan cast out Satan, he is divided against himself; how shall then his kingdom stand?"

We may therefore be sure that 'tis a good argument, otherwise Christ would not have made use of it as such with the Pharisees, to confute them. We may be sure that Satan won't be so divided against himself, as to cause those things that he knows are directly contrary to the interest {of his own kingdom}. Hence, he never does these two things:

1. He never convinces the mind of the truth of the things of the gospel. That would be most contrary {to the interest of his own kingdom}. 'Tis his interest to make man doubt to his utmost. And therefore, this is given as a sure sign of a righteous spirit, and a mark by which we may distinguish the true spirit from the spirit of the devil. I John 4:1–3, "Beloved, believe not every spirit, but try the spirits whether they are of God: because many false prophets are gone out into the world. Hereby know ye the Spirit of God: every spirit that confesseth that Jesus Christ is come in the flesh is of God: and every spirit that confesseth not that Jesus Christ is come in the flesh is not of God: and this is that spirit of antichrist, whereof ye have heard that it should come; and even now already is it in the world."

[The Spirit of God] teaches and confirms men in the truth of the same doctrines that Christ and his apostles taught, v. 6.[96] The devil is

---

95. MS: "that."

96. I.e., I John 4:6.

not[97] the prince of light, but of darkness; not a spirit of truth, but of error. Therefore the Apostle gives this reason.

The devil is a liar; he don't confirm men's hearts in the truth. Christ teaches us this; John 8:44, "He [. . .] abode not in the truth, for there is no truth in him. When he speaketh a lie, he speaketh of his own: for he is a liar, and the father [of it]."

The apostle Paul gives the same {reason}. I Cor. 12:3, "no man can say that Jesus [is the Lord but by the Holy Ghost]."

2. The devil never gives anything that has a tendency to stir men, and make 'em more concerned and careful to do their whole duty. {He} never {gives} that tendency to keep all God's means,[98] {never gives} such desires, {to have} concern and care about it.

The comforts and hopes that he causes never have that tendency. [They] tend to carelessness, {and} in the end to sin and wickedness. [The] devil's comforts are hardening comforts.

[The] devil's hopes tend to licentiousness. They are those hopes whence men flatter themselves in ways of sin. All is false {hope}. A true hope is sanctifying. Those comforts, that hope, that have this {tendency}, are undoubtedly from a right spirit, for the devil is not divided against himself. He is an unclean spirit, as he is often called in Scripture. Things that come from him, are like him.

Use III may be of *Exhortation*.

First. To those that are in a natural condition, {be exhorted} to seek this oil, seeing that 'tis the great thing wherein lies the most essential difference between saints and sinners, between the children of God and the children of the devil. It appears to be a thing of vast consequence indeed, and certainly must be of the greatest importance of anything in this world. You have heard how that this is the thing that renders anyone a true and real Christian, one of Christ's invisible church, and of God's family; and how that no profession of religion, no morality, no religious affections, no illuminations, will avail anything without it.

You have heard from sermon discourses from this parable how many other things men may have, wherein they may agree with the godly, and yet perish eternally. Therefore, let all other things be neglected and despised in comparison of this, and be esteemed as loss for the excellency of this, yea, esteemed as dung, that you may obtain this. Let

97. MS: "a."
98. Conjectural reading.

this oil be the very thing that you seek, laying aside all other pursuits, neglecting the world, neglecting the praise of men.

Let this be that one thing that your whole soul is bent to pursue after. You that have no reason to think that ever you felt anything of this divine principle in your soul, that never experienced a work of regeneration, never was born again, and so remain in the same miserable condition in which you came into the world: be entreated earnestly to seek after this precious oil that you have heard of. Here, I would offer several things to your consideration, to stir you up to seek this oil:

1. Without this, there never will, nor can be, any good thing in you, whatever natural endowments you may have. Though you may be a person of good natural abilities, and may have a comely body; and though you may have considerable acquired endowments, may have attained a good deal of knowledge in things of religion and in other things, and may be accepted as somebody more considerable among your neighbors than many others: yet God will despise you, and you will be abominable to him, without this oil. Yea, you will be the more hateful to him for these endowments; for the greater talents any person has that they misimprove, the more is God provoked.

And whatever moral attainments you may have, how just and how generous and how religious soever you may be, and whatever profession you may make, there is nothing good in you in the sight of God, without this.

As you are by nature, you have no good thing in you. Rom. 7:18, "For I know that in me, that is, in my flesh, dwells no good thing." You come empty of any good into the world, because you come without this holy oil in your heart; and however you may attain those things which may get you honor amongst men, and whereby you may set yourself off to their acceptance, yet unless you get this oil, you will be all together abominable in His sight, who sees things as they be. Luke 16:15, "That which is highly esteemed amongst men [is abomination in the sight of God]." There is nothing amiable or acceptable to God in the souls of them that are destitute {of this holy oil}. Man, when he fell, lost all his primitive excellency; his soul became totally empty of all that was good. And no good can ever be restored to him any other way, than by his receiving this anointing from above.

2. Consider what hateful principles reign in the hearts of all such as are destitute of this holy oil. As long as you are destitute of this, you are under the dominion of sin, and are a poor servant of sin.

Your heart now is full of darkness and wickedness; there is all filthiness and deformity, and may truly be represented as a hold of every foul spirit, and a cage of every unclean and hateful bird [Rev. 18:2].

You have those principles reigning in you that are your dishonor and disgrace. Man was set in honor in his first estate, but he is become like the beasts that perish.

Those principles that now reign in you make you very vile; otherwise, God in his Word would not call such as you are dogs and swine and vipers [Matt. 23:33], as he does.

Certainly, human nature is brought into very dishonorable and vile circumstances, if man is so debased as this comes to.

But this dishonor is owing to those vile principles that reign naturally in him, whereby he becomes like the beasts that perish, and wherein consists the image of the devil, that old and foul serpent.

Man is reduced to a sordid meanness and baseness by the loss of that image of God that was his glory, and by his being under the dominion of selfishness, pride, and earthly and carnal dispositions; and by a disposition that reigns in every natural man, whereby he delights to wallow in the mire of sin, and to feed like filthy vermin on things that are putrid and loathsome.

Such principles as these art, you under the power and dominion [of]. Such principles are you a slave to, as long as you are destitute of that divine principle that you have heard of.

And the principles that you are under the dominion of, are not only hateful in their nature, but dreadful in their consequences. They are as so many plague sores in the heart, and constitute a complicated mortal disease in the soul, that, unless it be healed by this holy anointing that you have heard of, will surely corrupt and destroy it, will bring it inevitably to eternal death. These corrupt principles that are in you, and are rooted in your heart, have all got hell in them; they are a seed of hell. You that have none of this oil in your hearts, you carry about hell in you, but only it is in its seed; it has not yet brought forth. But if it remains in reigning power, as it is at present, will more surely bring forth hellfire in your soul, than the seeds that are sown in the earth do bring forth the plants after their kind.

So that as you remain under the power of those principles, you are now a miserable creature. Your soul is in a corrupted, ruined state.

Now the only way that your soul can be healed of this noisome and dreadful disease, is by receiving an unction of this holy oil that you have heard of. This oil is the only antidote against that poison.

If you obtain this oil, it will prevail against those principles: it will destroy the dominion of 'em in your heart; it will by degrees root them [out]; it will gradually cleanse your soul from this filthiness; it will mortify that seed of hell in your heart, and will prevent it ever bringing forth its fruit, and so it will raise you up from the state of disgrace that sin has brought you into. It lifts the poor out of the dust, and the beggar out of the dunghill, and will deliver your soul from going down into the pit.

3. Consider the preciousness of this oil. It is far more precious than silver and gold and pearls. This oil, this is that wisdom, of which it is said, Prov. 3:14–15, "The merchandize of it is better than the merchandise of silver, and the gain thereof than fine gold. She is more precious than rubies: and all things thou canst desire."

Because the merchandize of it is so precious, then by all means go to them that sell, and buy it for yourselves, before the midnight cry. Hearken to that advice of the Wise Man, Prov. 4:5, "Get wisdom, get understanding"; and v. 7, "Wisdom is the principal thing; therefore get wisdom: and with all thy getting get understanding."

You are concerned about getting other things: how to get food and raiment, how to get money to support yourself, how to get these and those worldly comforts [and] enjoyments. But will all your getting get this oil? How much better is it to get this, than to get gold, and how much rather is it to be chosen than choice silver, as the Wise Man says, Prov. 16:16. This oil is the same with that wisdom that Job speaks of, Job 28:16, etc., "It cannot be valued with the gold of Ophir, with the precious onyx, or the sapphire. The gold and the crystal cannot equal it: and the exchange of it shall not be for jewels of fine gold. No mention shall be made of coral, or of pearls: for the price of wisdom is above rubies."

The preciousness of this oil may appear from the following considerations:

(1) It is[99] the life and health of the soul. Those souls that are destitute of it, are under the most dreadful disease in the world; but this holy oil, when infused into the heart, brings health with it. Therefore,

99. MS: "to."

the Wise Man says of it, Prov. 3:8, "It shall [be] health to thy navel, and marrow to thy bones."

Of old, while the gift of miracles was continued in the church, it was appointed that if anyone was sick, he should send for the elders of the church, and he should anoint him with oil in the name of the Lord, Jas. 5:14. Oil was not appointed to be used because of any natural virtue it had to restore the sick man to health, but probably because oil was typical of that spiritual anointing spoken of in I John 2:27, by which spiritual health is restored to sick souls.

The soul in its natural state is dead, but when this oil is obtained,[100] life is obtained. Therefore 'tis said of it, Prov. 8:35, "He that findeth me, findeth life." What is it that is esteemed more precious by men than life, especially when it is blessed with health?

(2) 'tis the glory of the soul. 'Tis a most excellent ornament to it. Therefore the Wise Man says of spiritual wisdom and instruction, Prov. 1:9, "They shall be an ornament of grace to thy head, and chains about thy neck." 'tis an ornament in the hidden man of the heart, in that which is not corruptible, that is in the sight of God of great price. And this is a more excellent ornament.

['Tis a more excellent ornament] than the wearing of gold, or putting on of apparel adorned with precious stones.

This is the glory of the soul, for 'tis the image of God in it. It will be a more excellent glory to you, to have this image of God in your heart, than if your face shone as Moses' did: for hereby your soul will shine with a spiritual brightness that is a greater resemblance of the glory of God, than any external shining can be.

This holy principle will be a reflection of the glory of the Sun[101] of righteousness. The glory of the Lord shall not only shine upon you, but it shall also shine in you, and you shall shine with it. Therefore 'tis said to the church, Is. 60:1, "Arise, shine; for thy light is come, and the glory of the Lord is risen upon thee."

This holy principle will be the bright and morning star [that] not only shines upon you, but rises in your heart, the morning star, taking place in your soul.[102] There shall be a little sun in your heart, to answer

100. MS: "obtain."
101. MS: "son."
102. JE deletes: "There shall be as it were a morning star in your heart, to answer the Christ, the morning star, that shines with [great luster]."

the Sun of righteousness, that shines out of heaven upon you. By this means, you will become heavenly; and how great an honor and glory is that to such a poor creature as man, to have something of heaven in him? This is the way that heaven and earth are united again after the fall, and something of heaven dwells on earth, viz., by giving them this anointing from above into the hearts of men.

This spiritual principle in the heart is the most glorious piece of God's workmanship in all the visible creation. There are many excellent pieces of the workmanship of God's hands we behold on earth, and in the heavens, the sun, moon, and stars; they are very glorious works of God. But there is none to be compared with the new creature, that divine principle wrought in the soul.[103] And 'tis this that all will honor you for, if you obtain it. You will be honorable in the eyes of good men, and even the saints and angels of heaven: for they can't but honor the image of God wherever they behold it.

And even wicked men, that don't love you for it, will honor you: for when the image of Christ seems to appear in the conversation of any person, it makes him appear honorable to all. Prov. 3:3–4, "Let not mercy and truth forsake thee: bind them about thy neck; write them upon the table of thine heart: so shalt thou find favor and good understanding in the sight of God and man."

Wicked men can't but in their judgments approve of Christian holiness, when they see appearances of it. Rom. 14:18, "For he that in these things serveth Christ is acceptable to God, and approved of men."

And if you have this principle in your heart, even the very devils, though they will hate, yet will fear you: for they know that they are to be subdued under the feet of[104] such, and that they are to be their judges.

(3)[105] This oil is precious on account of its sweetness. When God infuses this oil into the soul, it relieves it of its sorrow and pain. It has power, above all things, to comfort the wounded heart. We read, Job 5:18, that 'tis God wounds, and he heals. He heals the painful wounds that have been made in the soul, pains of a wounded conscience, with this oil.

---

103. In revising for repreaching, JE drew a closed bracket followed by the reference, "next p." referring to pt. 3, below.

104. MS: "as."

105. In revising for repreaching, JE drew a bracket at the beginning of this paragraph.

The heart that was bruised and broken and in great distress, by reason of its painful wounds, has ease and comfort and care by being anointed with this oil. It is said in Ps.[106] 147:3, that God "heals the broken heart, and bindeth up their wounds." This is the healing balm that he binds 'em up with. And none can express the ease and sweet quietness that it, as an sovereign remedy, gives to the soul.

We read in the 57th [chapter] of Isaiah, 15th verse, that God will revive the heart of the contrite ones. He revives it by diffusing the odors of this excellent oil that we have heard of.[107]

Ointments are made precious by the sweet perfumes with which they are mingled. There is no ointment that is tinged with so precious a perfume, and sends forth so excellent a savor, as this oil that we have heard of.

That holy anointing oil that we read of, Ex. 30, compounded and perfumed with all the sweetest spices by God's own direction, to be kept in the sanctuary, was a type of it, and was made for that end.

This[108] in Ps. 133 is called precious ointment, and grace is there expressly compared to it, especially the grace of love or charity. Vv. 1–2,[109] "Behold, how good and how pleasant it is for brethren to dwell together in unity! It is like the precious ointment upon the head, that ran down upon the beard, even Aaron's beard: that went down to the skirts of his garments."

'Tis some of that pure river of [the] water of life, that we read of in the beginning {of Rev. 22}, that is clear and crystal, proceeding from the throne of God, and of the Lamb. And though it be but very little of it, as it were a drop, yet that drop will abide, and become a little fountain or spring, a well of living water springing up, giving you some foretaste of the sweetness of everlasting life.[110]

(4) The preciousness of this oil appears in that, [that] it gives him that hath it, security from all evil. If there was any such sort of oil that you could purchase of any apothecary, or could obtain by sending for it

---

106. MS: "Is."

107. In revising for repreaching, JE drew a closing bracket followed by the reference, "next p." referring to the passage three paragraphs down, starting, "This in Ps. 133 . . ."

108. In revising for repreaching, JE drew a bracket at the beginning of this paragraph.

109. MS: "1. 2 v."

110. In revising for repreaching, JE drew a closing bracket followed by the reference, "next p but one," referring to pt. 7, below (p. 000).

unto any foreign country, that if you had it about you would defend you from all mortal sickness, and from all fatal and hurtful accidents, would effectually secure you from the bite of poisonous serpents when traveling in the woods, and from all danger of shipwreck or drowning when passing upon the water, and from all the power of the sword or weapons of enemies in war; not only so, but would defend you from poverty, and secure to you a plentiful supply of bread, and would give you light when travailing in the dark, and would keep you from all mortal diseases: I say, if you could by any means [purchase] such a sort of oil, or any medicine, or some precious stone of these virtues, would you not be willing to give a great deal for it?

But this oil that you have heard of, will do much greater things for you than these. It will secure you from more and much greater evils, and to which you are more exposed than you are to these. It will secure you from all evil. I Pet. 3:13, "who is he that will harm you, if ye be followers of [that which is good]?"

This oil is that which is spoken of, Prov. 3:23–26, "Then shalt thou walk in thy way safely, and thy foot shall not stumble. When thou liest down, thou shalt not be afraid: yea, thou shalt lie down, and thy sleep shall be sweet. Be not afraid of sudden fear, neither of the desolation of the wicked, when it cometh. For the Lord shall be thy confidence, and shall keep thy foot from being taken"; and ch. 4:6, "Forsake her not, and she shall preserve thee: love her, and she shall keep thee"; and v. 12, "When thou goest, thy steps shall not be straitened; and when thou runnest, thou shalt not stumble." If you have this oil in your heart, God will be on your side: and what then can do you any hurt? Surely if God be your protection, you'll be safe wherever you are.

And if any evil seems to befall, it will not be any real evil; it will only be so in appearance. For all things, by God's promise, shall work together for your good [Rom. 8:28]. So that though things seem to be evil to you for the present, yet nothing shall prove so in the end.

If you have this oil in your heart, it will secure you from the reigning and condemning power of all sin.

{It will} secure {you} from the sting of death. All hurt that death can do you {shall not touch you, nor} all the malice of the innumerable evil spirits that are the mortal enemies of your soul. {If you have this oil in your heart, it will} secure you from the wrath of God, and secure you from everlasting burning.

And when other things fail, other streams are cut off, by virtue of this you shall be supplied with bread. You shall surely have sufficient; your supplies now shall [not] fail. [In] Is. 33:15–16, the Prophet, speaking of the righteous man, him that has this oil, says, "He shall dwell on high: his place of defense shall be the munitions of rocks: bread shall be given him; his waters shall be sure."

And it will give you light in darkness. Ps. 112:4, "To the upright there ariseth light in the darkness." Yea, it has power to give light in the greatest darkness. It often keeps a little Goshen about, and even in Egypt, where there is such darkness as can be felt, and makes it light even in passing through the valley of the shadow of death.

(5) This oil is precious, because it is an incorruptible, unfailing treasure. 'Tis a jewel that can neither be corrupted nor lost. As to earthly treasures, the most precious of them, they are corruptible. Silver and gold and precious stones, are corruptible things, as 'tis said, I Pet. 1:18. But this precious jewel that you have heard of is everlasting; 'tis durable riches. Durable riches and righteousness: he that has this treasure, has a treasure in bags that wax not old.[111]

And it is that which never can be stolen or lost. If a man should find any very precious jewel, something that was worth a great many thousands, he would be in continual pain for fear of it being lost or stolen. He would he afraid to travel[112] about with it, for fear somebody or other, by fraud or force, should take it from him, and he would not know where to find a place safe enough to lay it up, to prevent his being robbed of it.

If he should find such a jewel, and at the same time could be sure he should never be deprived of it, he would set a much higher value upon it.

But there is this attends this precious treasure in the heart that you have heard of: that he that has it, has it everlastingly secured to him, out of all danger of being deprived of it. He that gives it, also undertakes to keep it for them.

He that bestows it, grants with it a safe repository, a cabinet that no man can unlock and open to take it thence, even Jesus Christ, through whom it shall be kept. This is that spiritual life that is hid with Christ in God, Col. 3:3. God that gives it, grants to him that has it, as it were to lay

<hr/>

111. In revising for repreaching, JE drew a closing bracket followed by the reference, "next p. but one," referring to the passage below (p. 182) ending, "because Jesus was not yet glorified."

112. MS: "travail."

it up safe in heaven, where it is out of the reach of thieves; and there it is hid with Christ.

(6) It shall not only be kept, but it shall be increased. Gold is much valued, but a man would value his gold much more, if it would grow and increase as it lay in his chest, if he could open his cabinet from time to time and see it grown and increased. But this precious oil is of a growing nature. We are told, Prov. 4:18, "that the path of the just is as the shining light, that shineth more and more unto the perfect day."

(7)[113] It is that which is most precious, because of the precious fruit[114] that it will produce. It will grow while in this world, but hereafter it shall yield abundant, sweet and excellent fruit.

If you could by any means purchase a seed to sow in your garden, that when sown would spring up and would bear plentifully of silver and gold and pearls, would you not esteem this precious seed? Would you not be very choice of it?

But then consider how infinitely more precious is the fruit of this divine seed that you have heard of, that he that is born of God hath remaining in him. Wherever this seed is, it will in due time bud and blossom and bear fruit more precious than if every branch were hung with diamonds and rubies, or kings' crowns.

The flowers that it shall yield will be eternal honor and glory, and the fruit shall be eternal life. Prov. 3:2, "[For] length of days, and long life, and peace, shall they add to thee." The seed, when it comes to spring up, shall become a tree, and the tree shall be a tree of life; the fruit of it shall be eternal life. It shall answer all the ends of the tree of life in the garden of Eden, which if our first parents had stood they would have eat of, and which afterwards there was a flaming sword to keep them off from. If they had stood and had [not] eat {of the tree of the knowledge of good and evil}, they would have lived forever. So this seed will become a tree of life. Prov. 3:18, "She is a tree of life to them that lay hold upon her: and happy is every one that retaineth her."

The fruit of this tree will be the light of glory. And therefore 'tis said, Ps. 97:11, "Light is sown for the righteous, and gladness [for the upright in heart]."

When the seed comes to bear, it will as it were bear crowns of gold, crowns more precious and excellent ten thousand times than the crowns

113. In revising for repreaching, JE drew a bracket at the beginning of this paragraph.
114. MS: "of it."

of all the kings of the world: for they will be crowns of glory, that fade not away. Prov. 4:8–9, "Exalt her, and she shall promote thee: she shall bring thee to honor, when thou dost embrace her. She shall give to thine head an ornament of grace: a crown of glory shall she deliver to thee."

This seed shall by no means fail of producing this fruit, either by any waters smiting of it, or by drought or blasting, or mildew or frost, or any accident whatsoever; but God, who hath planted it, will bring the fruit to perfection.

The fruit will be exceeding sweet and exceeding abundant; that will be a plentiful harvest indeed. "They that go forth, weeping, bearing this precious seed shall doubtless come again with rejoicing, bringing his sheaves with him" [Ps. 126:6].

There is no seed that will multiply in its fruit, like this little seed sown in the heart. It shall hereafter produce ten thousand fold.

Thus is that verified of Christ in Matt. 13:31–32, where he compares the kingdom of heaven in the heart to a grain of mustard seed, which a man took and sowed in his field; which, though it be the least of all seeds, yet "when it is grown, is the greatest of all herbs, and the fowls of the air come and lodge in the branches thereof."

So that little drop of the water of life, that becomes a little fountain in the soul, in time shall become a river. John 7:38–39, "He that believeth on me, as the scripture hath said, out of his belly shall flow rivers of living water. (But this spake he of the Spirit, which they that believe on him should receive: for the Holy Ghost was not yet given; because that Jesus was not yet glorified)."[115]

And now consider, will you not be persuaded earnestly to seek that which is so precious, as you have heard, and which you are in necessity of, and that which you have so much opportunity and advantage to obtain?

Consider, this precious oil is not a thing unattainable; 'tis really offered to you. There are means that God has appointed on purpose, that you might attain, which if you improve, as you may do, you may in all probability be successful. See what God himself says to you as well as others—and he doubtless represents things as they are—Prov. 2, at [the] beginning.

Consider how many advantages God is now giving you to obtain this advantage, above what many others have. And will you, after all,

---

115. In revising for repreaching, JE drew a bracket at the end of this paragraph.

continue to neglect it, following after worldly vanities, pleasures, trifles too, and shadows, to your eternal undoing? O, don't be so exceeding unwise! And be directed to two things:

1. Be seasonable in seeking it. Now [you] have an opportunity. {The} midnight cry is not come {yet}. If the foolish virgins had gone to buy before {the midnight cry, they would have entered into the banquet. But they} foolishly neglected, and soon it was too late. {You} know not how soon it may be too late. Therefore, now immediately be in good earnestness if you love life, love happiness; if you love your own soul, now be in good earnest: and be so from henceforward.

2. Don't grudge to be at the cost. Don't neglect to buy under a notion of the oil's being too dear {to buy}. Alas, how can too much be found out for that which is so precious? {Therefore,} don't begrutch to sell {all}. Don't stick at self-denial, and denying any appetite, {and} suffering anything in your carnal ease, worldly convenience, {and} profits and advantages. {And} don't begrutch hard and constant labor; willingly comply with any means {God provides}. O, how richly will you be requited for all {your labor to be rich} in this precious oil.

But I would now, in the

Second place under this *Use*, direct myself to the godly in two heads of advice:

1. Be exhorted and advised earnestly to labor, that this oil may be increased. In having that, wherein the great and essential difference between the children of God and the children of the devil consists, and its being of such an excellent and precious nature, may all be as well applied to you, to move you to get more of it, as to the ungodly, to stir them up to seek it. Men don't want urging to stir them up to labor to increase in silver and gold, and such like things, because they have a high value for those things, and look upon 'em precious: and will you need urging to {stir you up to labor for that} which is so much more precious?

'Tis Christ's advice to Christians to be adding to this treasure, to be laying up treasure in heaven, Matt. 6:20.

2. Seek much of the exercises of this divine principle. The excellent fruits and effects of it come by the exercises of it. A seed does nothing but as it acts, and its hidden virtues exert themselves.

Labor therefore to abound in the exercises of this seed. Exercise it towards men, and especially seek to exercise it towards him that gave it, in holy faith and love, humble praise and obedience towards Christ.

Thus pour this holy [oil] on Christ's head, as we read of Mary in Mark 14, that she poured very precious ointment on Christ's head as he sat at meat. So pour forth this precious oil that you have heard of, on the head of your Redeemer.

And pour it out of a pure heart, as she poured it out of an alabaster box, which is a sort of matter exceeding clear and white.

And also pour it out of an humble heart, a broken contrite heart, as she poured the ointment on Christ head out of a broken box. As we read, "she brake the box, and poured it on his head" [Mark 14:3].[116]

Thus, as you have received an anointing from above with this oil, so anoint Jesus Christ with it.

Anoint that Savior that you rest on by faith with this oil, as Jacob poured oil on the stone that he had rested on while he slept, Gen. 28:18. And anoint Christ, the spiritual David, to be king over you, joyfully yielding yourself up to him, to be his willing subject; as we read that the children of Judah anointed David to be king over them, II Sam. 2:7. And so let him who is the Lord's anointed, be also your anointed, chosen King.[117]

[DOCTRINE RESUMED.]

[The text is] Matt. 25:1–12, at this time especially, v. 8.

After having observed from this parable wherein true Christians and false agree, I proceeded to consider wherein they differ. And we observed that those things wherein they differ, might be referred to three heads:

1. The great and most essential difference consisting in that, [that] the one {have} oil {in their vessels, and the other have none}.

2. In the consequences of this.

3. In that general character that is manifest from the consideration of both.

Having spoken to the first of these, viz., their most essential difference, consisting {in the one having oil, and the other not}; I now proceed to the second, viz., the difference consisting in the consequences of this. As the difference between true Christians and false consisting in the one

116. See the sermon on this text, *Mary's Remarkable Act*, in WJE 22:378–99.

117. This marks the end of the seventh booklet, though the conclusion of the eleventh preaching unit occupies the first leaf and the first three lines of the second leaf in the next booklet.

having oil, {and the other not}, is very great, so the consequences are very great.

The consequences of this difference are twofold. They are either,

(1) Those things that are consequent upon it, with respect to their behavior; and,

(2) With respect to their state.

In the

(1) [First] place, I would take notice of the difference between true Christians {and false Christians}, appearing in the consequence of one's having oil, {and the other not}, with respect to their behavior. And under this head, the parable that we are upon leads us to observe this difference, viz., that the external religion of false Christians [is] wont to fail in times of trial, but that is not so with respect to true Christians.

Under this head, three things are to be shown:

12.1. *That false Christians' external religion is wont to fail in times of trial.*

13.2. *That it is not so with respect to true Christians.*

14.3. *That this difference is a consequence of the one having oil in their vessels, and the other none.*

1. False Christians' external religion is wont to fail in times of trial. What is principally signified by the lamps of the virgins, is their external religion. The oil signifies the religion of the heart, that is hid within the vessel, and is out of sight; but the lamps are outward and visible. With respect to the lamps of the foolish virgins, we are informed that they went out; and when the midnight cry came, they were found with their lamps gone out.

This external religion, signified by the lamps, includes all besides what is in the heart: all their religious practice—not only that which is open before the world, but their external behavior, though it may be secret and hid from the eye of the world—and also their profession of religion.

It has been shown that false Christians may make the same profession with the godly, and that they may in many things agree with the godly in their external practice of religion.

But their religious practice is wont to fail in times of trial, and in some sorts of trials their very profession of religion is wont to fail too.

Neither their profession nor their practice is to be depended on, nor are they built so that they will stand all trials that may come.

The religion of some false Christians fails under one trial, and others under another. But the religion of all such is liable to fail; it is none of it of that nature as to be suited to bear trials.

Here, I would mention several sorts of trials, under which the religion of false Christians is wont to fail:

a. In what respects their religion is wont to fail under such trials. I shall mention, and I would mention, but three sorts of trials:

(a) Length of time is a trial that the religion of false Christians is commonly wont to fail under. Time is that which will try the stability and durableness of things. That which in[118] its own nature is not solid and substantial, will be devoured by time; they will by degrees decay and molder, and wear away and come to nothing.

So it is with the religion of false Christians. They often, for a while, at first seem very religious and very strict in many duties. It may be, a little while after they have met with these common affections, when they have entertained hopes of heaven, they for a while will [have] seemed to be zealous and engaged in religion, but this don't hold. They in a little time grow weary of it. They'll quickly be tired of this exactness and care and pains, and will alter their hand; by and by, religion will be very much let alone by 'em.

They never had a preparedness of heart to endure to the end, and very commonly their religion vanishes away in a little time. Hos. 6:4, "O Israel, what shall I do unto thee? for thy goodness is like the morning cloud, and as the early dew it goeth away."

This was the case with the foolish virgins. While the bridegroom tarried, they slumbered and slept, and their lamps went out. The bridegroom tarried long, and the length of time tried their lamps; they by degrees burnt more and more dimly, till at length, before the bridegroom came, they totally went out.

(b) Another trial under which the religion of false {Christians} is wont to fail, is a time of general decay of religion. This again was the case with the foolish virgins. The time when their lamps went out, was a time of general decay of religion in the society to which they belonged; they all slumbered and slept. And we are taught in the foregoing chapter that at such a time, the love of false Christians is wont to wax cold, v. 12.

118. MS: "is."

False Christians, while it is a time of the flourishing of religion amongst the people where they dwell, many keep up a great deal of religion, and many appear well in their walk and conversation: for then there [are] a great many things to move 'em, that there are not at other times. There are many things then to work on natural principles, to induce 'em to behave themselves well.

But when such a time is past away, and there comes a dull and dead time in religion, and a time of the prevalency of many ill and corrupt things, then they have their trial.

And commonly, at such times, the religion of false Christians is wont to fail. Then they [are] wont to return, and appear as they used to do: to be careless of the practice of religion, to neglect God and Christ and holy things, and to pursue mainly after other things; and their old corruptions, their pride and their worldliness and their malice and the like, are wont to revive, [like] the snakes in the spring.

And sometimes, when they get amongst those that have religion in contempt, they are wont to grow ashamed of religion, ashamed of religious talk and of religious practice too, and, it may [be], ashamed of the very profession of religion; and so are ashamed of Christ in an evil generation, and therefore are of that number of whom he will be ashamed when he comes.

(c) Another trial[119] is when times and such changes come, wherein the practice of religion is attended with more than ordinary difficulty.

It may be, when the false Christian first sets out in religion, it is a smooth time, a time when the practice of religion was attended with no remarkable difficulty, and there was no occasion for any remarkable suffering or denying themselves.

But after a while, God in his providence brings a change of time and change of circumstances, so that now they can't be strict in the practice of religion with that ease and convenience that they could before: now, if they would hold on as they have begun, they must very much deny themselves; they must exceedingly cross some of their natural inclinations, and, it may be, must suffer much in their temporal interests; they must suffer in their honor, or in their estates.

Such a kind of trial as this had the virgins in this parable: it grew late in the night, and it was very difficult for 'em to keep awake.

---

119. MS: "under which."

When they first went out to meet the bridegroom, it was, we may suppose, early in the evening, when they could be concerned and engaged in such an affair with but little difficulty. But by and by the time altered; it grew very late, and they could not [but] attend it with much more difficulty and inconvenience. Midnight is a difficult time to be engaged in any earnest business: in this time, their lamps went out.

Such times of difficulty are [described] in the parable of the sower and the seed, "And when the sun was up, they were scorched; and because they had no root, they withered away," Matt. 13:6.

Such difficulties seem to be one thing meant by winds and storms arising, [and] rain descending. "And the floods came, and the winds blew, and beat upon that house; and it fell: and great was the fall of it," Matt. 7, latter end. Such difficulties are what are called in Ezekiel "the stumbling block" that God lays before hypocrites. Ezek. 3:20, "Again, When a righteous man doth turn from his righteousness, and commit iniquity, and I lay a stumbling-block before him, he shall die: because thou hast not given him warning, he shall die in his sin, and his righteousness which he hath done shall not be remembered; but his blood will I require at thine hand."

God commonly is wont to try professions in this manner. Sometimes God brings the trial of persecution, in which case the religion of false Christians is wont to fail, and commonly their very profession of Christianity.

[b.] Having thus observed of what kind the trials are, under which the religion of hypocrites is wont to fail, I now proceed, in the second place, to show how it is wont to fail. I would here mention several ways:

a. When they under trials cast off the profession of the Christian, as it has now been observed that false Christians are wont to do in times of persecution. Or,

b. When they become openly vicious and profane in their lives. So sometimes those, that for a while have the guise of saints, do become. There is soon a great alteration in them; they seem in a great measure to cast off religion and get into wicked ways, which they live in in an open manner, and sometimes prove some of the worst of men, the most intolerable in vice and wickedness.

So it was with many that the apostles speak of in their epistles. Particularly, the apostle Peter speaks much of them, in the second chapter of his second epistle; and the apostle Jude in his epistle.

c. When they by degrees grow into a distaste and dislike of religion. There are some that don't come to that, to be openly profane, being restrained from it for their credit's sake and from other selfish motives, that yet grow into a distaste of strict religion.

They get out with such a way of living: it seems to them a kind of bondage; one while, they seemed to comply with it, but they soon grow sick of it: since that, they have thought it was needless, and, it may be, [are] ready to call it by an evil name. It looks to them to be a needless, uncomfortable, over-precise way of living.

And as they dislike it for their own practice, so they have a distaste of it in others. When they see others that seem to continue zealous in such a way of living, they have a disrelish of them upon that account; they ben't suited in the company of such persons.

For a while, at first, they joined with them, and seemed to think it honorable and commendable; but now they have other notions. They are ready to despise such things, and it may be laugh at them, and speak contemptibly of them. They now like other sort of company a great deal better.

So Judas seemed to like the company of Christ and his disciples, and followed them a while; but at last he got out with them, he left 'em in a disgust, and turned a traitor.

d. When they are come to that, as to leave off the laborious parts of religion. There are some false Christians that don't turn openly vicious and profane, that will yet have done with the laborious parts of religion.

There are some parts of religion that are very laborious, and require[120] a great deal of watchfulness and pains: those, they are wont to forsake.

They may continue to go to meeting, and attend other things wherein the form of religion consists, and may keep from gross sins. But as for constant and daily reading, and strict prayer and meditation, watching against their constitution-sins, and fighting with temptations and corruptions, and such like laborious duties: they do but little of them. Of those things, they in their practice say as those, Mal. 1:13, "What a weariness is it!"[121]

---

120. MS: "requires."

121. JE deletes: "They do in a stated manner set their hearts more on worldly things, than things of religion."

e. When they come to that, as secretly to live in ways of known sin. Sometimes false Christians, while under some remarkable awakenings, or just while they are under the first impressions of their first affections and hopes, may be very careful to keep from indulging their lusts.

While under awakenings, they dare not do these and those things; and while under the sensible impressions of their first affections and false joys, they may seem to be very exact a while. But after a little while, they grow more bold. They begin to venture to taste their old, sinful sweets; they have been tied up a while, but they break loose again; and so it is with [them] as the apostle Peter says, according to the true proverb, II Pet. 2:22, "The dog is returned to his own vomit again." For a while, it may be, they seemed to be universal in their respect to God's commandments, but 'tis not so long: after a little while, they begin to make very free with some of the commands; and if they were observed in their dealings with their neighbors and in their talk in their chimney corners, and were followed into their families and secret places, and observed in the dark as well as the light, it would plainly appear that they lived with little regard to some of the holy communion of God.

f. [Sixth,] and lastly, when they begin a course to make use of their hope, to engage themselves in negligence and laxness in religion. At first, while their affections and impressions were new, it may be they thought they should be willing to do anything for God. Gal. 4:15, "I bear you record, you would have plucked out your own eyes, and have given them to me."

But after a while they learn another way; they begin secretly to think with themselves, Why, now, if they be converted, they are safe; what need they be concerned? They that are once converted shall certainly be saved, and if they don't take so much pains and put themselves to such difficulty, and if they take their ease more, it will be well with them at last.

When persons are got into such a way as this, and this is usual with them, then it may be said of 'em, that their lamps are gone out.

When it comes to that with them, that all their concern is to have just religion enough to carry 'em to heaven, and because they think they have so much set their hearts at rest about getting any more striving against sin, then they prove themselves to be some of that sort spoken of by the Prophet. Ezek. 33:13, "When I shall say to the righteous, that he shall surely live; if he trust to his own righteousness, and commit iniquity, all his righteousness shall not be remembered; but for his iniquity that he hath committed, he shall die for it."

[2.] I come now to the second[122] thing under this head we are upon, viz., that is not thus with true Christians; or thus, that the external religion of some Christians don't thus fail in times of trial. True Christians may be guilty of many failings, and they may greatly decline in times of trial [in] the practice of religion; but yet it never fails in the manner as has been spoken of, wherein the religion of false Christians is wont to fail. The wise virgins slumbered and slept as well as the foolish, but here was the difference: that while the foolish virgins slumbered and slept, the lamps went out; but it was not so with the wise: their lamps burnt dim, so that they needed trimming when they awaked, but they were kept alive, so that it could not be said of them that they were gone out. Not only their oil lasted, but also the flame of their lamps continued burning, signifying that not only shall religion always remain in the hearts of the godly, but also in their walk and practice. Though a godly person may be guilty of great declensions, yet God will never suffer their lamps [to] go out; he will watch and keep them alive while they sleep, for he is the watchman of Israel, who never slumbers nor sleeps [Ps. 121]. They are those spoken of, Matt. 24:13, "who endure to the end, and shall be saved"; and therefore are said, Luke 8:15, "to bring forth fruit with patience"; and are those spoken of, Rom. 2:7, "who by patient continuance in well doing seek for glory and honor and immortality, eternal life." It is said of the righteous, Job 17:9, that he "shall hold on his way." And we are told, John 15:16, that Christ has chosen 'em, that they should go and bring forth fruit, and that their fruit should remain: not only shall their seed remain, but their fruit shall remain.

Their seed's remaining is the reason why their fruit will remain; and therefore the apostle John says, I John 3:9, "Whosoever is born of God sinneth not," i.e., {continues to be fruitful}. They are those that so answer that precept of Christ in Rev. 2:10, in a measure of being fruitful unto death, and so at last receive "a crown of life."

Therefore, the Apostle speaks so positively of those that are indeed of the number of true Christians, that they will not[123] continue with them, and not go out from them, I John 2:19.

122. MS: "III."
123. MS: "no."

And though the godly may be guilty of great declinings in religion in times of trial, yet their religion can't be said to fail as the religion of hypocrites is wont to do at such times; because their declinings ben't of that nature as to carry in them a practical casting off God and religion, as those backslidings of hypocrites that have been mentioned do. As when a man comes to leave strict religion out of a real dislike and distaste of it, and to quit the laborious parts of religion and those things in it that are contrary to his own interest, or stand in the way of his idols: this shows that the man regards religion not for its own sake but only as a thing by-the-bye, and just to serve a turn, and shows him to be indeed no real friend to the thing itself. And so when he will live in known sins, and seeks to be religious no further than just so as to get to heaven, this implies a real casting off God and religion. And therefore, how far soever a godly [man] may decline, his religion never comes to fail in such a manner as this.

3.[124] This difference is the consequence of the forementioned difference, of one's having oil in their vessels, and the other not: and that, partly from the nature of the thing, and partly from the nature of God's covenant.

a. 'Tis partly from the nature of things. If there be no spiritual principle in the heart, or change of nature in the soul, 'tis the natural consequence that such a man's external religion should not be durable: as natural as that a lamp should go out that has no oil to feed it; or that a plant should die when the sun is risen upon it with a burning, but that has no root in the ground to support its life against the heat of the sun; and as natural as that a stream of water should fail that has no spring to supply it. The religion of false Christians may be compared to those puddles of snow water that run in our streets, in or near the spring. They run plentifully for a while; there seems to be as much water in them as in those streams that have a living spring at the head of 'em. But by and by they will dry up; drought and heat will consume those snow waters, because they have no spring to supply 'em.

The trials that professors meet with are like wind and water, that overthrows what is built on the sand, or like fire that burns up wood, hay and stubble, and such things as won't stand the fire.

b. ['Tis] partly from the nature of God's covenant. [The] religion of false Christians is not built on Christ, the mediator of the covenant, as

124. MS: "IV."

has been observed; and therefore has not the promises of that covenant to secure it, as the religion of true Christians {does}.

[There is that] great promise of [the] gospel covenant, Jer. 32:40. "And I will make an everlasting covenant with them, that I will not turn away from them, to do them good; but I will put my fear in their hearts, that they shall not depart from me."

APPLICATION.

Use I of *Self-Examination.* Many professors of religion [are] present. Many that set out in religion a little while ago, {they} seemed at first to be zealous {and} affectionate. {They seemed} strict to comply with [God's commands], to approve of and esteem [them].

How has it been since {then}? There have been trials, [and] length of time. [There has been a] general declension.

Doubtless, [they have] met with change and been in circumstances, one and another, wherein religion has been attended with special difficulty.

[The] circumstances of many of you [has] much changed. [Love of religion has] grown into distaste. [The] laborious parts of religion [have become too hard]. [You] begin to depart from universality [of obedience].

Let it be your manner to make use of your hope.

Perseverance in the practice of religion, through trials, is what is greatly insisted on in Scripture, as that which professors should try themselves by. Rom. 11:22, "Behold therefore the goodness and severity." John 8:31, "If ye continue in my ways, then are you my disciples indeed." Gal. 6:9, "Be not weary of well doing: [for in due season we shall reap, if we faint not]." Luke 14:29–30, "Lest haply, after he hath laid the foundation, and is not able to finish it, all that behold it begin to mock him, saying, This man began to build, and was not able to finish." Jas. 1:25, "Whoso looketh into the law of liberty, [and continueth therein, he being not a forgetful hearer, but a doer of the work, this man shall be blessed in his deed]." Ezek. 18:24, "But when the righteous turneth away from his righteousness, and committeth iniquity, and doeth according to all the abominations that the wicked man doeth, shall he live? All his righteousness that he hath done shall not be mentioned: in his trespass that he hath trespassed, and in his sin that he hath sinned, in them shall he die"; and ch. 33:12, etc., "Therefore, thou son of man, say unto the children of thy people, The righteousness of the righteous shall not deliver him in the day of his transgression: as for the wickedness of the wicked, he shall not fall thereby in the day that he turneth from his wickedness; neither shall the righteous be able to live for his righteousness in the day that he sinneth." "In those is continuance, and we shall be saved" [Is. 64:5].

[Perseverance is] so much insisted on probably for two reasons:

First. This is what is plain and visible, and can't be denied as to things internal. [It leaves no] room for many cavils and disputes.

Herein it, above all things, appears whether religion is effectual, has its thorough effect.

Second. This tends to convince the conscience how justly they may be disowned and repented of God.

[*Use*] II [of] *Exhortation.* If it be thus, will you seek earnestly to get into a better state?

First Motive. Commonly, such professors are surprised by the midnight cry in such circumstances.

Second [Motive]. Consider how you would accept a friend that should treat you as you do God and Christ.[125]

[DOCTRINE RESUMED.]

[The text we are upon is] Matt. 25:1–12, especially at this time, v. 8: "[And the foolish said unto the wise, Give us of your oil; for our lamps are gone out]."

Three things wherein they differed:

1. [That the one have] oil {in their lamps, and the other have none}.

2. [The] consequences [of this].

3. [That] general character [manifest from the consideration of both].

We were last on the consideration of the difference consisting in the consequences of the one's having oil, {and the other having none}.

We observed that those consequences are of two kinds: either with respect to their behavior, or their state. As to the difference between true

125. This point marks the end of the twelfth preaching unit and of the eighth booklet.

Christians' behavior [and false], they were considered in the former part of the day.[126] I come now,

(2) To consider those consequences of true Christians having oil, and the other having none, with respect to their state. And the consequences of this are twofold: the one is with respect to their hopes of a state of grace, and the other with respect to a state of glory. I would,

1. Consider the consequences of this with respect to their hopes of a state of grace. And the difference between true Christians and false, with respect to this, consists in this, viz., that when Christ comes, false Christians' hopes and seeming evidences of a state of grace, will at once totally vanish away. But with respect to true Christians, it will be far otherwise.

a. When Christ comes, [the] hopes and seeming {evidences of a state of grace in} false Christians will totally vanish away.

What is signified by the lamps of the virgins, as has been observed, is the appearances of godliness that are in them. And those appearances of godliness are either those whereby godliness seems to appear in them in the eyes of others, or in their own eyes.

The lamps of the virgins are either those by which they shine in the eyes of others, or in their own eyes.

So that one thing signified by the lamps of the foolish virgins, are the seeming evidences of their godliness, whence they have entertained an hope of their state as good.

And therefore by their lamps appearing to them to be gone out when the midnight cry was heard, we are taught that those things in them, that shined in their eyes like a bright lamp, and served to uphold light and comfort and hope in them before, won't shine then; but instead of appearing like a lamp that shines bright, will, when the midnight cry is heard, appear like a lamp that is extinct. There will be nothing to be seen there to give 'em any light, or to afford any hope or comfort. There will be all darkness then, without the least glimmering of the light.

The first that the foolish virgins saw that they were without any lamps, was when that cry was heard, "Behold, the bridegroom cometh."

They might have discerned it before, if they had been watchful, but till then they were asleep; they trusted to their lamps, that they presumed to sleep in the state they were in, and then when they were waked by this

126. This indicates that no. 461 was delivered during a morning service and no. 462 during the afternoon service on a sabbath day.

solemn cry, they at once saw that their lamps were extinct. Very often false Christians have a good opinion of themselves while they live here, and God lets 'em alone. It has been already observed, they may agree with the godly in that, that they think they are converted; yea, they may have a strong confidence of it.

But yet when Christ comes, they will have their evidences of a good estate to seek. They will look where they used to look, but they won't then find what they used to think they did find.

Those things that before used to look to 'em like burning lamps, will then appear as stinking snuffs. Those things that before glorified, and appeared as precious jewels, will now appear to be nothing but an heap of ordure and filthiness.

Before, when they heard awakening sermons, whereby they were told of hell, they had their refuges to fly to. They had met with these and those things, and these quieted them, and made 'em think themselves safe. The refuges they fled to then seemed strong to 'em, and for the present did their turn, and kept their minds in quietness and security.

And when they come to hear the awakening, awful cry, they will go to fly to the same refuges that they used to fly to, but they wont find 'em; they will be gone; their walls, that have been daubed with untempered mortar, will be fallen down. They will go to fly to their strongholds, but they will all vanish away before their eyes.

Then they will go catch hold on those things that they used formerly to hang by, to keep themselves from sinking, and they thought strong; but now they will find nothing to lay hold of.

Thus will it be with the hope of the hypocrite at that time, Job 27:8. All their foundation will then be gone, and they will be left in a dreadful state and condition. His "hope shall be cut off, and his trust shall be as a spider's web; he shall lean upon his hope, but it shall not stand: he shall hold it fast, but it shall not endure," Job 8:14–15. When that cry is heard, they will fly to their lamps in a great hurry, and they will fall to trimming their lamps to make 'em burn, and give 'em as much light as they used [to]: but it will all be in vain. They will soon see it is in vain. They won't be able to revive their old religious affections. They used to think themselves clothed in shining apparel, but now they will see themselves quite naked; and if they look about for their garments, they won't find 'em; if they strive to patch up something to cover their nakedness, it will be in vain. But they will then see and know that there is no other way but for 'em to walk naked, to be exposed in their nakedness and hideous deformity before God, angels, and men.[127]

There may be two reasons given of this. This will be brought to pass by the voice of a twofold judge.

a. Conscience, that before was stupefied and blinded, will then be thoroughly awakened and enlightened, to pass a right sentence concerning their seeming evidence of a good estate.[128]

b. They must then have their state tried by a Judge that searches the heart, and cannot be deceived. The Wise Man observes, in Prov. 16:2, "that all the ways of man are clean in his own eyes, but the Lord weigheth the spirits." Men may deceive others, and may deceive themselves, but they can't deceive God.

There is no hiding anything from God, no, not in the most secret corner of the heart. The eyes of the infinitely holy Judge will try men's hearts, as gold is tried in a furnace of fire; and therefore the Prophet, Mal. 3:2–3, when speaking of Christ's coming to judgment, he says, "He is a refiner fire, and like fuller's soap"; and 'tis said, Rev. 19:12, "His eyes are like a flame of fire." The eyes of this Judge are piercing, and pierces into the dark recesses of the heart; his eyes are more piercing than lightning, that is so quick and powerful in its effects.

Those eyes will try men's religion, of what sort it is. Men's religious affections and impressions that they have had, must come under the test of the piercing eyes of this Judge.

And he'll try the principles men have acted from; he'll discern whether there has been any sincerity in anything that men have met with. There is no deceiving this Judge with any paint, {or any} disguise whatsoever.

Alas, "who can abide the day of his coming, and who can stand when he appeareth?" [Mal. 3:2]. Surely none that are rotten at heart, whatever fair shows of piety they have had, and whatever false hopes and comforts they have entertained.

Everyone is to be as it were tried by fire. Every heart must come under the trial of that light, that is a thousand times more piercing than the fire of the fiercest furnace, or the keenest lightning.

127. JE's shorthand note at this point reads, "Second time from this place to the mark."

128. At this point in the MS, JE left a page blank.

And in such a trial as this, 'tis impossible any dross should pass for gold, or that any false covering should fail of being burnt up.

This omniscient and strict Judge will have no regard to the opinions of men, neither good, neither bad; he'll have no regard to the determinations men have formerly come to about themselves. But he will try how they are in reality; he [will] search and see what bottom men stand upon, and whether they are built on a rock or on the sand.

And therefore, 'tis impossible that it should be otherwise at that time, than that all the seeming evidences and false hopes of false Christians should then totally vanish away, and be as it were everlastingly consumed.

Thus the hopes and seeming evidences of false [Christians].

2. It will be far otherwise with true Christians, which may appear in these three things:

a. Then their hopes and evidences will not vanish away, but will endure. They will stand the trial of that day, and bear the test of that judgment. Those things that were the evidences that they depended on, will appear evidences still. Their comforts won't fail, and be turned into horror and despair, as it will be with false Christians.

Their consciences will not pass sentence against them. The light of the awful majesty and holiness of their Judge won't scare away all their hopes, and extinguish their lamps.

The wise virgins, when they were awaked with the midnight cry, they did not find their lamps gone out. But when the wind blows, {their lamps} won't shake,[129] {and} when the fire comes, {their foundation} won't burn up.

b. Their evidences will then be brightened, and their former judgment of themselves confirmed. The wise virgins, when the midnight cry was heard, arose and trimmed their lamps, and they burnt brighter than before. Some true Christians, before that time, are wavering in their hopes; they have often doubts and fears. But when that time comes, their doubts will be removed, and those evidences that before appeared dim and obscure, will then appear bright; the clouds that before hid them, will now all be scattered.

The light of the false Christians will then be removed, and nothing but darkness left. But it will be contrariwise with respect to true

129. Conjectural reading.

Christians: their darkness will then be all removed, and there will be only light, or light without darkness.

The light of that day will discover what is truth. And therefore, it will more clearly discover the goodness of the foundation of the godly, as it will manifest the badness of the foundation of the ungodly.

The more trying that time is, the more piercing and searching the eye of conscience and the eyes of the Judge will be, and the more like a refiner's fire, so much the more certain will it render the good estate of the true Christians.

That the eyes of the Judge will be as a flame of fire, will bring no danger to those that have a true hope, nor any tendency then to bring the godly to question their hope; but the effect will be, that their hope will be the more certain. And whereas now, many of the godly have only hoped with a fearful, trembling hope that their state was good, they will then know that their state is good; everyone will have assurance.

c. Then their hope will begin to turn into fruition. They shall not only have their hope strengthened to assurance, but they shall then begin to see and enjoy the things they have hoped for.

They shall not then only be confirmed in an opinion of their title to salvation, but they shall then begin actually to be made the subjects and possessors of eternal salvation, receiving the joy and issue of their faith and hope, and reign in life by Jesus Christ.

They shall not then merely have hope: "for that which a man sees, why doth he yet hope for"? Rom. 8:24. They shall be got beyond hope, to enjoyment.

When the godly at the day of judgment shall see Christ coming to be their judge, that sight will be a joyful, beatifical sight. They shall see him coming as their judge, and also as their food and portion, and shall then begin to receive the glorious tokens of Christ's everlasting love, in being caught up in the clouds to meet the Lord in the air. And thus it is that true Christians and false will differ in the consequence of the one's having oil, {and the other not}, as to what respects their hope of their state of grace.

[APPLICATION.]

The *Use* that I would make of what has been said under this head, is of *Exhortation* to all, to take thorough care that they have such evidences and such a hope as won't vanish away when Christ appears.

Are not some of you, that have entertained a good thought of your state, too careless and negligent of this matter? Are there none such that have in a great measure left off concern about things of this nature, and don't spend much time in exercising their minds about them, or concerning themselves about the state of their souls, whether it be good or bad; that of late han't much to do with their own hearts, in searching of it or inquiring into its circumstances, because their minds are taken up with other things, the vanities of this world?

If it be thus with you, surely it argues that you don't think much of that day that we have been now speaking of, when all persons' evidences and hopes will have such a trial, and when the hypocrite's hope shall utterly and eternally vanish away.

Or is it because you think you are so sure, that you think there is no further need of troubling your head about it? But you seem to be greatly mistaken concerning the nature of a true assurance: it is not the nature of it, to dispose persons to have their minds less taken up about the things of religion, and to be less earnestly engaged in heart-work, and more taken up about the vanities of the world.

But on the contrary, they that are most assured with a true assurance, have commonly their hearts, more than any, taken from all that is vain and trivial, and their minds most engaged about their heart's searching, their hearts and ways being conversant and taken up about those things that most immediately concern God and their own souls.

If that be the case with you, that you [are] quiet and easy about this matter, taking it for granted that all is right; and your quietness is of that nature, that the consequence of it is that you have but little to do with soul-concerns, and have your head and heart filled with other concerns: be assured that there is no sort of persons in the world have more need to look about you, and examine your evidences, than such as you.

Therefore let me exhort all, whatever they do, to be thorough now, while the day of probation lasts, in that great concern, to see [to] it that[130] their evidences are good, and the grounds of their hope sure, and such as will never fail. And be advised to attend the following *Directions*, concerning the manner in which persons should take care of this matter:

First. Never flatter yourself with anything whatsoever that you may call discoveries or spiritual experiences, when your own conscience testifies that your stated, allowed practice contradicts your hope. If it seems

130. MS: "that they."

to you that you have had something extraordinary, and something that you could not make yourself; and though others that you have told it to have thought it was right, {and that your experiences} seemed to agree very well with others' stories, {and you} thought you have felt 'em when you have heard 'em talk: let those things be how they will, yet if you would not have such an hope as will vanish away when Christ {comes}, flatter not yourself in any {way}, as long as your own conscience {testifies against you}.

This very rule I now give you, is very much insisted on [in] the Word of God. Why did Christ say with such emphasis, John 14:21, "He that hath my commandments, and keepeth them, he it is that loveth me: and he that loveth me shall be loved of my Father, and I will love him, and will manifest myself to him"?

And why did the apostle John say as he does, I John 2:4, "He that saith, I know him, and keepeth not his commandments, is a liar, and the truth is not in him"? "He that saith I know him": that is, that pretends he has had discoveries of God.

And why do you think it is the apostle Paul says as he does, I Cor. 6:9–10, "Be not deceived: neither fornicators, nor idolaters, nor adulterers, nor effeminate, nor abusers of themselves with mankind, nor thieves, nor covetous, nor drunkards, nor revilers, nor extortioners, shall inherit the kingdom of God"; as much as to say, "Let others[131] pretend what they will about what they experience, [they] do but deceive themselves."[132] If you, therefore, don't go to deceive yourselves, hearken to no pretenses in the world, as long as 'tis thus with you.

And again, Gal. 6:7, "Be not deceived, God is not mocked. For that which a man soweth, [that shall he also reap]"; as much as to say, "'Tis but a vain deceit, and a mere mockery, for a man to pretend that {he loves God but does not keep his commandments}." Eph. 5:5–6, "For this ye know, that no whoremonger, nor unclean person, nor covetous man, who is an idolater, hath any inheritance in the kingdom of Christ and of God. Let no man deceive you with vain words: for because of these things cometh the wrath of God upon the children of disobedience."

And why did the apostle James say as he does, Jas. 2:14, "What doth it profit, my brethren, if a man say thou hast faith, and I have works? Can faith save him?"

131. MS: "you."
132. MS: "yourselves."

Is any so vain as to think that Christ and his apostles did not know how to give rules for persons to judge of their condition by? Or what shall we make of those things?

Remember that this same Christ that says these things, either by his own mouth or his Spirit in his apostles, is to be your judge; 'tis his eyes, that are as a flame of fire, that is to judge: and do you think that in judging you, he'll depart from his own rules in judging, and make use of other means? Therefore, if you would not have your hope and evidences vanish away when you come to appear before this Judge, {do no flatter yourself in any way, as long as your conscience testifies against you}.

Second. Settle it with yourself, that that hope is always the most likely to be right, that is attended with a most sensible, tender and awakened conscience. {It is the} tendency of a false hope evermore to stupefy; [you are] more stupid with it than without it, more senseless about the dreadful nature of sin, the importance and worth of the soul, and the like.

[It is the] tendency of a true hope, on the contrary, to awaken, soften the conscience, and make it sensible.

If you find that when your hope is most lively at such times, [and you] seem to have most of a sense of the greatness of God, {the} dreadfulness of his wrath, {the} dreadful nature of sin against him, [and are] most afraid of sin: that at such time doth judgment and eternity seem to come with most sense of their greatness and weight on your mind. True hope is attended with an holy and religious fear, Ps. 33:18. [Ps.] 147:11, "Those that fear the Lord, they that hope in thy mercy."

Third. Remember that that hope is most likely to be right, the increase of which is attended with an increase of your conversation within, and softens conversation without. If at such times as when your hope is strongest, {you} find your heart most engaged about those things that are inward, observing what passes there, watching your thoughts, keeping a strict eye on your affections, God's principles, [and] motives of action; if you at such times find you have most of heart-work to do, most to do in those things that concern God and your own soul, and less to do with the world, [and your] thoughts [are] less taken up [with the world]: a true hope is heavenly; it takes the thoughts off from this world, and makes it more conversant in things spiritual and heavenly. Heb. 6:19, "And thus enters into that within the veil."

Fourth. Bear in mind that hope is most likely to be right, that when it is strongest, is attended with most of a disposition to self-abasement. Scripture teaches that the hope of the hypocrites exalts, and lifts him up. Is. 65:5, "Stand by thyself, come not near to me; for I am holier than thou." [In the parable of the] Pharisee and publican, [the] Pharisee thanked God {that he was} "not as other men are, extortioners, unjust, adulterers, or even as this publican" [Luke 18:11]. True hope [is] of a contrary nature: when they have most sense of God's favor, and his being pacified towards them, is their heart most agreeable to that in Ezekiel, "that thou mayest remember, and be confounded," Ezek 16:63.

Fifth. When you feel your hope most lively and strong, then remember and inquire whether you feel your heart most engaged to grow and make progress in religion.

[The] tendency of a true hope, [is] to seek after greater degrees of purity with the greatest labors and endeavors—I John 3:3, "He that hath this hope in him purifieth himself even, as he is pure"—with the greatest labors and endeavors.[133]

[DOCTRINE RESUMED.]

[The text is] Matt. 25:1–12, especially, vv. 10–12.

[We observed a] threefold difference [of consequences between true and false Christians]:

[*1.* A] difference in consequences with respect to a state.

[*2.* A difference that] attends hopes of [a] state of grace.

[*3.* A difference] with respect to [a] state of glory.

[The] difference with respect to a state of glory consists in this: that the one shall be admitted into it, and the other shut out of it.

a. True Christians shall be admitted {into a state of glory}. Concerning what is said of their admittance into a state of glory, [from] the words read in this parable, these things may be observed:

(a) That they shall enter in with the bridegroom. By which the following things seem to be taught us:

---

133. The thirteenth preaching unit ends here. JE closes with "ORDINATION," possibly announcing the ordination of William Seward (Yale, 1734) as pastor of the church in Killingworth, Conn., on Jan. 18, 1738. If that is the case, then the assumed dates for the final portions of the Virgins Series, February and March 1738, have to be pushed back so that the series ended in January.

a. That it shall be with the full approbation of Christ. [He shall] own them {and} confess their names, Rev. 3:5.

b. Christ will as it were lead them into his glory by his power, [by] his own right hand. He'll bestow it upon them, Rev. 7:17.

c. They shall there enjoy the presence of Christ in glory. John 17:24, "Father, I will that they also, whom thou hast given me, be with me where I am." I John 3:2, "It doth not yet appear."

d. [They] shall be made partakers with Christ of his glory. John 15:11, "My joy may remain in you, and that your joy might be full."

(b) Another thing to be noted, is that they shall enter in with him into the marriage, i.e., to be guests at the marriage feast, partakers of the joys and entertainments of that royal wedding. By which the following things are taught us: this denotes,

a. The heavenly union and love that they shall enjoy. Christ calls 'em his friends. Cant. 5:1, "Eat, O friends."

b. Their sweet communion and society. They sup with him, and he with them, Rev. 3:20.

c. Their rejoicing together. Is. 55[:2], "Delight itself in fatness." Rev. 19:9, blessed and holy is her. [Their rejoicing together is] compared to a banquet, Cant. 2:4.

d. The richness and fullness of their entertainment: exceeding costly, most excellent. "Eye has not seen, nor ear heard, neither have entered into the heart of man, the things which God hath prepared for them that love him" [I Cor. 2:9]. [They shall] partake to the full of the bread of life, John 6:48; drink of the water of life, Rev. 22, at [the] beginning; [of] that new wine, angel's food, Ps. 105:40. In the 25th[134] [chapter] of Isaiah [it says, they shall "make a] feast of fat things," [of] great fullness and abundance, all that is needed. [There shall be] enough for everyone, suited to every faculty of the soul, [enough to] satisfy every holy appetite. [There shall be] "twelve manner of fruits," [and] yields [of "her] fruit every month" [Rev. 22:2]. [They shall enjoy] inexhaustible plenty. [It is] called "a river" [Rev. 22:1].

b. False Christians shall then be shut out. Concerning what is said of false Christians being shut out, these things are taught us in the parable we are upon:

---

134. MS: "29."

(a) They shall be admitted to enjoy no part or measure of this glory, but shall be kept far from it. [They shall] not [be] suffered[135] to come nigh; [a] wall of separation [shall keep them out]. {False Christians shall} come to the door, and find it shut; shut on purpose to keep them out, that they might by no means enter. What is here represented by a door locked, or bolted, is elsewhere represented by a great gulf fixed, Luke 16:26. When that door is shut, the door of mercy shall be shut, [the] door of opportunity.

(b) [They] shall be shut out in darkness, expressed by Luke 13:28, by "wailing and gnashing [of teeth]." The whole representation [is] carried on by the similitude of a wedding, which used to be in the night; and therefore this, which is here understood, is elsewhere expressed. This intends misery in "blackness of darkness," Jude 13, [and] is the power of the prince of darkness.

(c) All requests to be admitted will be in vain. [They will] cry, "Lord, Lord." [They are] represented as using arguments and pleading. Matt. 7:22–23, "Lord, have [we] not prophesied in thy name? and in thy name have cast out devils? and in thy name done many wonderful works?" Luke 13:26, "We have eaten and drunk in thy presence, and thou hast taught in our streets."

(d) They shall be shut out with great manifestations of Christ's abhorrence. [They shall be] thrust out, bound[136] hand and foot, and cast out.

(e) All hopes of admittance will be dashed. Christ's answer will bring despair. They will be to show 'em that 'tis hopeless.

(f) Therefore, the same answer is elsewhere repeated to confirm it. Luke 13:25–27, Matt. 7:28, "Then will I profess unto them I never knew you: depart from me, ye that work iniquity." [It] signifies as much as Abraham's answer, Luke 16:25. When that door is shut, [the] door of hope [is] shut.

APPLICATION.

[The] *Use* I would make of what has been said upon this head, is of *Warning* to those here present, that are hitherto foolish virgins, to take

---

135. MS: "suffer."
136. MS: "bow."

heed that it don't come to this with you at last: that when true Christians are admitted into {a state of glory, you are cast out}.

But the more effectually to instruct you, [consider] more particularly:

First. How great the glory is that true Christians will be admitted into, which appears in the following things:

1. [They shall have a] perfect rest.
2. [They shall enjoy a] perfect bounty.
3. [They shall have a] kingly glory.
4. [They will have] perfect satisfaction.
5.[137] [They will be] in perfect assurance of the continuance [of their glory].

Second. You shall see them enstated in their glory.

Third. You shall see persons of all nations, and of all sorts. Luke 13:29, "And many shall come from the east, and from the west."

Fourth. Consider how great the misery is that will overtake you, particularly:

1. The misery your soul shall suffer after death.
2. The misery you shall suffer in body and soul after the day of judgment.[138]

[DOCTRINE RESUMED.]

[The text is] Matt. 25:1–12, especially v. 2, "And five of them were wise, and five were foolish."

Three things wherein they differ:

(1) [That the one have] oil {in their lamps, and the other have none}.
2. [The] consequences [of this].
3. [That] general character [manifest from the consideration of both].

I come now to the

3. [Third] and last thing wherein the difference consists, viz., their general character, which is manifest from both the foregoing things: and that is, that the one are wise, and the other foolish. This indeed appears

137. MS: "6."

138. This point marks the end of the fourteenth preaching unit and the end of the ninth booklet.

by all that we are taught of them in this, by all those things that have been observed of each; but especially from those different qualifications, that different behavior, and that different issue of things with respect to them that has been taken notice. This is what every particular declares, and especially is this manifest from all particulars together.

In discoursing of this point I shall only,

[(1)] First, show how this difference in the general character of true Christians and false, appears from the consideration of those points of difference that have been already spoken of.

[(2)] And secondly, I would show how that those opposite characters are emphatically ascribed to them, and do belong to them above all persons in the world.

[(1)] But in the first place, I would [show] how that this difference in their general character, viz., that the one sort are wise and the other foolish, appears from the two sorts of difference forementioned, viz., that one has oil and the other none, and in the consequences of it.

1. This appears from the consideration of that difference, that the one has oil in their vessels, or grace in their hearts, and the other none; and that, either in the different conduct of each that respects the obtaining grace, or in the difference that consists in the one's having it, and the other being without.

a. The wisdom of the one, and the folly of the other, appears in their different conduct with respect to obtaining of it. The one took thorough care to obtain oil in their vessels before they went out to meet the bridegroom, the other neglected.

We are told that the one took oil in their vessels with their lamps, but that the other took their lamps and took no oil with them.

The one wisely considered what they should stand in need of, in that undertaking that they were setting out upon it. They considered that it was of necessity that they have their lamps continued burning till the bridegroom come, that they might meet him with lights in their hands, to put proper honor upon him, and that they might be accepted of him; and they considered that it would not be expected that the flame of their lamps should hold, without oil to feed them.

And therefore they took care, before they set out on this undertaking, to have all things in readiness, that they might be acceptably received by the bridegroom, and not be put to shame when he came.

On the contrary, the other never wisely considered this matter. They had lamps, and they hoped that would be sufficient, not considering how little lamps would signify without oil.

They see that their lamps burnt and gave light for the present moment, and so they[139] set their hearts at ease, and never considered with themselves that, however their lamps flamed now, it was impossible that the flame should last without oil to feed it; and so they foolishly neglected to take any care to get oil. For the present, their lamps gave light as well as those of the other; they made as good a show outwardly, and they contented themselves with that.

But [they] acted like madmen, or persons bereft of their reason, to expect a fire could be continued without fuel, or that the flame of a lamp could be upheld with nothing but a wick without oil.

The wise virgins considered of what great importance the errand was that they went forth upon, viz., to meet the bridegroom, and how much it concerned 'em to have success in it; and therefore, like wise persons, they spared no pains nor cost, that they might be so provided as to be safe in this matter, and secured from such a dreadful calamity as failing in this undertaking.

The other, on the contrary, foolishly begrutched the trouble of going after oil, and the cost that must be expended, and so sottishly ran the venture of greatest interest—yea, their all—upon no better security than the flame of a burning wick without oil to feed it.

The wise virgins were seasonable in their care to obtain oil; they took care of that matter in the first place, before ever they set out to meet the bridegroom. The other very foolishly put it off to the very last, till it was too late.

They were not willing to put themselves to the trouble of going after oil, or the expense of buying of it, when they might have done it to good purpose and had a fair opportunity for it: and so they foolishly put it off till all their opportunity was gone.

And then at last, when it was too late, and it would be to no purpose to seek it, then they are willing to be at the trouble, and go in a great hurry to buy oil, at the time when they should have gone forth with the rest to meet the bridegroom with lamps in their hands.

Alas, what did it signify to go after oil to feed their lamps to meet the bridegroom with, and put honor upon him, when the bridegroom is

139. MS: "their."

already gone by with his attendants, and has entered into the marriage? Now, they are sensible, 'tis of great import to have oil.

Now they are in distress for some: they see now by experience that lamps won't continue burning without oil, and how dull and foolish were they, that they could not be convinced of this before they saw it.

Now they are sensible that to have oil in their vessels, is well worth the price {to buy it} and expense {of time}. Alas, where were their thoughts, that they were not sensible of this before? They had time enough to bethink themselves. What were they doing, what were they employed about, that they never in all that time considered those things before?

The wise virgins acted wisely, in that they did not depend on uncertainties in so great an affair. When they were about to go forth in this great undertaking, they wisely considered that they did not know how long the bridegroom might tarry; and therefore, that they might be provided against the worst, they took oil sufficient to keep their lamps a long time burning.

But the other foolishly neglected to make any provision for this. When they set out, they never prepared to meet with difficulties; and therefore, when difficulties came, they were overthrown. They never sat down to count the cost, and so, though they began to build, they never finished, and so exposed them[selves] to be mocked and derided for their folly.

They foolishly depended on the greatest uncertainties; when they went forth to meet the bridegroom, they thought nothing of future difficulties. And when the bridegroom tarried, instead of improving that opportunity that he by tarrying gave them to go and buy oil, [they] but seem to act as if they concluded that because he was not come yet, that he never would come at all, and so went to sleep instead of going to buy oil; and while they were sleeping, taking their slothful ease, their lamps went out. These things are a lively representation of the foolish conduct of sinners under means of grace and opportunities for salvation.

But that true Christians are wise, and others foolish, don't only appear in that one have been thorough in seeking grace, and the other neglected it; but,

[b.] Secondly, the wisdom of the one and the folly of the other appears in that, [that] the one have grace, and the other are without it. And that, for this reason, viz., because that grace is the greatest and the only true wisdom, and that sin that graceless persons are under the dominion of, is the greatest folly. Here,

[(a)] First, grace is the greatest and only true wisdom. The word "wisdom" is commonly used in Scripture for grace, because herein consists the only true wisdom; and so sin is commonly called "folly," and wicked men and "fools" are terms used synonymously in Scripture. And the Scripture does directly teach us that godliness is the greatest and only true wisdom. Prov. 1:7, "The fear of the Lord is [the beginning of wisdom]." Job 28:28, "The fear of the Lord, that is wisdom; and to depart from evil is understanding." And that it is so, that grace is the greatest and only true wisdom, if we considered wherein wisdom consists. It consists in two things, viz.:

[a.] First, in the knowledge and right understanding and judgment of things.

[b.] Second, in a prudent determination of the mind in it designs and pursuits.

And,

a. If we consider the first thing that belongs to wisdom, viz., {knowledge and right understanding and judgment of things}, it will appear that those have the greatest and only wisdom, that have grace in[140] their hearts. Grace gives a true knowledge. I John 2:27, "Anointing teacheth you of all things, and is truth, and is no lie."

[Grace is] knowledge of the most excellent and important objects. They only have a true knowledge of, or judgment about, anything, {who have grace}. They only have the right knowledge of God, {or} of themselves, or of other things, {who have grace}.

b. Grace influences the mind to a prudent determination in its designs and pursuits. Prov. 8:12, "I, Wisdom, dwell with prudence, and find out knowledge of witty invention." {Grace influences them to make a} prudent choice. They only {who have true grace know the} right end, true happiness, prudent means, wise ways, {and} wise behavior.

(b) That sin that false Christians are under the power of, is the greatest folly.

a. [They have the] most wrong and foolish notions of things, [and] blindness and darkness of the soul. II Cor. 4:4, "In whom the god of this world [hath blinded the minds of them which believe not]." [They have the] most foolish notions of God. [They thought God was] altogether

140. MS: "& th."

such an one as themselves. In their thoughts, [they] rob God of the glory of his perfections.

[They have] foolish thoughts of themselves, high [thoughts] of other things; [they] deify the world. [They have] foolish thoughts of time and eternity.

b. [That sin that false Christians are under the power of,] is an habitual inclination of heart to a most imprudent and foolish determination in its designs. [It inclines to a] foolish choice, [a] foolish course, [so that they] pursue even [their own] misery. Prov. 8:36, "All that hate me love death."[141]

I proceed now to show,

b. That this different and opposite character is manifest from the consequences of the one's having oil, {and the other not}. It appears in the consequence of it that respects their behavior, viz., in the one's being steadfast and persevering in the profession and practice of religion, and in the unsteadiness and fickleness of the others.

Steadiness in conduct in temporal affairs, especially those that are of great weight, is looked upon as a great part of wisdom, and instability and fickleness a great evidence of weakness and folly.

And above all things is it so in affairs of such vast concern as that which we are speaking [of], that concerns the honor of God and our own eternal interest.

How wisely do they act who, when they have once begun in religion, so hold on and follow God and Christ and their own soul's salvation, in the ways of universal obedience to God's commands, however they may be flattered to draw them away, and what opposition soever they may meet with from those enemies that seek to fright them from their duty and the way of their happiness. How much is it a man's wisdom to

---

141. This portion of the MS (L. 5) is made from a fragment of a child's response to a biblical question:

The answer to my Question is this
viz in Nahum 1 Ch & 4. v: He Rebuketh [the sea]
and maketh it dry & Isaiah 50: Ch 2 [At my]
Rebuke I dry up the sea & Psalms 10: [. . . Thy way]
is in the \<sea\> and thy Path in the Great water [Psalms 29]
3 the voice of the Lord is upon the waters [the God of glory]
thundereth the Lord is upon many wat[ers.]
Psalms 100: 7: vrs: 29: He maketh the S[torm a calm]
so that the waters thereof are stil[l.]

disregard all the scarecrows that the devil can lay in his way, to fright him back or hinder his going on heavenward, and to disregard those light afflictions that are but for a moment in comparison of that far more exceeding [happiness].

But then [there is] the wisdom of the one and the folly of the other in all these, from the consideration of the final issue of things, with respect to the state of both: and this is the most lively mirror in which we may behold the wisdom of true and the folly of false Christians, when we come to see the issue of the different choice that they make, and behold the exceeding different ends to which the opposite courses they take lead them to.

When the false Christians' lamps are totally and eternally gone out, then will their folly appear in not taking oil. When their good opinion of their own state and all their hopes, come utterly to vanish away then, and their hope turns into disappointment and confusion, issues in everlasting shame, then will be seen most clearly the folly of their hopes, and the foolishness of all their presumption and false dependence.

Then will appear their folly of building their house on the sand, in making a spider's web their trust, in satisfying themselves with shadows, and clothing themselves with such fig leaves.

And on the contrary, when the hope of the godly at Christ's appearing comes to be confirmed, and {their hope turns into joy}; and when that time comes, when true Christians are admitted {into the eternal wedding banquet}: then will it be most abundantly manifest how wise {are those who had oil in their lamps}. Then the truth {of true Christians' hope} will be manifest, {and the} falsity of the surmises {of false Christians, and their vain} imaginations, {will be known}. Then the vast importance {of having oil in their lamps} will be manifest.

Then will the wicked themselves be all convinced of the wisdom of the godly in {getting oil, and} in {being ready for the bridegroom}, in those things that formerly they were ready to wonder at them and despise them for. Then [will they] see their own folly [in] not improving opportunities, {and} not taking pains to get oil {in their lamps}, not harkening to counsel.

Then will their folly appear and be declared by the voice of their own consciences, {and by the} voice of the Judge, {and by their} own voice, crying out of their folly.

Having thus shown how the wisdom of true Christians and {the folly of false Christians appears}, from the one's having oil and the other having none, and the consequences, I proceed now, in the

[(2)] Second place, to show those opposite characters are emphatically ascribed, and do belong to them eminently and above all persons in the world. Here are two things:

1. That there are no other wise persons in the world, but only true Christians.

There are those that are called wise men [among the] heathen philosophers. Now are men of great learning {accounted wise persons, and} many great politicians, {and there are wise persons} among the great divines.

If natural men are not wise men, {who have} no true knowledge {of divine things, no} right judgment {in the} main things, things of greatest importance, {then they have} no true prudence and discretion, {that belong to true Christians}.

[The] weakest Christian, the little child, [is wiser than they]. Eccles. 4:13, "Better is a poor and a wise child than an old and foolish king, who will no more be admonished." {A child} knows more of [the] important truth, {and has} greater prudence.

I Cor. 1:25, "[The] foolishness of God is wiser than man." This appears in God's choosing the foolish things of this world, to confound the wise. True wisdom is not attained by learning, by education in colleges, {by study with} learned tutors, {and by reading} many books. {True wisdom is} not gotten for gold. Job 28:14–[15], "[The depth saith, It is not in me: and the] sea saith, It is not with me." Prov. 2:6, "[For the Lord giveth wisdom: out of his mouth cometh knowledge and understanding]." True Christians are the only truly wise persons. {They are truly wise,} not only as their spiritual wisdom excels human learning and policy, but all moral virtue, [the] virtue of philosophers and great men. {Thus} many men have been eminent for virtue, and called wise on that account, yet know not God. The world by wisdom knows not God, don't know Christ and him crucified—I Cor. 1:20, "God makes foolish [the] wisdom of this world"—because it is foolish.

2. False Christians are the greatest fools of all persons in the world; not the only fools, {but the greatest}.

[The heathen,] they han't such an opportunity, such light and instruction; [they have not been] told how they may obtain, [or] told the necessity of it. [They] han't such warning; {they} are not told of the bridegroom's coming. {They know not} the blessings he will bestow on the wise, and the misery [he will bestow on the foolish]. Their hope is not so foolish a hope, their trust not so foolish. They are more willful.

[APPLICATION.]

Use of *Exhortation,* to those that are in a Christless condition. Foolish virgins, forsake your folly and seek spiritual wisdom! To leave the folly of neglecting and preparation for {eternal misery}, wisely consider the absolute necessity you stand in of oil. Don't trust in external appearances; consider how unreasonable [it is] to expect that they should be continued without oil.

Don't begrutch the trouble. Be seasonable.

Don't depend on uncertainties. {Be exhorted to} seek the true wisdom, [the] right knowledge of things.

Consider,

First. How much bodily sight is prized.

Second. How much pains many take for learning and worldly wisdom, [as] education {in colleges, and} universities, {and} travelling[142] [to distant places].

Third. How long you have been in the school of Christ. II Tim. 3:[6–]7—silly ones, lead away, never learning, and never coming. "O fools, when will ye be wise?" [Ps. 94:8]. Prov. 27:22, "bray a fool in a mortar [among wheat with a pestle, yet will not his foolishness depart from him]."

Fourth. What would you think of any that you saw, so foolish in temporal affairs as you are in spiritual things of such importance, so slack, negligent of opportunity? [What would you think of one who would] run such great ventures, give away his life for a song?

Fifth. You sink yourself below the brute creatures in folly. Is. 1:3, "[the] ox knows his owner." Jer. 8:6–7, "I hearkened and heard, but they spake not aright: no man repented him of his wickedness, saying, What have I done? every one turned to his course, as the horse rusheth into the battle. Yea, the stork in the heaven knoweth her appointed times; and the turtle and the crane and the swallow observe the time of their coming; but my people know not the judgment of the Lord."[143]

142. MS: "Travailing."

143. This point in the text coincides with leaves 10 and 11, which contain parts of a

Sixth. As those sinners that {continue Christless} under the gos-pel [are the] greatest fools, so [the] greatest among false Christians {are those} that are under the greatest advantage {to leave their folly}. This place {in Scripture shows this}.

*

Thus I have finished my discourse from this parable. [I have] shown that there are those two sorts [of Christians, wise and foolish].

[I have shown] in many particulars how they may agree, {and how they may} differ.

What an idea will these things [give], if they [have] been duly at-tended, to give of both {kinds of believers}. How much tending to instruct, and to convince and affect. How nearly do all these things concern us.

We are the persons {spoken of in the parable}. All of us [are] con-vinced one way or the other. {We are} all either true or false Christians.

How full are[144] the holy Scriptures of instruction {and warning}, especially that revelation given by Christ, {as} appears by the abundant, familiar instruction and warning given in this one parable.

Let us take heed to ourselves, lest all things should be written in vain as to us, and all that has been spoken, spoken in vain. How inexcus-able {will we be}, if we continue in the way of the foolish virgins, after so much plain instruction and such abundant warning. What shame and everlasting contempt and aggravated punishment shall we expose our-selves to, as not only foolish virgins, but some of the most foolish[145] and inexcusable [of] all mankind.

---

child's response to a biblical question.

> How often was the Temple Pillaged of its treasure
> from the Time that it was built Till it
> was burnt by the Chaldeans
> The Answer is 7 Times:: once
> By Shishak which we Have an
> account of in the 12 of the 2 of Chron
> att 9 verse Again we Have an account in the
> 25v of 2 Chron att: 23 24 verse of Joash
> [. . .] the Temple
> [. . .]

This answer corresponds to no. 33 in "Questions for Young People," WJEO 39.

144. MS: "is."

145. MS: "fool."

INDEX